# THE COACHING BUYERS' HANDBOOK

# THE COACHING BUYERS' HANDBOOK

## A practical guide for HR managers, coach commissioners and coachees to get the best from coaching

Jonathan Passmore and Sam Isaacson

First published in 2023 by Libri Publishing

Copyright © Libri Publishing

Contributors retain copyright of their chapters.

The right of Jonathan Passmore and Sam Isaacson to be identified as the editors of this work has been asserted in accordance with the Copyright, Designs and Patents Act, 1988.

ISBN: 978-1-911450-96-2 (Hardback)
ISBN: 978-1-911450-97-9 (Paperback)

A CIP catalogue record for this book is available from The British Library

Cover and Design by Carnegie Book Production

Libri Publishing
Brunel House
Volunteer Way
Faringdon
Oxfordshire
SN7 7YR

Tel: +44 (0)845 873 3837

www.libripublishing.co.uk

# Editors

## Jonathan Passmore, DOccPsyc

Jonathan is Professor of Coaching and Behavioral Change at Henley Business School, UK, Senior Vice President at CoachHub, the digital coaching platform, and Chair of the Division of Coaching Psychology, British Psychological Society. Prior to these roles he worked at PricewaterhouseCoopers and IBM. He is a chartered psychologist, EMCC Master Coach, ICF PCC, holds qualifications in team coaching and coaching supervision, and five degrees including an MBA and doctorate in psychology. He is the executive editor of the *International Coaching Psychology Review* and has written and edited over 30 books including *The Coaches' Handbook* and *Becoming a Coach: The Essential ICF Guide*. He has also written over 200 scientific papers and book chapters, making him one of the most widely published coaching researchers.

## Sam Isaacson

Sam is an accredited coach and coach supervisor, Global Director of Consulting at CoachHub and Chair of the Coaching Professional apprenticeship trailblazer group in England. He plays roles in several coaching professional bodies and industry thinktanks, with a particular focus on coaching with technology, and has written an Amazon number-one bestseller. He is the first person in the world to offer coaching in virtual reality. Prior to taking up his current role, he spent several years advising organizations on technology risk, digital transformation and coaching.

# Contributors

**Omar Alaoui**

Omar has a background in business and organizational consulting. He is a certified coach and works with public and private organizations to help them design the most effective coaching programs for their leaders, managers and individual contributors.

**Emily Barber**

Emily is a project and program manager, with substantial experience in both the private and public sectors, delivering everything from technology infrastructure projects to large-scale transport reconfiguration. She is a qualified coach and mentor, and has worked providing advice to government and coaching senior leaders.

**Laura Chapin**

For over 20 years, Laura has helped leaders reach their potential and organizations achieve results through leadership and consultant roles in talent management, organizational effectiveness, L&D and coaching. Her experience includes global Fortune 100 organizations, technology start-ups and consulting across multiple industries.

**Jule Deges**

Jule is an organizational psychologist with an MSc in positive and coaching psychology. She has extensive experience in designing employee experience solutions that help organizations grow happier and healthier workforces.

**Rosie Evans-Krimme**

Rosie Evans-Krimme is a psychologist, coach and mindfulness practitioner. Rosie holds an MSc in Mental Health Studies and has published research on the coaching industry, ethics of coaching and wellbeing coaching. Rosie applies insights from positive psychology and coaching psychology into the world of work.

### Eliana Gialain

Eliana is a multicultural HR executive with extensive experience in leadership development. Her academic background includes a master's degree in Business and Psychology. She is certified in systemic, strengths-based and neuroscience-based coaching.

### Morgan Hyonne

Morgan has a background in business psychology and learning and development. He is a certified strengths-based coach, engages with C-suite and VP-level executives at Fortune 1000 companies to design and evaluate novel, transformational coaching programs for their employees.

### Naila Abdul Karim

Naila is a business psychologist and an ICF coach with years of experience in the talent management and human resources space. She has worked across various industries and regions across the globe helping people navigate their careers and achieve their career and life goals while unlocking their ultimate potential.

### Qingsong Ke

Qingsong is a career coach and psychologist working in digital coaching, based in Shanghai, China. She is an avid reader with a fascination for psychology, history and economics.

### Qi Liu, PhD

Qi is a mixed-methods professional researcher who has conducted extensive research in industry and academia on human behavior and attitudes in the learning process, as well as possessing many years of experience in curriculum design.

### Windy Tshepiso Maledu

Windy is passionate about developing human and leadership potential. She has spent her career as a leadership development specialist and certified coach, using her honors in dramatic arts and MSc in coaching and behavioral change from Henley Africa to liberate the best in others.

### Laurène Mayer

Laurène worked as a social entrepreneur and as an HR innovation consultant. She is a certified coach from HEC Paris and builds coaching programs aiming to fit both the human and business stakes of organizations.

### Laurel McKenzie

Laurel is a behavioral science expert with eight years of specialized experience in cognitive performance and coaching. She holds an MA degree in clinical and counseling psychology and is currently studying for a PhD.

### Rui Munakata

Rui is a coach and behavioral scientist based in Japan. She finds joy in movies, cats, and moments with friends and family by the beach.

### Anna Pachenkova

Anna is a researcher with a background in social and occupational psychology, experience in policy consultation and applied science and social projects. She is passionate about evidenced-based practice in coaching and the potential that it brings for personal and organizational development.

### Dr Naeema Pasha

Naeema is Principal Practitioner, Association of Business Psychologist and Leadership Fellow at Windsor Castle Leadership Society. She has researched and written widely about technology and the future of work.

### Elizabeth Pavese, PhD

Liz is an organizational psychologist and certified coach with extensive experience working with organizations to design evidence-based employee experience solutions that help people and organizations thrive.

### Valeria Cardillo Piccolino

Valeria is a certified coach and business psychologist, with experience in learning and development in both HR and consultancy, across different countries and industries (from the United Nations to retail). She is strongly committed to building inclusive organizations, and is a board member and mentoring program director of the Professional Women's Network Milan.

### Roxane Rath

Roxane Rath is a business psychologist with vast HR consulting experience. She advises organizations worldwide in establishing personnel development programs that provide behavioral solutions to organizational challenges and change.

### Patrick Rütten

Patrick is a business psychologist with a master's degree in work and organizational psychology and with a passion for transformation and people development, using his broad expertise to bring evidence-based coaching to organizations.

### Miriam Schneider-Tettenborn

Miriam is a certified coach and organizational psychologist who blends her scientific acumen with business expertise in sales and innovation programs to support companies in their striving towards building better workplaces.

### Yu Dan Shi

Yu Dan is an author, executive coach and practice leader. Outside of work, she enjoys bushwalks, reading books and the amazing beaches in Sydney.

### Gill Tanner

Gill is an accomplished human-resources professional, a fellow of the CIPD and holds an MSc in coaching and behavioral change from Henley Business School.

### Shammy Tawadros

Shammy is a psychologist and behavioral scientist. Outside of work she enjoys food, weight lifting and art.

### David Tee, PhD

David is a chartered psychologist, coaching psychology researcher and author, as well as editor of the peer-reviewed British Psychology Society's journal, the *Coaching Psychologist*. He holds a PhD from South West Wales University.

### Lisa Tomlin

Lisa is an experienced consultant and accredited ICF coach based in the United States.

### Andreas Weber

Andreas has an MSc in cognitive science and is a certified coach with extensive experience in the development of audio-, video- and text-based coaching materials.

# Glossary

**Coach**: a trained and accredited professional who works with the coachee, helping them on their journey of development. The coach is responsible for managing the process, but not deciding the content, focus or direction for the conversation.

**Coachee**: the individual who participates in the coaching issue, who is responsible for the topic of conversation and who benefits from that conversation.

**Coaching**: coaching involves partnering with clients to help them reflect on themselves, their situation and context, and identify new insights and actions to unlock potential, enhance wellbeing and improve performance.

**Digital coaching**: digital coaching is a technology-based, live coach–coachee collaboration, enabled by secure digital communications involving both audio and visual channels, which is scalable and has measurable outcomes for individuals and organizations.

**Line manager**: the person who has management responsibility for the coachee.

**Organizational client**: the individual who acts on behalf of the organization to commission the coaching service from the coaching supplier – sometimes also known as the 'coach commissioner'.

**Supervision**: supervision is a formal, reflective and confidential process used by coaches, working with a qualified supervisor, combining support and challenge, to enhance the coach's confidence, competence and creativity in their practice.

**Team coaching**: team coaching is a partnering process with a group who share a common purpose, to help them reflect on themselves, their relationships and context, and to identify new insights, actions and ways of being to achieve their common purpose.

# Acknowledgements

As editors, we owe a debt of thanks to many people, including the contributors for sharing their expertise, and especially to Emily Barber for her input on the manuscript. We would also like to thank the wonderful people at Libri Publishing, with whom we have worked before and whose expertise, guidance, advice and general loveliness make publishing with them a pleasure.

Finally, a thank you to you as readers. We hope that we have produced a useful guide which can inform your journey, whether you are buying coaching for your organization or planning on hiring a coach for your own personal development.

We would welcome your feedback as you apply the insights and guidance in this book so we too can continue to learn and improve.

# Contents

# Introduction

Coaching has grown over the past 30 years from being a side hustle to being a professional service, from being delivered by individuals who were on the margins to being delivered by billion-dollar businesses, from only being available to the privileged few to being available for the many.

Over this period, I have also witnessed the growth of coaching science, with an explosion of coaching books and research articles to support coach development. I should know, as I have written many of them. But what we have seen very little of is advice, guidance and support for those tasked with the responsibility of buying coaching, either as an individual client (coachee) or those responsible for buying coaching services on behalf of their organization.

For individual buyers seeking a personal coach, it can be a tricky process. The individual coachee is likely to have lots of questions: what should they look for in a coach? How can they judge in advance what might be right for them? And what can they expect from a coaching relationship?

For line managers who have team members engaging in coaching, they too have questions. How can they best support their direct reports who are receiving coaching? What should they expect in terms of reporting back from the coach? And how will coaching help their team to improve its performance?

Organizational buyers often receive the least support. Buying coaching services is different from most other procurement decisions. Coaching is different to buying a software system or leasing new offices, where it's possible to calculate a return on the investment (ROI). Humans are far more complex than that and, as a result, using ROI can only ever provide a starting point for a discussion about the full impact of coaching. In most large organizations, the buy decision often involves half a dozen people, sometimes as many as a dozen, from HR and Talent Management to Finance and Procurement. While some may have had experience of coaching, others will have had little experience or knowledge of 'what good looks like'.

So why this book? This book is designed to help all three groups: individual coachees, line managers and organizational buyers of coaching. By engaging with stakeholders in all three groups, we have compiled the 50 most popular questions asked by them, and drawn together a panel of experts – coaches, psychologists and behavioral change specialists – to provide short, crisp and clear answers to help each stakeholder group improve their understanding and their decision making.

We believe helping users and buyers make better decisions is just as important as helping improve the quality of coaching. In what is still an unregulated market, sometimes called the 'wild west of coaching', it's easy to be duped by the high-pressure sales tactics and expansive claims of 'fairy dust' coaching.

While there are many great coaches across the world, there are also lots of pretty average coaches and still far too many examples of bad or unethical practice. By helping create smarter, more informed buyers, we believe we can contribute to driving up standards throughout the coaching industry.

We hope you find the book useful. We are always delighted to hear from coachees, line managers and coaching buyers about their experiences so that we can continue to learn and improve, and hopefully make the second edition of this book even more useful than the first.

**Professor Jonathan Passmore**

London, UK

# SECTION 1

# The coachee's guide to coaching

In this section, we focus on the individual user of coaching: people considering whether coaching will be right for them or who want to start the process of finding the right coach, but are nervous about what to look for or how to set up a coaching program. In this section of the handbook, we introduce coaching and consider some of the key questions a coachee should consider before embarking on a coaching program.

In Chapter 1: 'What is coaching?' Jonathan Passmore explains what coaching is and what it is not, and how it compares to alternative interventions. In Chapter 2: 'How do I know if I'm ready for coaching?' Laura Chapin discusses how you will know you are ready for coaching through a coaching readiness questionnaire. By completing the questionnaire, you will have a much better insight as to whether coaching is right for you. In Chapter 3: 'How can coaching help my performance at work?' Qi Liu explores how coaching can help with individual and organizational performance, as well as how research and psychological theories support coaching interventions. In Chapter 4: 'How can coaching help my health and wellbeing?' Jule Deges considers how coaching can help with health and wellbeing, and where having a positive coaching mindset can result in a multitude of personal and professional benefits. In Chapter 5: 'When is coaching the best choice to help my personal and professional development?' Gill Tanner discusses how coaching can support career development and professional growth through training, mentoring and reflective practice.

In Chapter 6: 'How can I select the best coach for me?' Yu Dan Shi explores what to consider in choosing a coach, such as language, time zone, sector knowledge, gender and race. In Chapter 7: 'How should I approach my coaching relationship?' Valeria Cardillo Piccolino considers how commitment to coaching, willingness to trust, a supportive environment and feedback can help the coaching process. In Chapter 8: 'How can I make the most of each session?' Laurène Mayer discusses how to prepare for coaching, how to get the most out of coaching sessions and the work which can happen in-between sessions. In Chapter 9: 'Why should I have a contract with my coach?' Liz Pavese discusses coaching contracting, the benefits of setting boundaries and how to approach digital coaching. In Chapter 10: 'What should

I do after my coaching ends?' Windy Tshepiso Maledu explores how to sustain the positive effects of behavior change found through coaching.

In Chapter 11: 'Are my coaching sessions confidential?' Naila Abdul Karim discusses what confidentiality means in a coaching relationship, why it is important and how coaches are held accountable. In Chapter 12: 'Why does my coach invite me to do work between sessions?' Patrick Rütten discusses the importance of actively engaging in the coaching process in-between sessions through knowledge acquisition and experimentation. In Chapter 13: 'How can I set up my home office for an online coaching session?' Lisa Tomlin discusses how to get online, how you might want to set the scene for your online calls, including body language, and how to make online coaching successful. In Chapter 14: 'How can a support team help me in making the most of coaching?' Eliana Gialain explores how to identify and build a support team, and how having a reliable source of support can help with the coaching journey.

In Chapter 15: 'Why should my coach have supervision?' Patrick considers what coaching supervision is, what the benefits are and what the supervision process involves. Finally in this section, in Chapter 16: 'Where should I meet my coach?' Jonathan explores what is involved with in-person coaching sessions, such as the issue of where to meet, before examining digital coaching, its benefits and the things to consider when coaching online.

# CHAPTER 1

# What is coaching?

Jonathan Passmore

## Introduction

Coaching has become one of the fastest-growing organizational interventions of the past 20 years. The simple reason for this is because it works (Jones et al., 2015; Theeboom et al., 2014). Back in 1999 an internet search for the word 'coach' may have brought back a few thousand responses. Most of these would have been connected to sport. Over the subsequent two or so decades coaching has undergone a transformation. Coaching has become an essential ingredient for most modern organizations' learning and development (L&D) strategies. Now, virtually every organization is using coaching to support their employees and to develop their talent. But in spite of this, there remains confusion in some quarters about what exactly 'coaching' is, and how organizations can optimize their use of coaching. In this first chapter we will explore these questions to provide greater clarity on coaching and its uses.

## What is coaching?

At its most basic, coaching is a developmental technique which can be used in a wide variety of ways to help people to learn. This learning can help people to develop new skills, insights or coping methods which contribute towards enhanced performance and wellbeing. John Whitmore (1992), the originator of the GROW model, suggested that coaching was about encouraging an individual to develop greater self-awareness and take more personal responsibility in their lives, becoming more 'choiceful' in the process. These ingredients, while helpful, may not precisely clarify what happens in a coaching conversation.

To start our exploration, we have included some popular definitions in Table 1.1.

**Table 1.1: Popular definitions of coaching**

**Practical definition**

Coaching is unlocking a person's potential to maximize their own performance. It is helping them to learn rather than teaching them.

(Whitmore, 1992)

**Practitioner's definition**

Coaching involves partnering with clients in a thought-provoking and creative process that inspires them to maximize their personal and professional potential.

(ICF, 2021)

**Process definition**

A Socratic-based, future-focused dialogue, between a facilitator (coach) and a participant (coachee/client), where the facilitator uses open questions, active listening, summaries and reflections which are aimed at stimulating the self-awareness and personal responsibility of the participant.

(adapted from Passmore and Fillery-Travis, 2011)

These three definitions offer different perspectives on what coaching is. The last of these three definitions seeks to create a unique definition clearly distinguishing it from other types of conversations by exploring the process of coaching: who is involved (a facilitator–coach and a participant–coachee/client), what coaches do (use open questions, active listening, summaries and reflections) and what they are working to achieve (stimulating the self-awareness and personal responsibility of the coachee). Even with such a detailed descriptive definition there is sometimes confusion. As a result, it can sometimes be helpful also to explain what coaching is not, and how it compares with other interventions.

## Coaching is not...

It often helps to think about what coaching is not. In Table 1.2 we have suggested ten things which coaching is not.

**Table 1.2: Ten things coaching is not**

1. Telling people what to do

2. Providing a wholly positive, affirming relationship

3. Sharing wisdom and experience through multiple personal stories

4. Instructing someone about a topic

5. Observing and giving feedback on performance

6. A single model or framework – such as positive psychology coaching, co-active coaching or cognitive behavioral coaching

7. A single technique or tool

8. Learned in one weekend

9. Available to fix people

10. The solution to every problem

## Coaching and other interventions

Finally, in considering what coaching is and is not, it can also be useful to compare it briefly with other interventions used in the workplace. Here we compare coaching with mentoring, management and therapy.

*Mentoring versus coaching*

Mentoring and coaching can often be confused, as both are typically 1:1 conversations and involve learning. While coaching tends to focus on a short-term relationship between equals, mentoring is more typically a longer-term relationship in which one of the parties is sharing their superior knowledge or experience. In terms of process, while coaching is almost always about asking open questions which prompt deep reflection, in contrast mentoring can often involve providing helpful answers.

In practice, many coaches and mentors work along the 'coaching–mentoring continuum'. They may be drawing on their skills in coaching to encourage reflection, while also providing some content for personal development, such as suggesting a book or article as background reading, or a video to watch, which helps provide greater knowledge for their coachee.

*Management versus coaching*

While coaching can certainly be used as one style of managing a team, it should be remembered that managers (and leaders) should be drawing on a wide range of styles. They will need to set a vision for the future, they will consult team members, they will set goals as well as tell or instruct people what to do in some situations, such as compliance with health and safety practices or with diversity and inclusion. While many managers (or leaders) may use a coaching style, this is not the same as being an independent coach, outside the line-management chain. The independence of the external coach encourages greater self-disclosure, and research evidence confirms that it leads to better outcomes (Losch et al., 2016). In addition, the external coach is more likely to offer greater confidentiality, while supporting the individual's development.

*Therapy versus coaching*

There is sometimes confusion between psychotherapy, counseling and coaching. While each is a 1:1 conversation which uses questions and listening, the primary focus and topics of these three interventions are different. Psychotherapy tends to focus most frequently on dysfunction and diagnosed conditions, for example clients with clinical depression or bi-polar disorder. Counseling is more likely to focus on supporting people during times of distress, for example during bereavement or the emotions associated with relationship breakdown. In contrast with these two approaches, coaching is focused on desires, enabling the client to become the best version of themself, through a future-focused dialogue.

Of course, coaching also overlaps with many other organizational practices including training, appraisals and performance management. We will explore some of these differences in other chapters. However, it differs from each of these. While many of these have developmental aspects, in coaching the learning is driven exclusively by the agenda set by the client.

**Table 1.3: Definition of coaching**

Coaching involves partnering with clients to help them reflect on themselves, their situation and context, and identify new insights and actions to unlock potential, enhance wellbeing and improve performance.

(CoachHub, 2021)

## But does coaching work?

During the early development of coaching, it was hard to provide categorical evidence that coaching worked. Many coaches had seen positive results from their work and coachees were very positive about their experience, but warm feelings and personal experience are not scientific evidence. Over the past decade, however, research studies have provided the evidence that coaching can have a positive impact on performance and wellbeing (Theeboom et al., 2014; Jones et al., 2015; Grover and Furnham, 2016; Athanasopoulou and Dopson, 2018).

This evidence from a wide range of studies has confirmed that coaching is a highly effective intervention that can be useful for a range of common workplace challenges, including:

- Transition to a new role

- Knowledge transfer from leadership classroom to workplace role

- Stress management

- Career choice

- Assessment preparation

- Strategic decision making/reflection

- Goal-setting and goal attainment.

However, while coaching is a highly effective intervention, it is not the solution to every workplace problem. The outcomes of coaching conversations are dependent on a range of factors: the skill of the coach, the willingness of the coachee to engage, the quality of the coach–coachee relationship, the suitability of the topic being discussed, and the organizational or cultural context in which the coaching is occurring. In short, coaching is a social process and the outcomes are moderated by a multitude of external factors. There are many occasions when alternative interventions would be better, such as: when the individual needs to learn a technical skill (for example, how to use a new software application being introduced to an organization), where training would be a better option; when the person is seeking to develop their long-term career within an organization, where mentoring might be a better choice; or when a manager wishes to address under-performance, where feedback and performance management may be required.

What we can say is that coaching is a distinct, evidenced-based intervention that should form part of a wider range of tools used by an organization in developing, managing and supporting its workforce to achieve their full potential.

## Conclusion

In this chapter we aimed to clarify the nature of coaching, offering definitions and comparisons. Coaching at its simplest is a developmental conversation which supports individuals to become more self-aware, and helps them to take greater personal responsibility and become more choiceful. It works best in helping individuals achieve the best version of themselves and fulfil their future goals. There is strong evidence that it works to help employees in a wide range of circumstances, and thus should form an integral part of any modern organization's learning-and-development strategy. But like all interventions, it is best used alongside other interventions including leadership development, appraisal, performance management and training.

## References

Athanasopoulou, A., and Dopson, S. (2018). A systematic review of executive coaching outcomes: Is it the journey or the destination that matters the most? *Leadership Quarterly* 29(1): 70–88. https://doi.org/10.1016/j.leaqua.2017.11.004.

CoachHub (2021). *Definitions, Processes and Models*. Internal Document. Berlin: CoachHub.

Grover, S., and Furnham, A. (2016). Coaching as a developmental intervention in organizations: A systematic review of its effectiveness and the mechanisms underlying it. *PLoS ONE* 11(7), Article e0159137. https://doi.org/10.1371/journal.pone.0159137.

ICF (2021). ICF Definition of coaching. Lexington: ICF. Retrieved 3 January 2022 from: https://coachingfederation.org/about.

Jones, R.J., Woods, S.A., and Guillaume, Y.R.F. (2015). The effectiveness of workplace coaching: a meta-analysis of learning and performance outcomes from coaching. *Journal of Occupational and Organizational Psychology* 89(2): 249–77. doi: https://doi.org/10.1111/joop.12119.

Losch, S., Traut-Mattausch, E., Muhlberger, M.D., and Jonas, E. (2016). Comparing the effectiveness of individual coaching, self-coaching, and group training: How leadership makes the difference. *Frontiers in Psychology* 7: 629, doi 10.3389/fpsyg.2016.00629.

Passmore, J., and Fillery-Travis, A. (2011). A critical review of executive coaching research: A decade of progress and what's to come. *Coaching: An International Journal of Theory, Research and Practice* 4(2): 70–88. https://doi.org/10.1080/17521882.2011.596484.

Theeboom, T., Beersma, B., and van Vianen, A.E.M. (2014). Does coaching work? A meta-analysis on the effects of coaching on individual level outcomes in an organizational context. *Journal of Positive Psychology* 9(1): 1–18. https://doi.org/10.1080/17439760.2013.837499.

Whitmore, J. (1992). *Coaching for Performance*. London: Nicholas Brealey.

# CHAPTER 2

# How do I know if I'm ready for coaching?

Laura Chapin

## Introduction

In Chapter 1: 'What is coaching?', we defined coaching and shared a number of common workplace challenges where coaching can be useful. No matter the challenge or reason for engaging with a coach, 'coachee readiness' is a key factor in how useful and effective coaching will be for the individual. Before deciding to work with a coach, it's essential that the coachee honestly assesses their readiness to ensure coaching is the right fit for them at this moment in their development, life and career. In this chapter, we'll explore what it means to be ready for coaching and share a short questionnaire that a coachee could use to help them assess their readiness for coaching.

## What does it mean to be ready for coaching?

'Readiness' has been defined as a state of preparedness, mentally or physically, for some experience or action. An individual contemplating coaching needs to consider whether they are ready, or mentally prepared, for the challenge.

**Table 2.1: Points for reflection**

A coachee who is ready for coaching:

1. Is well informed about coaching (e.g. what it is and isn't) and has a good understanding about the coaching process

2. Views coaching as important, relevant and beneficial

3. Has the motivation, willingness, desire and positive energy to engage in a process of change

4. Believes they have the ability to change and grow (growth mindset)

5. Is committed to the process (e.g. time and attention) to be successful

6. Recognizes one or more challenges or goals to work on

7. Feels safe to explore who they are and where they want to go

8. Is flexible and adaptable in their thinking

9. Is willing to be solution focused

10. Is willing to explore their emotions

11. Is prepared to be uncomfortable at times as they are challenged with new ways of thinking and behaving

12. Is open to experimenting with new behaviors that may not initially go as planned

13. Is willing to reflect on and make sense of their thoughts and feelings, and the nature of their challenges

14. Will take active steps towards addressing their identified challenges and goals

15. Is responsible for their own behavior (vs. defaulting to blaming others) and change

16. Is persistent when faced with setbacks or failures

17. Is able to ask for support and constructive feedback from others (e.g. managers, peers, direct reports, mentors, family or friends)

18. Welcomes the coach as their supportive, encouraging and challenging partner.

(Kretzschmar, 2010; Passmore and Fillery-Travis, 2011; Caley et al., 2002; Franklin, 2005; Steinber, 2020)

## Why is coaching readiness important?

Pausing to consider and confirm whether we are ready to engage in the coaching process is essential. Coachee readiness affects coaching effectiveness (Kauffman et al., 2008; Dawdy, 2004; Singh and Vinnicombe, 2005; Lambert and Barley, 2001) and increases the likelihood of successful coaching outcomes (Kretzschmar, 2010). The coachee's behavior and motivation level can impact the coaching process and the effectiveness of the coaching interaction (Caley et al., 2002).

## How can a coachee assess their readiness for coaching?

An individual considering coaching can reflect on the items below in the questionnaire to help determine if coaching is the right intervention at the right time to support their development.

**Table 2.2: Coaching readiness questionnaire**

Rate your level of agreement (high, medium or low) with each of the following statements:

|   | Question Item | High | Medium | Low |
|---|---------------|------|--------|-----|
| 1 | I am well informed about coaching (e.g. what it is and isn't) and have a good understanding about the coaching process. | | | |
| 2 | I see coaching as important, relevant and beneficial. | | | |
| 3 | I have the motivation, willingness, desire and positive energy to engage in a process of change. | | | |
| 4 | I believe I have the ability to change and grow. | | | |
| 5 | I am committed to the coaching process (e.g. time and attention) to be successful. | | | |
| 6 | I recognize one or more challenges to work on and am committed to setting specific goals. | | | |

| | Question Item | High | Medium | Low |
|---|---|---|---|---|
| 7 | I feel safe to explore who I am and where I want to go. | | | |
| 8 | I am flexible and adaptable in my thinking. | | | |
| 9 | I am solution focused. | | | |
| 10 | I am willing to look into the emotions related to my behavior, recognizing that simply 'knowing' what to do doesn't guarantee behaving in alignment with what is rationally understood. | | | |
| 11 | I am prepared to be uncomfortable at times as I am challenged with new ways of thinking and behaving. | | | |
| 12 | I am open to experimenting with new behaviors that may not go perfectly as planned. | | | |
| 13 | I am willing to reflect on and make sense of my thoughts, feelings and the nature of my challenges. | | | |
| 14 | I will take active steps in the direction I set for myself. | | | |
| 15 | I am responsible for my own behavior (vs. defaulting to blaming others) and change. | | | |
| 16 | I am persistent when faced with setbacks or failures. | | | |
| 17 | I am able to ask for support and constructive feedback from others (e.g. managers, peers, direct reports, mentors, family or friends). | | | |
| 18 | I welcome the coach as my supportive, encouraging and challenging partner. | | | |

After rating yourself on the questions above, what do you notice about your readiness level? If your ratings are mostly medium and high, you are more likely to benefit from coaching.

If you rated more of your scores as medium or low, coaching may not be the right step for you now. However, with further time, reflection or preparation, this may change. Review your answers to assess what might need to change to help you move forward.

(Questionnaire adapted from concepts contained in Kretzschmar, 2010; Passmore and Fillery-Travis, 2011; Caley et al., 2002; Franklin, 2005; Steinber, 2020)

## Conclusion

Engaging in coaching can be a meaningful and impactful way of developing, identifying new insights, pursuing goals, enhancing wellness and improving performance. It is easy to assume that anyone can engage in coaching at any time, yet research and experience show that readiness for coaching is important to the success of the coaching relationship and overall outcomes. In order to reap the benefits of coaching and make the most of the investment, the coachee needs to fully lean into the coaching process.

## References

Caley, L., Reynolds, J., and Mason, R. (2002). *How do people learn?* London: CIPD. Retrieved 8 January 2022 from: http://www.cipd.co.uk/podcasts.

Dawdy, G.N. (2004). Executive coaching: A comparative design exploring the perceived effectiveness of coaching and methods. *Dissertation Abstract International Section B: The Sciences & Engineering* 65 (5-B) 2674.

Franklin, J. (2005). Change readiness in coaching: Potentiating client change. In M. Cavanagh, A.M. Grant and T. Kemp, *Evidenced-based coaching, Vol. 1. Theory, research and practice from the behavioural sciences*, pp.193–200. Bowen Hills: Australian Academic Press.

Kauffman, C.M., Russell, S.G., and Bush, M.W. (eds) (2008). *100 coaching research proposal abstracts*. International Coaching Research Forum, Cambridge, MA: The Coaching & Positive Psychology Initiative, McLean Hospital, Harvard Medical School and the Foundation of Coaching. Retrieved 5 January 2022 from: www.coachingresearchforum.org.

Kretzschmar, I. (2010). Exploring client's readiness for coaching. *International Journal of Evidence Based Coaching and Mentoring, Special Issue* 4: 1–20.

Lambert, M.J., and Barley, D.E. (2001). Research summary on the therapeutic relationship and psychotherapy outcome. *Psychotherapy: Theory, Research, Practice & Training* 38(4): 357–61. https://doi.org/10.1037/0033-3204.38.4.357.

Passmore, J., and Fillery-Travis, A. (2011). A critical review of executive coaching research: A decade of progress and what's to come. *Coaching: An International Journal of Theory, Research and Practice* 4(2): 70–88. https://doi.org/10.1080/17521882.2011.596484.

Singh, V., and Vinnicombe, S. (2005). *The Female FTSE Report.* Cranfield: Cranfield School of Management.

Steinber, B. (2020). Are you ready to be coached? *Harvard Business Review* 30 October.

# CHAPTER 3

# How can coaching help my performance at work?

Qi Liu

## Introduction

Multiple research studies have confirmed that coaching is an effective intervention to improve performance at both individual and organizational levels (see, for example, Athanasopoulou and Dopson, 2018). Coaching, when done well, enhances the knowledge, skills and abilities of individual employees, and also contributes to the positive development of organizational performance. But performance at work is a tricky concept, and varies between jobs and sectors. In what ways can coaching enable coachees to improve? This chapter will explore these questions, and aims to broaden our understanding around how coaching can help in the arena of performance improvement.

## Individual performance at work

People are the most valuable and difficult-to-control element at work. But they can also be the most important factors affecting business success. Developing a high-performance culture is the goal of most modern organizations. But as we noted, 'performance' is not as straightforward as we'd like it to be.

Performance can be thought about at three levels:

(i)   The individual level

(ii)  The team level

(iii) The organizational level.

Koopmans et al. (2011) reviewed the results from research across different sectors, and at the level of individual performance suggested the following four dimensions:

- Task performance refers to how well primary work tasks are completed
- Contextual performance relates to actions that support the technical core within the organizational, social and psychological environment
- Adaptive performance refers to an employee's competence to adjust to changes in a work system or role
- Counterproductive work behavior is activity that negatively affects the organization's wellbeing.

When combined effectively together, these aspects generated high performance at the individual level.

**Table 3.1: Four-dimension framework of individual work performance**

| Dimensions | Examples |
| --- | --- |
| Task performance | Work quantity, work quality, job knowledge, productivity |
| Contextual performance | Communication competence, leadership, organizational citizenship behavior, teamwork |
| Adaptive performance | Change management |
| Counterproductive work behavior | Absenteeism, being late for work, engaging in off-task behavior, theft, substance abuse |

(Adapted from Koopmans et al., 2011)

While coaching may focus primarily on the individual level, organizations are made up of teams, and ultimately what matters is how these teams collaborate to deliver organizational performance. Although the focus of this chapter is the individual, it's worth recognizing that coaching also contributes to the achievement of team and organizational performance. For example, the development of leadership behaviors will contribute to team performance, and working across the organization, collaborating with colleagues is likely to contribute to organizational performance.

## What is the process of measuring performance?

As we're seeing, there are different aspects to job performance, varying between roles, industries and national contexts. These each demand different tools to define, measure and track performance. Some examples are key performance indicators (KPIs) and metrics, which are ideal for roles where clear processes and tangible targets exist, such as in sales teams. But alternative measures such as attitudes or alignment may be more appropriate in more creative roles, like research and development, where setting a target for the number of new inventions would be counterproductive.

Thus, there is no simple, universal way to measure employee performance. In order to define an employee's performance given their specific role and organization, we need to consider the organizational vision and goals, the role of their team in the organizational structure, critical success factors, strategic planning and execution, and individual strengths.

## In what aspects of performance can coaching help?

Now we know the different dimensions of individual job performance and their relationship with the organizational vision, the next step is to consider how coaching can make a difference. As discussed in Chapter 1, coaching is not an instructional approach, but a facilitated learning approach, helping the coachee to discover from themself what works in a given task and context. And while there is no direct teaching of job-specific skills, coaching outcomes cover all dimensions in the individual work performance framework we discussed above. Numerous studies have proven that coaching helps to enhance performance in the aspects of goal-setting, productivity, time management, assertiveness, confidence, role-clarity, cognitive flexibility, learning and goal-oriented behaviors (Theeboom et al., 2014; Jones et al., 2016).

Secondly, research shows that the influence of coaching frameworks on objective work performance (for example, 360 feedback) is stronger than the impact on coachee self-reported performance (Wang et al., 2021). This is possibly because the aspects of performance improvement brought about by coaching are not easily quantifiable. Coachees will inadvertently improve some of their abilities through greater self-awareness and self-efficacy, and these competencies can sometimes be hard to prove through productivity but may be simply observed by other stakeholders (for example, in the case of increased confidence). That's what makes coaching so special. It doesn't give the coachee a direct knowledge boost like a training course, but rather makes the coachee a better version of themselves by stimulating their potential.

## How does coaching work to enhance performance?

Research over the last 20 years has equipped coaching with a solid theoretical foundation from psychology, which helps us to understand the mechanisms of coaching interventions. Coaching practitioners borrow a collection of psychological theories to support their coaching practices. These theories include goal-setting (Locke and Latham, 2019), self-determination (Ryan and Deci, 2000), self-regulation (Berkman, 2016), grit (Duckworth et al., 2007), self-efficacy (Bandura, 2000) and cross-cultural competence (Bennett, 2013). Table 3.2 describes how coaching draws on these theories to help to enhance different aspects of performance.

**Table 3.2: Psychological theories, coaching and performance**

| Psychological theories | Theories in practice | Examples of outcome/ performance |
| --- | --- | --- |
| Goal-setting (Locke and Latham, 2019) | Support on search for and definition of goals; planning of and support for their achievement, as well as their adjustment and evaluation | Goal-setting, planning |
| Self-determination (Ryan and Deci, 2000) | Working with/activating intrinsic motivation to fulfil needs and increase individual engagement and satisfaction | Productivity |
| Self-regulation (Berkman, 2016) | Coach supports the process of successful self-regulation (planning, implementation, evaluation and adaptation of action to achieve goals) | Time management, assertiveness |
| Grit (Duckworth et al., 2007) | Four assets to increase grit: interest, practice, meaning-fulness (intrinsic motivation) and confidence | Confidence |

| Psychological theories | Theories in practice | Examples of outcome/ performance |
| --- | --- | --- |
| Self-efficacy (Bandura, 2000) | Coaching helps, for example, to increase the perception of competencies, and to integrate mastery experiences and physical and affective states to increase self-efficacy | Self-efficacy |
| Cross-cultural competence (Bennett, 2013) | Facilitates acquisition of intercultural competence and understanding cultural differences | Awareness of DE&I |

## Does coaching always work to enhance performance?

It's important to keep in mind that no intervention is 'fairy dust', useful on all occasions. In order to maximize the role of coaching to improve employee performance, the coach and coachee need to agree realistic goals. Coaching can have a negative impact on job performance if the coachee establishes unrealistic goals or lacks motivation (Bozer et al., 2013). This means that coaching goals must be realistic. While they should be a stretch, they should not be too tough to attain, and should remain relevant to the coachee's motivation, with the opportunity to review and revise goals as the journey progresses. Finally, they must also be appropriate for a facilitative intervention which is about contextual deployment of a skill, as opposed to learning a new skill.

## Conclusion

In this chapter, we have discussed the different dimensions of job performance and how coaching can help. By making use of research and psychological theories, coaching can help the coachee to maximize the positive outcomes. At the same time, we need always to keep in mind that coaching interventions are only one of many useful interventions in organizations, and make the greatest difference when used at the right time, as part of a wider learning and development strategy.

## References

Athanasopoulou, A., and Dopson, S. (2018). A systematic review of executive coaching outcomes: Is it the journey or the destination that matters the most? *Leadership Quarterly* 29(1): 70–88. https://doi.org/10.1016/j.leaqua.2017.11.004.

Bandura, A. (2000). Self-efficacy: The foundation of agency. *Control of human behavior, mental processes, and consciousness: Essays in honor of the 60th birthday of August Flammer*, 16.

Bennett, M. (2013). *Basic concepts of intercultural communication: Paradigms, principles, & practices*. Boston: Intercultural Press.

Berkman, E.T. (2016). Self-regulation training. *Handbook of self-regulation: Research, theory, and applications*, 440–57.

Bozer, G., Sarros, J.C., and Santora, J.C. (2013). The role of coachee charac-teristics in executive coaching for effective sustainability. *Journal of Management Development* 32(3): 277–94.

Duckworth, A.L., Peterson, C., Matthews, M.D., and Kelly, D.R. (2007). Grit: Perseverance and passion for long-term goals. *Journal of Personality and Social Psychology* 92(6): 1,087–101. https://doi.org/10.1037/0022-3514.92.6.1087.

Jones, R.J., Woods, S.A., and Guillaume, Y.R.F. (2016). The effectiveness of workplace coaching: A meta-analysis of learning and performance outcomes from coaching. *Journal of Occupational and Organizational Psychology* 89(2): 249–77. https://doi.org/10.1111/joop.12119.

Koopmans, L., Bernaards, C.M., Hildebrandt, V.H., Schaufeli, W.B., de Vet Henrica, C.W., and van der Beek, A.J. (2011). Conceptual frameworks of individual work performance: A systematic review. *Journal of Occupational & Environmental Medicine* 53(8): 856–66. https://doi.org/10.1097/JOM.0b013e318226a763.

Locke, E.A., and Latham, G.P. (2019). The development of goal setting theory: A half century retrospective. *Motivation Science* 5(2): 93.

Ryan, R.M., and Deci, E.L. (2000). Self-determination theory and the facilitation of intrinsic motivation, social development, and well-being. *American Psychologist*, 67.

Theeboom, T., Beersma, B., and van Vianen, A.E.M. (2014). Does coaching work? A meta-analysis on the effects of coaching on individual level outcomes in an organizational context. *Journal of Positive Psychology* 9(1): 1–18. https://doi.org/10.1080/17439760.2013.837499.

Wang, Q., Lai, Y.-L., Xu, X., and McDowall, A. (2021). The effectiveness of workplace coaching: A meta-analysis of contemporary psychologically informed coaching approaches. *Journal of Work-Applied Management*. https://doi.org/10.1108/JWAM-04-2021-0030.

# CHAPTER 4

# How can coaching help my health and wellbeing?

Jule Deges

## Introduction

Wellbeing is of interest to everyone. We all want to be well, and we want to do well. Organizational leaders recognized the connection between wellbeing and performance as early as the nineteenth century. Titus Salt created a model village for his workers, with a library to improve their learning, high standards of sanitation and no public houses (to reduce alcohol consumption and accidents when operating equipment). The ideas of the early pioneers of workplace wellbeing have become mainstream. Most organizations now invest in the health and wellbeing of their employees through a variety of interventions, from gym membership to employee assistance programs and coaching. In this chapter, we will explore what health and wellbeing is, and how coaching might help contribute towards healthier and happier work.

## What is health and wellbeing?

Before we look at how coaching can contribute towards health and wellbeing, it is important to first explore what we mean by these terms. According to the World Health Organization, "health is a state of complete physical, mental and social wellbeing and not merely the absence of disease or infirmity. Mental health is [thus] a state of wellbeing in which an individual realizes his or her own abilities, can cope with the normal stresses of life, can work productively and is able to make a contribution to his or her community" (WHO, 2018).

Rather than see mental wellness as an either/or, it's more helpful to view mental wellbeing as a continuum. A useful tool to help us understand where someone sits on this continuum is the wellbeing and engagement framework

(Grant et al., 2010). The framework consists of a mental-health dimension and a workplace-engagement dimension. The ideal state is considered to be in the top-right quadrant, 'Thriving' (see Chapter 27: 'When should we use counseling or occupational health rather than coaching?' for more details).

**Figure 4.1: Mental wellbeing and engagement**

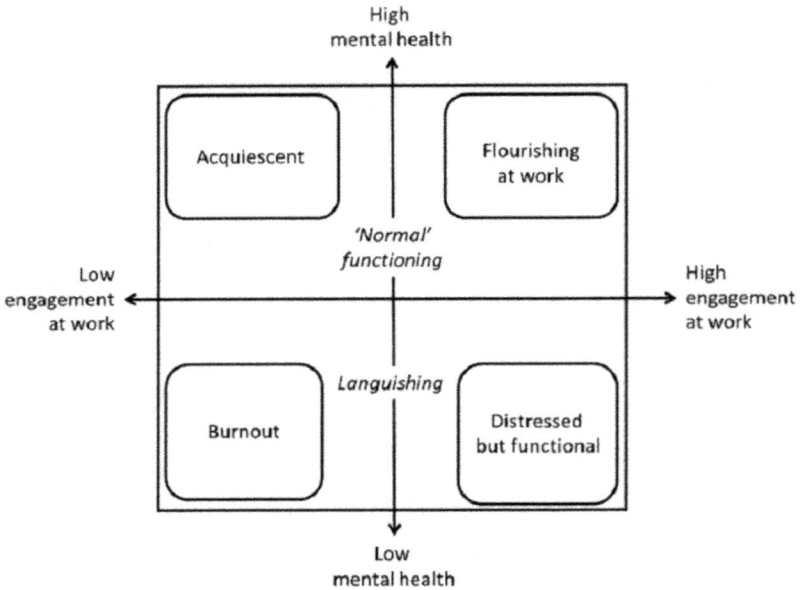

(Adapted from Grant et al., 2010)

So, how can individuals achieve a state of thriving? Seligman's (2012) PERMA model offers one way to progress towards this state. The model captures the following five domains, which individually and in combination have positive effects on wellbeing outcomes:

- Positive emotion

- Engagement

- Relationships

- Meaning

- Accomplishment.

More recently, others have added the element of health (PERMA-H) to the model, which expands the notion of wellbeing to include important aspects of physical health, such as good sleep, nutrition and physical exercise.

We know from research that wellbeing interventions are most effective when the person–activity fit is high (Lyubomirsky and Layous, 2013). Working with a coach is a highly individualized and targeted intervention that will allow the coachee to focus on their growth and move closer towards a state of thriving.

## How might coaching help a coachee in experiencing more positive emotions and fewer negative emotions?

Positive emotions are linked to a number of desirable wellbeing outcomes, including optimism, self-efficacy, prosocial behavior, physical wellbeing and effective coping with challenge and stress (Lyubomirsky et al., 2005). Coaching can help identify ways in which we can experience more positive emotions. One example is the practice of gratitude, which has been found to be strongly related to all aspects of wellbeing (Wood et al., 2010). Practicing gratitude can be an active element during a coaching conversation, and the coach can help build a habit of gratitude by inviting you to undertake tasks between sessions (see Chapter 12: 'Why does my coach invite me to do work between sessions?'). Examples of this might include the 'three good things' exercise (Passmore and Oades, 2016a) or a 'gratitude visit' (Passmore and Oades, 2016b; Passmore et al., 2021).

Coaching can also help decrease negative emotions. Practices such as acceptance and commitment coaching and self-compassion can help the coachee to be more accepting of them, and to let go of negative thoughts and emotions. Examples might include 'Sky and Weather' or 'Leaves in a Stream' (Passmore et al., 2021).

## How might coaching help me in increasing my engagement?

Engagement, as defined by Schaufeli et al. (2006), is a state of wellbeing in the work context characterized by vigor, dedication and absorption. Engagement has much in common with flow, a state in which we find ourselves fully engaged by the task and time passes without awareness. In order to have more experiences of flow and to increase engagement at work, the coach might work to explore the coachee's personal strengths, helping them to make best use of them in the role. Alternatively, the coach might explore the coachee's values with them, checking their alignment and resonance with how they perceive their role.

## How might coaching help me in developing positive relationships?

Relatedness is one of our basic psychological needs as human beings (Ryan and Deci, 2000), and the quality of our social relationships is one of the most important predictors of wellbeing (Diener and Seligman, 2002). At the workplace, colleagues and in particular positive supervisor–employee relationships can be a source of meaning, and an anchor of support and comfort during stressful times. Coaching can help coachees identify and nurture positive relationships that give them stronger feelings of vitality, positive regard and mutuality (Dutton, 2003). A coach might explore the coachee's role and help them to make sense of it, and to better understand their network of support and how they can foster this within a workplace context.

## How might coaching help me in developing meaning in the work that I do?

As the world of work continues to undergo change, this offers both challenges and opportunities for employees to re-think their relationship to work. Individuals who report a high presence of meaning in their lives and work are more likely to report higher levels of wellbeing. Conversely, a lack of meaning is correlated with negative emotions, such as high anxiety and even depression (Steger et al., 2006). In other words, knowing what makes their work and life meaningful is an important factor in a person's health and wellbeing. Coaching can help coachees appreciate how they bring value to their role, enabling them to build a stronger sense of meaning and purpose. Ways of doing this include using techniques such as the meaningful photos exercise and personal values exploration.

## How might coaching help me in reaching my goals and feeling accomplished?

The process of goal-setting and goal attainment sits at the very heart of the coaching process and is linked to greater performance and also greater wellbeing. Research shows that the process of goal pursuit alone, reaching small steps and achievements along the way of goal attainment, is linked to greater wellbeing (Lyubomirsky, 2008). So coaching can help individuals achieve goals, and in doing so, contribute to improved wellbeing.

## How might coaching help me in taking care of my body?

Physical activity, balanced nutrition and sleep have all been linked to a number of positive wellbeing outcomes, such as positive emotions and cognitive functioning (for example, Hefferon and Mutrie, 2012). Coaches, while not trained as mental-health specialists or therapists, can help individuals to think about these aspects of their lives and, as with other aspects, develop a personal plan which contributes towards improved sleep, improved diet and greater physical activity.

## Conclusion

Each person may have their own wellbeing challenges. The coach can work with the individual to help them identify their goals and then, using a range of evidence-based approaches, help the individual to plan, prioritize and implement their plan to move towards a state of thriving.

## References

Diener, E., and Seligman, M.E.P. (2002). Very Happy People. *Psychological Science* 13(1): 81–4. https://doi.org/10.1111/1467-9280.00415.

Dutton, J. (2003). *Energize Your Workplace: How to Create and Sustain High-Quality Connections at Work*. Jossey-Bass.

Grant, A., Passmore, J., Cavanagh, M., and Parker, H. (2010). The State of Play in Coaching Today: A Comprehensive Review of the Field. *International Review of Industrial and Organizational Psychology* 25. https://doi.org/10.1002/9780470661628.

Hefferon, K., and Mutrie, N. (2012). Physical Activity as a 'Stellar' Positive Psychology Intervention. In E. Acevedo (ed.), *The Oxford Handbook of Exercise Psychology*. Oxford University Press. https://doi.org/10.1093/oxfordhb/9780195394313.013.0007.

Lyubomirsky, S. (2008). *The how of happiness: A scientific approach to getting the life you want*. Penguin Press.

Lyubomirsky, S., King, L., and Diener, E. (2005). The benefits of frequent positive affect: does happiness lead to success? *Psychological Bulletin* 131(6): 803–55. https://doi.org/10.1037/0033-2909.131.6.803.

Lyubomirsky, S., and Layous, K. (2013). How do simple positive activities increase well-being? *Current Directions in Psychological Science* 22(1): 57–62. https://doi.org/10.1177/0963721412469809.

Passmore, J., Day, C., Flower, J., Grieve, M., and Moon, J. (2021). *We coach: The complete handbook of tools, techniques, experiments and frameworks for personal and team development.* London: Libri.

Passmore, J., and Oades, L.G. (2016a). Positive psychology coaching techniques: Three good things. *Coaching Psychologist* 12(2): 77–8.

Passmore, J., and Oades, L.G. (2016b). Positive psychology coaching techniques: Gratitude. *Coaching Psychologist* 12(1): 43–5.

Ryan, R., and Deci, E. (2000). Self-determination theory and the facilitation of intrinsic motivation, social development, and well-being. *American Psychologist* 55(1): 68–78. https://doi.org/10.1037/0003-066X.55.1.68.

Schaufeli, W.B., Bakker, A.B., and Salanova, M. (2006). The measurement of work engagement with a short questionnaire: A cross-national study. *Educational and Psychological Measurement* 66(4): 701–16. https://doi.org/10.1177/0013164405282471.

Seligman, M.E. (2012). *Flourish: A visionary new understanding of happiness and well-being.* New York, NY: Atria Paperback.

Steger, M.F., Frazier, P., Oishi, S., and Kaler, M. (2006). The meaning in life questionnaire: Assessing the presence of and search for meaning in life. *Journal of Counseling Psychology* 53(1): 80–93. https://doi.org/10.1037/0022-0167.53.1.80.

WHO (2018) Mental health: Strengthening our response. Retrieved 20 May 2022 from: https://www.who.int/news-room/fact-sheets/detail/mental-health-strengthening-our-response.

Wood, A., Froh, J., and Geraghty, A. (2010). Gratitude and well-being: A review and theoretical integration. *Clinical Psychology Review* 30: 890–905. https://doi.org/10.1016/j.cpr.2010.03.005.

CHAPTER 5

# When is coaching the best choice to help my personal and professional development?

Gill Tanner

## Introduction

Coaching is a powerful form of development. Numerous research studies have shown how it can contribute to new behaviors and mindsets. But how can we get the most from coaching to achieve these benefits? In this chapter, we will explore how coachees can use coaching alongside other developmental approaches to help achieve their personal and professional development goals.

## Personal and professional development

Coaching is one of a variety of different approaches. Despite the rise of coaching, training remains the most popular approach for development. Training is most effective when the individual wishes to acquire new knowledge, including everything from technical knowledge to the organization's recruitment processes or what to do in the event of a fire. Many organizations will have an active annual training catalog and a training policy outlining how training can be accessed.

Alongside training, mentoring is another popular tool. This involves a more experienced individual providing advice and guidance, usually through an informal relationship, sometimes extending over a significant period of time. Mentoring is excellent at helping people navigate their careers, supporting their progress in a specific sector or discipline, or in understanding how to navigate a particular organization. Evidence suggests that mentoring is also highly effective for supporting underrepresented groups to overcome sector or organizational inequalities (Tong and Kram, 2012; see also Chapter 25: 'When should we use coaching rather than mentoring?').

Many have also recognized the value of reflective practice, such as journaling. This approach can be taken alone, whereby the individual reflects on their day or week, focusing on a specific incident and exploring more deeply their reaction to it. There are many examples of structured reflective frameworks available, such as the Henley 8 (Passmore and Sinclair, 2021), which guide individuals through the process of reflection.

Coaching complements these practices, helping coachees to personalize and apply the theories taught in training. Coaching can also be used to help build on reflective insights to develop personal plans of action, while also challenging and supporting coachees as they seek to implement these new plans and test out new ways of being. As we have already discussed in this book, coaching is less about advice, and more about the individual discovering for themself the best approach to take. This is particularly helpful when the changes required are at an unconscious, mindset level; it's one thing to be taught a good model for providing feedback, and quite another to be good at it. With that in mind, let's look at how to use coaching in more detail.

## How do I use coaching?

Coaching can be used in a variety of ways. It might:

- Help coachees develop leadership skills such as delegation, communication and conflict management

- Help develop general skills such as problem-solving, time management and network building

- Help challenge thought patterns, develop new mindsets, overcome limiting beliefs and self-doubt, and enhance self-awareness.

In exploring professional development goals, a good place for the individual to start is to think about how they would like to grow as a professional, and for what purpose. Are they looking for promotion, to change careers or to perform better in their current role? The coach can help them assess where they are now and where they would like to be, breaking this down into goals and identifying ways to monitor progress and stay on track. It may be that they haven't yet crystallized their thinking in terms of career aspirations, in which case the coach can help them understand this too.

One useful tool when initiating coaching is a strengths questionnaire, such as the VIA Survey of Character Strengths or CliftonStrengths, which can provide a helpful structure for considering how to optimize the use of personal strengths. This could be supported by an understanding of personal values, using tools such as the Barrett Values Centre Personal Values Assessment. Using coaching to get to grips with how our values influence our emotions and behavior can help in deepening our self-awareness, and also helping align our career goals and personal values.

Once we have an idea of our destination, we can set intermediate goals with our coach to move closer to the goals. We have offered an example in the table below. It's not unusual for people to work towards a career goal over 10 or 15 years. In fact, I have worked with clients who recognized that their ultimate goal would be 20–25 years away. In these cases, they needed to identify four or five main steps to take them towards each intermediate objective, and in each case determine a series of actions or plans to enable them to prepare for the next step in their journey.

In some cases, coaching may end up being less about linear, goals-driven actions and more about a coachee exploring themself and their worldview. At these times, coaching becomes more about the coach asking questions to deepen an understanding of the assumptions and beliefs the coachee holds. In these instances, the outcome is not an action plan, but a deeper understanding of the self.

In reality, success is largely dependent upon grit (Duckworth, 2016). You must be proactive in undertaking the tasks, and show persistence and determination to move forward, whatever the circumstances or events that present themselves along the way. If a coachee's goal is around a promotion, for example, being clear about why this is important to them will provide stronger motivation to achieve it.

**Table 5.1: Goals and milestone tracker**

| Goal | Become a team supervisor | Become section manager | Become Area Sales Manager | Become Sales Director |
|------|--------------------------|------------------------|---------------------------|------------------------|
| Time | 1 January 2024 | 1 January 2026 | 1 January 2031 | 1 January 2034 |

## Conclusion

Coaching is a useful tool when used to best effect. Coaching can play a role alongside training, mentoring and reflective practice to enable individuals to move forward towards personal and professional development. When used in the right way, it can become an essential ingredient to enable coachees to deepen their understanding of themselves, as well as develop action plans that best position them for success.

## References

Duckworth, A. (2016). *Grit: The power of passion and perseverance.* New York: Simon & Schuster.

Passmore, J., and Sinclair, T. (2021). *Becoming a Coach: The Essential ICF Guide.* Shoreham on Sea: Pavilion Publishing.

Tong, C., and Kram, K. (2012). The efficacy of mentoring: The benefits for mentees, mentors, and organizations. In J. Passmore, D. Peterson and T. Friere (eds), *The Wiley Blackwell Handbook of the Psychology of Coaching and Mentoring,* pp.217–42. 10.1002/9781118326459.ch12.

# CHAPTER 6

# How can I select the best coach for me?

Yu Dan Shi

## Introduction

The relationship between the coach and the coachee is one of the most important factors influencing the outcomes from the coaching assignment. A positive relationship contributes towards higher levels of trust and greater openness, enabling deeper and more meaningful conversation. But in a globally connected world which offers so much choice, how can individuals choose the 'right' coach for them? In this chapter, we will consider a few factors to consider, helping individuals navigate their way through the selection process, and avoiding pitfalls and errors which can lead to disaster.

## The coach–coachee relationship

Coaching research has identified that the relationship, or 'working alliance', is an important aspect of coaching (see Chapter 28: 'How can we help our staff to prepare for coaching sessions?'). The coachee needs to respect and trust their coach. The coach needs to feel they have the skills to support their coachee and needs to be committed to working in their coachee's best interests. These factors support the openness and trustworthiness which make for an effective partnership. But sitting behind this relationship are a host of obvious – and some not so obvious – factors.

## Getting to choose

In many internally managed coaching programs, the match between the coach and coachee is undertaken by the coaching program manager. It's not uncommon for a single coach to be introduced to the coachee, as their 'best fit'. The evidence, however, suggests that giving choice to the coachee is an important factor. Choice empowers the coachee to decide for themself who is their best fit, increasing their commitment to both the process and their individual coach (Tong and Kram, 2013). But how much choice is helpful? There is some evidence that too much choice is also bad. Research indicates that individuals overloaded with options suffer from "choice paralysis" (Schwartz and Ward, 2004). The coaching program manager thus needs to find the Goldilocks range: "not too few to restrict a genuine choice, not too many to create choice paralysis". The optimum choice range depends on the product but, for coaching, having between three and six coaches to choose from is the Goldilocks range for most people.

## Language and culture

A second factor to consider is language. It may seem obvious that the coach needs to speak the preferred language of the coachee, but linguistic skills need to extend beyond a competent grasp of a language. In a globally connected world, there are many coaches who speak English, Spanish, French or Chinese, who may be scattered geographically. But just speaking a language is not the same as being fluent in how the language is being used right now, today, in organizations in that country. The coach needs not only to have an understanding of words, but to be able to build a relationship with their coachee through a deeper connection, engaging in culturally appropriate humor, making use of culturally situated references from literature or sport, and able to draw on metaphor and examples from politics or current events. This deeper level of communication builds the feeling in the coachee that their coach understands them and the cultural context in which they operate.

## Time zone

The next factor is time zone. Having a coach based in a different time zone can present challenges. If the gap is small, calls can still take place at times required by the coachee and when the coach is at their most effective. But as the time difference increases, the available options to meet will decrease – or worse still, the coach will try to accommodate their client but turn up tired, and less able to function at the level that their coachee deserves.

## Sector knowledge

One factor often discussed is sector knowledge. Some coaching practitioners have argued that people can coach across different sectors, relying on the main argument that the coach is an expert in the process, not the content. Others, however, argue that while the coach will not be providing advice, it is helpful for the coach to understand the basic issues, language and sector norms. This may come either from having worked in the sector or from experience of coaching clients. Coaches can also bridge the knowledge gap by doing some basic research about the sector or receiving a good coaching debrief. This can be taken at face value or, when interviewing the coach, a coaching commissioner could ask some questions to explore the depth of their understanding about the current issues in the sector.

## Gender and race

While often unspoken, coachees seem to have a preference in terms of the gender and/or race of their coach. We often assume, rightly, that coachees want to be coached by people like themselves, but the evidence is more complex. In terms of race this seems to be the case, with Black and Asian coachees favoring people of color as their preferred coach. This matches evidence from mentoring, in which mentees in US-based research studies have identified racial identify as an important factor in their choice of mentor (Tong and Kram, 2013).

In terms of gender, a different pattern emerges. While women strongly favor women coaches, men also seem to favor women coaches, although to a slightly lesser extent. Of course, different geographical territories may observe different preference patterns, reflecting their own racial diversity and attitudes towards race and gender. What is most important is that each coachee has the ability to choose someone who is like them, or someone who is different to them, whether this is in terms of nationality, race or gender.

## Chemistry

The final factor we will consider is chemistry: the personality match between the coach and the coachee. This can be assessed through a questionnaire or through a chemistry meeting. For some people, being alike with their coach is important, helping them to feel understood. Others, however, may be looking for someone with a different worldview, who can bring a different perspective to the fore. Using an assessment coach-matching tool can help, but we often don't know this until we start the working relationship. Thus, the final factor is what I call the 'no-fault divorce' clause. This is the right for both the coach and the coachee to say 'thanks, but this is not for me', without any blame being attached to that decision. The coachee is then free to look again, and find someone who is a better match for them.

## Conclusion

Selecting the right coach is an important step in the process. While there are some obvious aspects about the type of coach that will work best with a coachee, taking into account some of the less obvious, but still important, elements will help the coachee to find the best coach for them.

## References

Schwartz, B., and Ward, A. (2004). Doing better but feeling worse: The paradox of choice. In A. Lindsey and S. Joseph (eds), *Positive Psychology in Practice*. Hoboken. New Jersey: Wiley.

Tong, C., and Kram, K. (2013). The efficacy of mentoring: Benefits for mentees, mentors and the organization. In J. Passmore, D.B. Peterson and T. Freire (eds), *The Wiley Blackwell Handbook of the Psychology of Coaching and Mentoring*, pp.217–42. Hoboken. New Jersey: Wiley.

# CHAPTER 7

# How should I approach my coaching relationship?

Valeria Cardillo Piccolino

## Introduction

The beginning of a coaching relationship represents, for many, the start of a journey of discovery. We get the chance to reflect on who we are and how we show up in life and at work. Before coaching, many people have never given this a second thought. Psychologists Joseph Luft and Harrington Ingham (1955) defined 'blind spots' as those areas of ourselves known to others but invisible to us. One important purpose of coaching is to shed light on these blind spots. In this chapter, we will consider how to make this relationship as effective as possible by developing a shared commitment to growth, establishing a clear purpose for the work, and being willing to be open and adopt a growth mindset.

## The ingredients of the coaching relationship

If you have ever organized an adventurous trip, you might remember the moment you decided where you wanted to go, the excitement of imagining the landscapes, the food and the general sense of discovery. During the trip you might have encountered difficult moments as well: confronting your own limits, the inconvenience of being away from home, the lack of control – all sources of frustration that contribute to the whole. Metaphorically, a coaching journey does not differ much from this type of experience. Starting a coaching journey can be an exciting, challenging and rewarding experience. Four key ingredients can help make the most out of this adventure.

*1. Commitment*

Commitment in a coaching relationship is the "intention to remain in a close relationship that lasts" which both members (the coach and the coachee) pursue with their time and energy (Jowett et al., 2012). In a coaching relationship, while the coach might sit in the driver's seat as they manage the process, the coachee is responsible for pointing out the way to go. The coachee sets the direction, provides the content for discussion and evaluates success. For example, the coachee will select the objectives for the assignment, choose a topic for each conversation, determine how they wish the coach to work with them on their goal, and decide how they evaluate their progress. It is essential that the coachee is prepared for the commitment this kind of relationship requires.

The bulk of the mental effort required from coachees is to approach the coaching journey with a so-called 'growth mindset'. Carol Dweck, who coined the term, studied thousands of children in a learning environment to come up with the distinction between fixed and growth mindsets. The underlying belief of students who thought they could improve their skills and become smarter was a powerful engine inducing extra commitment in their learning process and, consequently, better results. This is exactly what happens during a coaching journey, in which the mental effort required of coachees is to overcome those limiting beliefs that are preventing them from learning, growing, changing or simply living the same situation from a different perspective.

The role of the coach, in contrast, is to support and challenge by asking open questions, listening, reflecting and, at times, disrupting the coachee's thinking. The coach will select different models, frameworks and tools based on their training, experience and intuition to facilitate the coachee in developing new insights about themselves and also moving towards their goals.

Misalignment of expectations can result in frustration or disappointment from the coachee. If they expect an expert who will give advice, make suggestions or tell them what to do, this is not a coach's role. In such cases, the coachee may be better attending a training course if they seek knowledge about how to do something, or a mentor if they want guidance. The coach's role is that of an enabler, helping the coachee to reflect, to think for themself and to develop the muscles they already have.

Consequently, during the first session and throughout a coaching relationship, it is important to 'contract'. Contracting provides the opportunity for the coach and the coachee to discuss the relationship, clarifying roles, expectations and boundaries. During the contracting, in addition to defining issues such as confidentiality, the working method, the logistics and duration of the sessions, it will become clear that the coaching relationship is "an equal one, neither participant being superior nor subordinate to the other" (Wilson and Bressler, 2021).

## 2. Focus

A coachee with a clear idea of what they want to achieve from their coaching relationship is more likely to achieve something tangible; without a direction to travel, the journey risks becoming a directionless ramble. Anthony Grant goes so far as to say that "a goal-focused coach–coachee relationship is a unique and significantly more powerful predictor of coaching success" (2013). For the coachee, deciding the topic to focus on in their coaching journey might involve a discussion with their people manager. This can ensure the needs of both the coachee as an individual and their employer are reflected in the goals set for the coaching journey.

The questions that a coachee can ask themselves before starting on their coaching path might include:

- What is the area I would like to change?

- How would I like to act or feel differently?

- On which specific occasions would I like to act or feel differently, or obtain a different result?

- What would I like to be, feel or think at the end of my coaching journey?

- How will I know that it worked (what measures will I use to judge my success)?

- When do I want to have achieved this goal?

These questions prepare for the initial phase, but there are some valid and interesting variations on how a coachee might approach goals; they might not have a clear idea of the goal, or simply want to explore around an idea without feeling restricted. In this case, gaining clarity could become a goal in itself, creating a progressive development of new habits to improve a skill in the longer term, rather than limiting oneself to achieving a single, limited goal based only on one's present understanding.

A final note on the area of focus for the coaching path would be that it's important to consider whether the coaching is taking place within an organizational context, particularly if it is sponsored by the employer. In these cases, the coachee needs to understand the purpose of the program in order to consider the organizational objectives that form the basis of the investment.

For this reason, it can be useful to prepare the coachee prior to starting the journey "to define a 'learning agreement', which may include: company aims; business goals (for example, team, career); development areas; desired outcomes; any previous assessments/feedback".

### 3. Willingness to trust

At first glance, it may seem paradoxical to ask a coachee to prepare for this relationship by trusting the coach, and yet this attitude can have a significant impact on the results of the journey. The best coaching relationship is one in which the client feels both full acceptance and absence of judgment on the part of the coach. This is especially crucial when parts of the Self come to light of which the client may feel anxious or ashamed. According to de Haan and colleagues (2016), in fact, feeling accepted and understood, and moving into a relationship based on warmth and respect, are critical elements as much as good contracting and definition of goals.

Coaches can actively work towards increasing their trustworthiness and stimulating trust in the coachee by demonstrating competence, integrity and ability (Terblanche and Heyns, 2020). At the same time, the more coachees predispose themselves to be vulnerable with their coach and accept a good degree of challenge, demonstrated through openness to thought-provoking questions that shed light on new perspectives and awareness, the more they can benefit from the power of the coaching relationship to help them discover new solutions and enhance their potential.

### 4. Support network

Coaching results don't take place in a vacuum; coachees are immersed in a network of relationships, which will have an impact on the ease with which they can progress and change. As coachees are immersed in a system, engaging with a surrounding 'support system' will often help in progressing towards goals. Partners, colleagues, managers and friends can all be helpful resources that the coachee might decide to involve.

One of the best ways coachees can increase the impact of their coaching is to ask people in their network to hold them accountable for progress. Coachees can ask these 'accountability allies' to check in regularly with simple questions such as 'How is X going?', and to provide feedback on the behaviors or mindsets that are the objects of the coaching journey. For more information, see Chapter 14: 'How can a support team help me in making the most of coaching?'

## Conclusions

The coaching relationship is a complex and adaptive system (Cavanagh and Grant, 2006) co-created by both the coach and the coachee. The more a coachee approaches it with commitment, a sense of focus and a willingness to 'trust the process', enhanced by a strong support network, the more likely it is that the coaching journey will be transformative, with outcomes of meaningful change.

## References

Cavanagh, M., and Grant, A.M. (2006). Coaching psychology and the scientist–practitioner model. In D. Lane and S. Corrie (eds), *The Modern Scientist–Practitioner: A Guide to Practice in Psychology*, pp.143–57. Hove: Routledge.

de Haan, E., Grant, A.M., Burger, Y., and Eriksson, P.O. (2016). A large-scale study of executive and workplace coaching: The relative contributions of relationship, personality match, and self-efficacy. *Consulting Psychology Journal: Practice and Research* 68(3): 189–207.

Grant, A.M. (2013). Autonomy support, relationship satisfaction and goal focus in the coach–coachee relationship: which best predicts coaching success? *Coaching: An International Journal of Theory, Research and Practice* 7(1): 18–38.

Jowett, S., Kanakoglou, K., and Passmore, J. (2012). The application of the 3+1Cs relationship model in executive coaching. *Consulting Psychology Journal: Practice and Research* 64(3): 183–97.

Luft, J., and Ingham, H. (1955). *The Johari Window: A Graphic Model for Interpersonal Relations*. University of California Western Training Lab.

Terblanche, N.H.D., and Heyns, M. (2020). The impact of coachee personality traits, propensity to trust and perceived trustworthiness of a coach, on a coachee's trust behaviour in a coaching relationship. *SA Journal of Industrial Psychology* 46(1), 1–11.

Wilson, C., and Bressler, F. (2021). What is coaching? In J. Passmore (ed.), *Excellence in Coaching* (4th edition), pp.13–33. London: Kogan Page.

# CHAPTER 8

# How can I make the most of each session?

Laurène Mayer

## Introduction

Coaching sessions should not be seen as isolated interludes in the coachee's busy week, but rather as interdependent and part of a journey. In this journey, the coachee is an actor of their own development: their willingness to start the coaching, their proactivity and commitment throughout all the sessions are key to achieving their goals. In this chapter, we will explore how the coachee can make the most of each session by preparing before the session, taking full advantage during the session and extending the benefits of coaching after the session.

## Before a session

Engaging in a coaching path begins before the session. This time can be used by the coachee to prepare themself, mentally and physically, and also to prepare the session content. It also offers valuable time to reflect.

A coaching session is a privileged time for the coachee to refocus on themself and move forward in achieving their goals. Making this time sacred is therefore important to make the most of each session. Coachees could take the following four steps to increase the value they will get from coaching:

1. Choose the right timing for the session – The coachee should avoid booking sessions at times when they may feel pressured, stressed or tired, instead selecting times when they have higher levels of energy. It is also good practice to keep a minimum of ten minutes (more if possible) free just before the session, to have a transition time between the previous activity and the coaching session.

2. Choose a safe and peaceful environment – The coachee should choose a space without distractions, in which they feel comfortable and can express themself freely. If the coachee has arranged an online session from home, it's also important to ensure they set up their equipment to make best use of the session (see Chapter 13: 'How can I set up my home office for an online coaching session?' for more insights on this point).

3. Focus by disconnecting – Turning off all digital signals and notifications that could interrupt the session (email, phone, etc.) will also help ensure that the coachee remains focused. Any pings and ringing phones can act as a significant distraction when trying to think deeply about an issue, and can detract from the overall value gained through a coaching session.

4. Focus physically and mentally – Exercises that help to center an individual's focus can also be helpful. This can be done in a variety of ways, such as by initiating breathing exercises or doing a 'body scan', which Passmore (2017) says can be useful "to create the appropriate mental space for the session to come".

5. Reflect on the upcoming conversation – Once the coachee is calm and centered, they can gather several elements to effectively prepare for the topics to discuss. For example, they can return to the list of coaching objectives and the notes taken during previous sessions to take a step back and evaluate the path already taken. They can also review the exercises and experiments carried out between the previous session and the upcoming one, in order to extract all the learnings. Finally, they can recall their emotional state during the last days or weeks. This time of introspection will help the coachee decide what they want to share with their coach, and identify what the coaching outcomes should be for the session.

Getting ready mentally and physically right before a coaching session encourages complete preparedness, much like an athlete would warm up physically and prepare themselves mentally prior to a competitive sporting event.

## During a session

As well as getting prepared before the session, the coachee can ensure they make the most of each session through a few simple, disciplined steps. The attention invested in the coaching session itself can make a difference between a good session and a great session.

1.  Express feelings – As a coachee enters the coaching conversation, expressing how they are feeling can help them to begin forming their experience into words, and provides the coach with important contextual information.

2.  Define needs – On the basis of their preparatory work before the session, a coachee should share with their coach what they wish to work on. After a few clarifying questions, the coach and the coachee establish a session contract. The coach and coachee should reach an agreement about how they will work together and the respective roles they will play.

3.  Adopt an attitude of curiosity – To make the most of a session, the coachee is invited to adopt a posture of openness, and to have an open mind towards new experiences. The coach's role is not only to be supportive and affirming, but also to encourage reflection and exploration. To achieve this, the coach may need to ask challenging questions, which may touch the coachee deeply and could stimulate feelings of discomfort; the coachee should always feel these questions are generated from a place of positive intent within their coach.

4.  Consciously experience 'presencing' – Senge and Scharmer (2004) have highlighted the importance of presencing, a state of heightened awareness in which we connect to the deepest sources of self. This is a time of letting go, of deep listening, requiring the opening-up of mind, heart and will. If this state is hard to reach for the coachee, the coach can help them through exercises or reflection to connect with these deeper parts of themselves.

5.  'Meta-communicate' with the coach – Sonesh and colleagues (2015) found a strong relationship between a coachee's tendency to share information and their perspective on the coaching relationship. In order to have a productive session, it is important that the coachee raises any concerns, so that they can be openly discussed and addressed within the coaching session. On the one hand, doing so will help the coachee alleviate any tension they are feeling, and on the other hand, what happens during a coaching session can be a reflection of other situations which the coachee experiences in their everyday life, creating interesting material for the coach and coachee to work with.

6.  Define an action plan – Making commitments about what the coachee wants to do and experience by the next time they meet their coach is an important part of any coaching session. To help the coachee to craft action steps and commit to goals, models such as GROW can be useful (Whitmore, 1992).

**Figure 8.1: The GROW model stages**

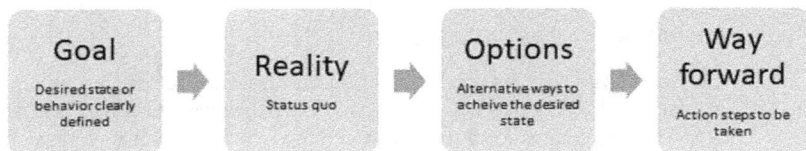

This last step is very important, because words have a performative dimension, and saying out loud one's commitments can help. In order to set a clear action plan, the coach might ask the coachee questions such as:

- What specifically are you going to put into action and when will you do this?

- What resources or support do you need to put into place to ensure you succeed?

- What is likely to stop you? How will you overcome this?

- Who will support you or hold you accountable?

## After a session

For coaching to have a long-term, sustained and significant impact, the coachee also needs to plan time after the session for reflection and action. Several steps can be taken after the coaching session.

1. Take a transition break – Similar to the way a coachee can prepare, taking a moment to pause after a session can also be helpful. This can take different forms, such as breathing exercises or reflecting on the session takeaways (writing down actions, insights and reflections). This is why many coaches leave time after a session for the coachee and the coach to reflect and capture insights. These reflections might also extend to reflecting on how the coachee feels, and why the session has provoked these responses. Some coachees find that a simple ritual helps to make a clear transition between the coaching session and their shift back to their day job. This might be as simple as making a drink and looking out of the window for two minutes, or going out for a short walk. This transition marks the calm of a session as different from the rush of the working day.

2. Evaluate the coaching session – With digital coaching in particular, coachees might receive short questionnaires immediately following the session, asking for feedback on several dimensions such as the relationship with their coach, the perceived usefulness of the session

and so forth. It is a good way for the coachee to take a step back and reflect on their session. It's also important for the coach to receive feedback on what the coachee found most useful, and what the coach could do to make the session even more productive next time.

3. Book the next session – When the coaching session is drawing to a close, it is important for the coach and coachee to arrange their next meeting. They might even include some notes in their diary about what they want to focus on, or thoughts from the session which has just passed, to help them connect next time.

4. Extend the work outside of the sessions – This is possibly the most important step. By sharing with a trusted friend or colleague their actions, plans or ideas, a coachee increases their accountability and enhances the chances of actions being taken. The coach might also invite the coach to undertake an exercise or some reading; the coachee should plan these actions in their diary, or set a reminder to help them check on their progress.

## Conclusion

The time before and after each session is just as important as the session itself in making coaching effective. If the coachee invests time preparing for each session and plans time after each session to draw out the insights and actions, coaching can offer a transformational experience, which produces sustained results. However, if the coachee sees the coaching as a remote island of calm in their day, disconnected from their everyday work and activities, it is likely the impact will be more muted. For this reason, investing time before and after each session, as well as committing fully to the sessions, are vital ingredients for an effective coaching session.

## References

Passmore, J. (2017). Mindfulness in coaching. *Coaching Psychologist* 13(1): 27–30.

Senge, C.O., and Scharmer, S. (2004). *Presence: Human Purpose and the Field of the Future, Exploring Profound Change in People, Organizations and Society.* London: Nicholas Brealey.

Sonesh, S.C., Coultas, C.W., Lacerenza, C.N., Marlow, S.L., Benishek, L.E., and Salas, E. (2015). The power of coaching: A meta-analytic investigation. *Coaching: An International Journal of Theory, Research and Practice* 8(2): 73–95. https://doi.org/10.1080/17521882.2015.1071418.

Whitmore, J. (1992). *Coaching for Performance.* London: Nicholas Brealey.

# CHAPTER 9

# Why should I have a contract with my coach?

## Elizabeth Pavese, PhD

## Introduction

With the internet boom in the late 1990s, the advent of social media through the 2000s and ever-increasing digitization, the way people connect and communicate has changed. The use of audio, video and text-based messaging provides a multitude of synchronous and asynchronous ways for engaging in a coaching relationship. This increasing flexibility for how and when a coachee can interact with their coach allows an even greater personalized approach for meeting coachee needs. However, this can present some challenges in negotiating the right boundaries between coach and coachee. In this chapter, we'll talk about the coach–coachee relationship and the importance of the contracting process, as well as explore potential questions that are key for a coachee to ask when entering a coaching engagement.

## Why create a coaching contract?

Establishing boundaries is a critical part of the coaching process. Having a mutually agreed contract can help us to do this and to ensure that coaching is positioned in a professional setting. If a coachee has been diligent in their coach selection and chosen an accredited coach, the coach will work within a code of ethics that informs how they will approach the relationship. These 'rules of engagement' will ensure a healthy and productive relationship. For example, one of the coach competencies outlined by the ICF is 'Establishes and Maintains Agreements', which sets out the way ICF coaches should work with their coachees (ICF, 2019).

**Table 9.1: Ways of working**

| ICF Coach Competency: Establishes and Maintains Agreements |
| --- |

| | |
| --- | --- |
| Establishes agreements for the overall coaching engagement as well as those for each coaching session. | 1. Reaches agreement about what is and is not appropriate in the relationship, what is and is not being offered, and the responsibilities of the client and relevant stakeholders. |
| | 2. Reaches agreement about the guidelines and specific parameters of the coaching relationship such as logistics, fees, scheduling, duration, termination, confidentiality and inclusion of others. |

A clear outline of what to expect through the coaching process, and a mutual agreement of what each party will bring to that relationship, helps to set the coaching relationship up for success. Specifically, outlining when and how communication should happen in and outside of the coaching relationship is extremely important to help avoid blurred lines. Coaching agreements, among many other benefits, do the following:

- Create clarity for all parties involved in an organizational context. When coaching is secured by a company, they are the sponsor of the coaching engagement. Here, contracts help to clarify the scope, the duties, and what can and cannot be communicated with the sponsor, while establishing the expectations on coach, coachee and sponsor.

- Foster greater trust and chemistry. Contracting enables trust to be built by emphasizing confidentiality (see Chapter 11: 'Are my coaching sessions confidential?') and reinforcing the roles of coach and coachee. Understanding and mutually agreeing upon the expectations of what each party will bring sets the stage for honest work towards achieving goals. It also helps to set the right expectations for the other.

## Defining coach–coachee engagement within the coaching contract

The coaching engagement is much more than what takes place during a coaching session. It should cover how to navigate the coaching engagement before, during and in-between sessions, as well as what happens after a coaching engagement ends. Once session frequency, duration and contact information are shared, there are other opportunities for communication that can arise. The following few situations are possible occurrences that a coach should outline in the contracting, and the coachee can ask about, to establish mutually agreed upon ways to engage.

- An emergency issue arising that requires a session cancellation or reschedule.
- The coach wanting to share information with the coachee.
- The coachee having a new insight or critical question in-between sessions
- A time-sensitive situation emerging that impacts coaching goals.

For all of the scenarios outlined in the coaching contract, coach and coachee should also agree on timing for a response. It is at the coach's discretion to set their own service-level agreements, and agreeing to these ways of working means there is a shared understanding between all parties.

## Does digital coaching lead to more blurred lines?

The advent of digital coaching has changed our ability to connect and communicate in near real time. As such, there is a more blended and dynamic way for coachees to be supported in their coaching journey. With options from telephone conversations to video-enabled sessions, and even email and instant messaging (via text messages or within web applications), coaching can happen in the moment, as well as in the session. With this in mind, is it okay for a coachee to communicate outside of the coaching session? The answer, of course, is: it depends.

Life is not linear, and the work that occurs in coaching doesn't stop when a coachee leaves the session. Issues can arise between coaching sessions that might call for additional support and exploration in order to move forward. Likewise, successes and progress will happen along the way, and a coachee sharing those achievements with their coach can be meaningful. A coachee referring back to the coaching agreement to identify what was agreed upon, then contacting their coach accordingly, is the right way to go. And it's important for coachees to acknowledge that even if a coach is not receptive, it's not that they don't care or aren't invested in the journey. It's their role to maintain objectivity and ensure that there is a healthy working relationship, not a dependent one.

**Table 9.2: Five tips for communications with a coach**

1. Check the coaching contract and review what was agreed upon.

2. Consider the context and issue of the situation that has emerged between sessions.

3. Be mindful of service-level agreements or response times when reaching out.

4. Respect when boundaries are held by the coach.

5. When in doubt, ask.

## Conclusion

A coaching relationship is a powerful one when there is trust and respect. A risk with a trusting relationship that is focused on helping someone achieve their goals is that over-dependence or blurred lines can happen. With a clear coaching contract that outlines agreed ways to connect inside and outside of the coaching sessions, coachees can be certain that they have the support they need, when they need it.

## References

International Coaching Federation (2019). ICF Core Competencies. Retrieved 1 February 2022 from: https://coachingfederation.org/core-competencies.

# CHAPTER 10

# What should I do after my coaching ends?

Windy Tshepiso Maledu

## Introduction

A coaching journey can be exhilarating and fulfilling, but coaching is a time-limited process, and the benefits should not stop with the final coaching session. Many coachees ask: what should I do next? How can I best continue my personal journey of development? In this chapter, we will first discuss the process of change, then think about how coachees can be sustained on their development journey into the future.

## Sustainable behavior change

For most coachees, the purpose of coaching is to help them make changes in behavior or thinking; although, over time, coaching can have an even more profound effect than on today's thinking and behaviors. Over time, coaching helps the individual develop a greater sense of who they are, leading them to take more personal responsibility for their lives, whilst also accepting the things they cannot change (Brent and Dent, 2015). As the coaching assignment draws towards a close, it's important to explore the learnings which can be applied going forward.

One way to think about this is to use a model to help us simplify the process of change. One commonly used model for understanding how we change is the Transtheoretical Model of Behavior Change, or TTM (see Table 10.1). This model suggests that when we make a change, we go through a number of stages.

**Table 10.1: The Transtheoretical Model of Behavior Change**

| Stages | Application to coaching |
| --- | --- |
| Precontemplation is the stage where individuals are unaware that their behavior is problematic or not as effective as it could be. In short, they don't know what 'better' looks like. | The coachee identifies behaviors from their coaching journey that they could improve. |
| Contemplation is the stage in which the individual is getting ready to change. | The coachee sets a goal. |
| Preparation (or 'ready') is where individuals are intending to take action in the immediate future. | The coachee identifies account-ability partners that can provide support along the way. |
| Action is the stage where individuals make specific overt modifications in modifying their problem behavior or in acquiring new healthy behaviors. | The coachee takes steps that drive positive behavior change, for example by writing actions in a place that will be visible each day. |
| Maintenance is when individuals have been able to sustain action for at least six months, and are working to prevent going back to the old behavior or habits. | The coachee asks for feedback from others to track progress, and support and accountability to help them overcome times when they might slip back to old habits. |
| Termination is the last stage and is where individuals feel confident that their new way of thinking/behaving is part of who they are. | This stage is not the end of the process! Future behavior gradually builds unconscious competence. |

(Adapted from Prochaska and Velicer, 1997)

## Continuously increasing self-awareness

Changes in behavior generated from coaching interactions often come about due to increased self-awareness, so let's now explore a tool that shines a light on how coachees can continue this process after the coaching has concluded. The Johari Window (Figure 10.2) is a model designed to help people better understand their relationship with themselves and others. The framework was created by two psychologists, Joseph Luft and Harrington Ingham (1955), who named it 'Johari' using a combination of their first names.

**Figure 10.2: The Johari Window**

|  | Known to Self | Not Known to Self |
| --- | --- | --- |
| **Known to others** | Open area | Blind area |
| **Not Known to others** | Hidden area | Unknown area |

(Adapted from Luft and Ingham, 1955)

The first 'pane' in the window is the open area, incorporating those aspects of a person known to them and also known to others, such as an awareness of one's preference for extroversion. It's also called the 'free area', the 'free self' or the 'open arena'. Following a coaching experience, the coachee can continue to increase this area through self-discovery, through disclosing appropriately to others and through asking for feedback.

The second pane is the blind area, incorporating those blind spots known to others but not to the person, like when someone has parsley on their teeth that other people can see, but they themself can't. This is an important area to reduce, as much as possible, through asking for feedback.

The third pane is the hidden area, also called the 'avoided self' or the 'façade'. This captures those aspects that the person knows about themselves that others do not know. For example, when a family emergency leads to a missed train and late arrival to a meeting, all good intentions remain hidden behind the effects of our actions. While concealing elements of ourselves can sometimes be appropriate for various reasons, it can often be helpful to reduce the size of this pane through disclosure.

The final pane is the unknown area, which covers those elements unknown to both the self and others. When a person's unconscious behaviors influence others in unconscious ways, the results become inherently unpredictable, which is not a helpful place to be in. This arena of mystery can only be discovered through adventurous exploration that pushes at the very edges of the known, for which coaching provides a safe space. After coaching has finished, a coachee continuously reflecting on the ambiguity of what they do not know, in combination with feedback and disclosure, can generate positive ideas around what else they need to learn.

## Practical actions following coaching

By considering these two helpful models, a coachee can develop an action plan to follow after coaching ends. This would begin with consciously adopting an ever-present mindset of continuously increasing self-awareness. Developing habits of self-reflection and self-observation are invaluable, as a coachee consistently self-reminds of what was discussed in coaching; the effects of coaching are often not fully seen until months or years after it has concluded.

A second step would be to identify accountability partners who can support, challenge and celebrate with the coachee. As Isaacson (2021) says, "When awareness and an attempt at effort don't have an effect, accountability tends to do the job."

A third step would be to recognize that forward is forward, no matter the pace. Trying and failing is not a final act, so a coachee should be kind to themselves when they 'fail', and be grateful for the small changes that they are making. Celebrating each milestone and self-congratulating on the fact that they're no longer where they used to be can serve as fuel for continued positive momentum.

## Conclusion

The challenge following coaching is to sustain behavior change. In this chapter, we have explored the Transtheoretical Model of Behavior Change and the Johari Window as tools that can enable the coachee to reflect on their behavior and deepen their self-awareness, increasing the likelihood that behavior and mindset change will be successful and sustainable.

Coaching as an intervention is coachee-centered, empowering the coachee to unlock internal and external resources to identify and maintain the desired change. The long-term, sustainable outcomes of coaching will always rely on the self-efficacy of the coachee, and with structured effort this is more likely to be achieved.

## References

Brent, M., and Dent, E. (2015). *The Leader's Guide to Coaching & Mentoring: How to Use Soft Skills to Get Hard Results.* New York: FT Publishing International.

Isaacson, S. (2021). *How to Thrive as a Coach in a Digital World.* London: Open University Press.

Luft, J., and Ingham, H. (1955). The Johari Window: A graphic model of interpersonal awareness. In *Proceedings of the Western Training Laboratory in Group Development.* Los Angeles: University of California.

Prochaska, J.O., and Velicer, W.F. (1997). The transtheoretical model of health behavior change. *American Journal of Health Promotion* 12(1): 38–48.

# CHAPTER 11

# Are my coaching sessions confidential?

## Naila Abdul Karim

## Introduction

Confidentiality is a key component in the coaching relationship. Coaches are taught to respect the confidentiality of the information which is shared with them. But what is meant by the term 'confidential'? Do we mean the coach treats absolutely everything as confidential or are there limits? Do all coaches work to the same limits? What are these limits and how does a coach manage them? In this chapter we will explore the nature of confidentiality, its limits and how coaches navigate the often complex and dynamic world of managing confidentiality.

## What is confidentiality?

In common language, 'confidentiality' means treating information shared with us as not to be shared with others. It's a common principle in counseling. It is also the cornerstone of a successful coaching relationship. Confidentiality enables greater trust, openness and insightful discovery between the two parties in a conversation, and thus facilitates deeper and more meaningful discussions.

## What does confidentiality in coaching mean?

Coaching is considered to be a safe space where a coachee is able to express their thoughts candidly and explore new possibilities without judgment or risk. This requires a certain level of trust for the coachee to be fully open, disclosing their weaknesses and their thoughts about possible plans. Without such trust, conversations can become superficial or limited in scope. The greater the level of trust, the more open the coachee – and the deeper the coach can work with them and enable truly transformational change.

In coaching, confidentiality is commonly explored while contracting. The coach is likely to make a specific commitment not to disclose information acquired through the coaching engagement, which includes the results of assessments as well as specific details about the individual coaching conversations. As a general rule, this information belongs to the coachee and would not be shared without their express permission.

This approach is endorsed by the main professional coaching associations and is enshrined in the two main global codes of ethics (ICF, 2017; EMCC, 2022). Accredited coaches can be held to account should they break these codes of practice.

## Why is confidentiality important in a coaching relationship?

A coach is responsible for ensuring that confidentiality is upheld during and after the coaching engagement. What's important to note here is that the confidentiality rule extends beyond the life of the coaching relationship, in perpetuity. Individuals can thus be assured that their personal information will not be shared.

The freedom granted by confidentiality enables the possibility for better insights. A coach can probe further to highlight potential blind spots, challenge the coachee's thoughts, actions or goals, and help them to identify potential areas of future growth and learning. Like in other aspects of life, these rules of confidentiality help the coach build trust, and create an environment of psychological safety.

## How are coaches being held accountable for confidentiality?

Coaches are held accountable through professional coaching bodies. The main bodies, such as EMCC Global and the ICF, have ethical codes of conduct that govern their members' coaching practices, and robust standards for investigation and resolution of complaints. Members can be struck off or suspended if their conduct is found to be in breach of these codes.

## When might confidentiality be broken?

A common misconception around confidentiality is that coaching is completely confidential, which cannot be true. Under certain circumstances, confidentiality can be broken. These limits to confidentiality can generally be considered under three headings (Passmore and Sinclair, 2021):

- Serious illegality
- Where there is a serious risk of harm to self or others
- When required by law.

For instance, a coach may be compelled to disclose confidential information by a court of law, relating to a specific individual or incident. Professional coaches are obliged by their code of ethics to uphold the law in the countries and states in which they work, and thus must comply with such an order, even when not a resident of that country. In contrast, great care is taken to honor confidentiality and not to provide information requested by a line manager, an HR manager or even the police unless backed by a court order (Turner and Passmore, 2017).

The coach may also have a legal responsibility to break confidentiality in cases of serious illegal activity, for example insider dealing, financial fraud or money laundering. Serious illegality may be considered to be where the unlawful act carries a custodial sentence in the state or country. Thankfully these are rare events, but they have happened in the past.

The third criteria where confidentiality may need to be broken is in cases where there is a risk of serious harm to an individual. Such circumstances might involve where children or vulnerable people are being abused, for example in a children's or care home, or where there is a risk of harm to the coachee, for example if the individual is talking actively about taking their own life.

In such cases, the coach needs to make a judgment about if, when and how to act. In most cases the situation is not clear-cut. The coach, for example, might discuss the case with the coachee, asking them for more information about the situation and encouraging them to disclose the illegality or risk issue themselves, through the organization's whistleblowing policy, to a regulator or to the police, depending on the individual circumstances. The coach might also discuss the case, in an anonymized way, with their supervisor. This is one of the reasons why coach supervision is recognized as an essential ingredient in high-quality coaching, as it provides a way to protect both coaches and coachees, providing space for reflection, advice and guidance.

There are often situations when the coach, with their supervisor, will consider the ethical implications of any action. In doing so, it is likely they will discuss with their supervisor the legal implications and the code of ethics, considering multiple perspectives before coming to a decision. This is one reason why having an emergency supervisor who is on call 24 hours a day, seven days a week and 365 days a year is important, as whilst such cases are rare, they are also unpredictable and may require immediate action to protect individuals. Given this, it's important that the coachee's organization is made aware of confidentiality and its limits, and that supervision should be part of the coaching contract.

## Different standards

Not all coaches work to the same standards, just as not all coaches are accredited by a professional body or have committed to following a code of ethics. Coachees should raise with their coach which professional body they are accredited with, which code of ethics they follow and what their approach is to coaching ethics.

There are some coaches in operation today who openly discuss the names and details of their clients. There are some digital coaching platforms outside of Europe recording all coaching calls as part of their approach to conversational analytics. Only by asking the coach or the digital coaching platform what their policy is can one find out what is happening. In Europe, data-privacy regulations make such practices illegal without explicit, opt-in consent from coach and coachee. For coachees, it is important to ask and find out how the provider is treating their data and what they mean when the say "it's confidential".

## What to do if your coach breaches the confidentiality rules

Coachees have the right to complain to the coaching provider and to the professional body. Most providers and professional bodies have procedures to manage complaints (EMCC, 2022; ICF, 2017). In the first instance, the coachee can raise the complaint directly with the coach or with the coaching provider. This may lead to the coach being removed from the coaching directory, and in more serious cases being referred to the coach's professional body, who can also take action, including suspending or removing the coach's accreditation or coach credentials. Most professional bodies publish a report each year on complaints. While such cases are rare, it is important to know that coaches, as professionals, just like doctors and lawyers, can be held accountable for their actions.

## Conclusion

Confidentiality is a crucial aspect of any successful coaching relationship. It is important for the coach to set up a coaching contract that clearly states what confidentiality means and the exceptions when confidentiality may be broken, and for coachees to explore during the contracting phase what the coach means by confidentiality.

## References

EMCC (2022). EMCC Complaints Procedure. Retrieved 10 January 2022 from: https://emccuk.org/Public/About/Policies/Complaints_Procedure.aspx.

ICF (2017). ICF Complaints Procedure. Retrieved 10 January 2022 from: https://coachingfederation.org/app/uploads/2017/12/ECRProcess.pdf.

Passmore, J., and Sinclair, T. (2021). *Becoming a Coach: The Essential ICF Guide*. Berlin: Springer.

Turner, E., and Passmore, J. (2017). *Confidentiality, record keeping and ethical decision making: What to do when the police come calling?* Conference Paper: EMCC Conference, Edinburgh, 1–3 March 2017.

# CHAPTER 12

# Why does my coach invite me to do work between sessions?

Patrick Rütten

## Introduction

Organizations may have the best intentions of providing their people with access to the development opportunities they deserve, but such desires are balanced against workload, cost and responsibilities. This results in a dilemma, a constant act of balancing the time invested in development for future readiness with the time available to get things done now. In this chapter, we will explore how coaching can stimulate development 'on the job', through the use of activities between coaching sessions, which together enhance the overall contribution of coaching to both future readiness and delivery of current objectives.

## Learning at work

As we explore the coaching domain and discuss it with our colleagues, we may come to wonder what coaching requires in terms of energy and effort. As with other development interventions, the amount of time that is invested may depend on multiple factors. For example, if we look at training, we start with a concrete idea of what a trainee should learn over the course of the program. We will also know how the training will achieve the desired results, as outlined in the number of training days, the breakdown of the syllabus, and the required reading. But what is rarely taken into account is the time taken to learn on the job, the additional time for conscious experimentation so that the trainee can apply what they've learned in the training environment to their real-world challenges.

The lack of these opportunities to apply knowledge to the real world is a significant factor in why training often fails to deliver, and is known as the 'transfer problem' (Baldwin and Ford, 1988). Without the time to reflect on the new knowledge, to set a plan to experiment, to reflect on its impact and to be both supported and held accountable, the new knowledge often slips through the learner's fingers like sand.

With coaching, the process works differently – for two main reasons. Firstly, instead of placing predefined learning objectives with the trainer at the steering wheel, coaching targets the specific needs of the coachee. Coaches do this by inviting coachees to set direction and limits, and by managing the pace and flow through a collaborative partnership. Secondly, the work between sessions is just as important as the conversation within the session.

The session itself might be spent setting or re-evaluating goals, exploring how one might bring about the desired changes and reviewing the consequences, benefits and risks of the options, but also discussing ways to apply these insights while benefiting from reflective and accountability mechanics. After the coaching session, the coachee ideally pursues opportunities to apply their insights and experiment with new behaviors, gaining new insights and awareness, which in turn lend themselves for potential revisiting in the next session – and so the cycle continues.

To harvest the full potential of the time in-between sessions, the coachee might be invited by their coach to explore complementary exercises or good-quality content from sources such as the *Harvard Business Review*, MIT Sloan or a TED talk.

With all these resources readily available, the challenge and key for coachees is to create sufficient time to engage with them, as well as to think about the new insights this material offers. Of course, the latter often forms part of the next coaching conversation, with the opportunity to discuss and discover learnings from both the content and its application in the workplace.

## Experimenting between coaching sessions

In a coaching session, a coachee is exposed to an interpersonal dynamic that is hard to replicate in a different environment. After the session, the coachee has the opportunity to use the real world to experiment and reflect. One way to look at it could be to compare it with moving from exercising with a personal trainer at the gym to working out alone for a period; the coachee has experienced deep self-reflection, and now needs to experiment and practice by themselves before returning for a check-in. The check-in reviews what was hard, what was easy, and what lessons and insights have been gained.

While the preparations during the coaching session are valuable parts of the process, in the real world the coachee is likely to encounter hurdles, barriers and challenges, as well as personal slips and relapses; a coachee's commitment to a change is not a guarantee that they will not return to their old habits after a short period of time. By helping the coachee identify these hurdles, they can anticipate them and make concrete plans to overcome them, and increase their acceptance that slips and relapses occur. This positions the coachee well to continue their journey.

With this in mind, it's also important to remember the valuable role that colleagues and others in the coachee's network can play. This network can support, encourage, challenge and hold the individual to account (see Chapter 14: 'How can a support team help me in making the most of coaching?' for more details).

## Why does this matter?

This in-between session activity is extremely important – in some ways, more important than the coaching conversations themselves. The reason for this is the temptation that can exist in some coaching conversations to drift towards the theoretical and abstract, rather than the tangible. A good coach should manage this tension, but even the most insistent coach will find at times that coachees will commit to actions and simply not follow through with them.

It can be helpful to think in terms of Honey and Mumford's (1992) unfortunately titled learning styles. While their original suggestion was that each individual has a preference for learning in one particular style, which is not backed up by evidence, the model still offers a helpful cycle of learning:

- Activist – During this stage, a coachee simply acts, perhaps trying out a new behavior identified in a coaching session.

- Reflector – In a follow-up coaching session, the coachee might discuss what happened and decide upon a new action to perform.

- Theorist – With a bigger population of activities to analyze, the coachee might identify patterns and construct a grander narrative around what other factors might be affecting their own behavior and the effectiveness of their actions.

- Pragmatist – Empowered by both their deepened awareness and experience, the coachee confidently establishes new, more effective habits.

## Conclusion

This chapter underlines the importance of undertaking activities between coaching sessions. These fall into two broad categories: knowledge acquisition and experimentation. The former provides the opportunity to explore new knowledge, reading and other sources of material to fill gaps in understanding or build upon existing knowledge, but doing so in a highly personalized way. The second provides the opportunity to experiment with new behaviors or approaches, and to reflect on these experiences, working with the coach to refine and incorporate these into a new way of being through a coach–coachee relationship that offers encouragement, support and accountability. By undertaking this work, the coachee ensures that the investment of time and money in coaching delivers the maximum value.

## References

Baldwin, T.T., and Ford, J.K. (1988). Transfer of training: A review and directions for future research. *Personnel Psychology* 41: 63–105.

Honey, P., and Mumford, A. (1992). *The Manual of Learning Styles* (3rd edition). Maidenhead: Peter Honey Publications.

# CHAPTER 13

# How can I set up my home office for an online coaching session?

Lisa Tomlin

## Introduction

Increasing globalization has led to an increase in the use of digital platforms for meetings and coaching. These platforms offer convenient, secure spaces for people to meet, with the facility to use supporting technologies such as integration to manage diaries, access to whiteboards and multiple other tools. In this chapter, we will review best practices for those setting up their home office to make use of online meetings and online coaching.

## The impact of globalization

The last few years have seen a continued growth in online platforms such as Microsoft Teams, Zoom and Google Meet, along with tools such as Slack and Mural. This trend was accelerated by the impact of the global pandemic since 2020. Most managers now use these platforms daily. They are highly familiar with the technology and the benefits it offers, from reduced travel time and cost, to more frequent opportunities for synchronous communications. Coaching too has gone online and most coaches and clients seem to prefer the convenience this offers (Passmore, 2021). For most managers, hybrid working has now become common, with many workers spending two or three days working at home and some now permanently working from home (WFH). But how much thought have people given to how they have set up their home office? What works and what should be avoided?

## How do I get going online?

In most workplaces, the employer will determine the digital platform, although sometimes we need to connect via other platforms to meet customers, suppliers or trade organizations. When it comes to selecting which platform to use, it's worth reviewing the market. While Zoom is perhaps the most universally popular choice, there are other providers too. A key consideration when deciding is to ensure that the online communications platform provides a stable and secure connection, and that all data is protected securely.

The next consideration is to check out devices, equipment and connection, and consider the following:

- All video conferencing relies on internet access, which can be unreliable if accessed through a mobile hotspot or even some wireless networks. The best advice is to connect via an ethernet cable, to limit the number of times the connectivity is lost.

- Particularly given the sensitivity of some coaching conversations, the connection should always take place via a private rather than public network. The use of a VPN (virtual private network, which encrypts the data from end to end) is best where possible, especially if the data is commercially sensitive.

- Some coachees may suffer from low broadband speeds, so activating airplane mode on mobile devices and either switching off or limiting any other connected devices in the home can maximize the bandwidth available for coaching.

- It's helpful to close down other communication software that may be running on the machine, such as email or social-media apps, in order to reduce interruptions.

- Using a separate, high-quality microphone and camera can be helpful if those built into the device are of low quality.

- Using an LED 'ring light' attachment to the camera can lighten the face of the user; this is particularly good if it replicates natural light.

- Using headphones is especially helpful to ensure confidentiality or if background noise might be distracting. On this point, full headsets that land somewhere between call-center operator and airline pilot can be visually distracting and introduce active audio compression, making the sound more intense and less dynamic; a simple, discreet earbud designed to be used with a mobile phone works well in most cases.

## Setting the scene

The next step is to consider the visual appearance of the video. What appears behind the person's head – for example, a tidy bookcase or a jumble of 'yet-to-be-organized' items – communicates something about the person. If in doubt, the various background effects and green-screen functions of video-call platforms help to create a neutral environment. These work best when in front of a flat surface like a blank wall, and the image selected will have an impact on the session. Light sources, such as a large window, directly behind the person on screen can turn them into a silhouette, while lights that are too bright shining onto a person's face can wash out the color and play havoc with spectacles wearers. Awkward camera positions can lead to poor posture, sending unintended visual signals and wellbeing concerns; sitting up straight, around an arm's length away from the camera works best. The optimal position means the viewer can see the eyes as well as the hands.

Eyes are important on a call as these often communicate our changing emotions. The amount of moisture, the dilation of the pupil and sustaining or breaking of eye contact all communicate messages to the listener. Even simply seeing the whites of the other person's eyes activates more advanced social intelligence (Aeria, 2016), giving even more reason for glasses wearers to pay attention to what any reflection might be doing to the look of their eyes.

Hands are also important, as most people communicate with their whole body, not just the words they say. Our hands communicate four broad types of messaging. 'Battle signaling', such as pointing or chopping actions, places emphasis on specific words or phrases. 'Illustrative signaling', such as using the gap between our hands, can help communicate size or illustrate differences, such as a growth in sales. 'Self-soothing', or comfort stroking, often undertaken unconsciously, can reveal anxiety or sadness in the speaker. Lastly, 'moderating signals' indicate to the listener when the speaker is finishing. These tend to be culturally situated, which partly explains why speaking with non-native speakers can generate more cross talk than we might find when speaking with colleagues who share cultural backgrounds (see Chapter 6: 'How can I select the best coach for me?').

Finally, while most laptop screens are arranged so they tilt back, coaching is much more about personal connection, and so angling the screen to be more upright can help build rapport. Repositioning a laptop on a stand or box brings the camera level with the user's eyes. Trying to ensure both parties can see one another's hands, arms and shoulders, as well as face, helps with non-verbal communication and will enhance the digital presence of those involved.

## Documentation

Before launching into an online meeting or coaching session, the following checklist may help ensure everyone is prepared:

1.  How long is the session or meeting? This may need to be reduced, given that concentration spans are more limited online.

2.  Is the meeting or session being recorded? Recording an event can be a really useful source of data. Some coaches like to record sessions to watch back and improve their coaching, just like call centers record all calls. If the session is being recorded, permission should always be gained first, in writing from the client, instead of this being an opt-out.

3.  Is there an agenda or any notes for the session? This allows for both parties to prepare appropriately.

## The coaching relationship

One of the key concerns for many is how technology may impact on outcomes. There is little research into online coaching, although much has been written about its potential over the past few years (Ribbers and Waringa, 2015; Berninger-Schäfer, 2018; Kanatouri, 2020). The few studies that have been published confirm that there is no difference between face-to-face and online coaching in terms of the outcomes (Berry et al., 2011).

To make online coaching successful, it can help to pay attention to some of the small details in setting up the session. The following are particularly important:

1.  Contracting – Agree with others to allow more pauses than in normal conversation, to ensure the person has finished speaking.

2.  Eye contact – Maximize eye contact by positioning the window containing the streaming video directly under the camera. When viewed from a distance, this gives the impression of eye contact.

3.  Silence – Silence can be impactful in negative ways online; it can sometimes be misinterpreted as a fault with the technology, or as an adverse reaction to what has just been said.

4.  Mute off – For 1:1 coaching sessions, hearing all sound is important. For larger meetings, clarify protocols around muting at the outset.

5.  Cameras on – Seeing faces makes it feel as if everyone is present and everyone is listening.

6.    Movement – Be mindful of movement, particularly when using a green screen. Excessive or exaggerated movement can be distracting, while no movement may make it appear as if the screen has frozen.

## Using online tools

Many platforms have embedded features such as mute, record, screen share, whiteboards and breakout rooms. There has also been a growth in supplementary tools, which offer more functionality than the embedded products, from multi-function whiteboards to diary booking systems and more. These can be useful features to research, to discover what will be most useful for meetings. As these tools are constantly changing, staying up to date and trying out new products as they emerge will ensure that the most appropriate technologies are available.

## Conclusion

The future of work has changed. Remote meetings and online coaching are here to stay. To make the best of technology, all users need to stay up to date not only with the psychology of operating in online spaces, but also with the technology that allows these spaces to become useful tools for everyone.

## References

Aeria, G. (2016). Why we show the whites of our eyes. *Go Figure*. University of Melbourne. Retrieved from: https://pursuit.unimelb.edu.au/articles/why-we-show-the-whites-of-our-eyes.

Berninger-Schäfer, E. (2018). *Online Coaching*. Berlin: Springer.

Berry, R.M., Ashby, J.S., Gnilka, P.B., and Matheny, K.B. (2011). A comparison of face-to-face and distance coaching practices: Coaches' perceptions of the role of the working alliance in problem resolution. *Consulting Psychology Journal: Practice and Research* 63(4): 243–53. https://doi.org/10.1037/a0026735.

Kanatouri, S. (2020). *The Digital Coach*. Abingdon: Routledge.

Passmore, J. (2021). *Global Coaching Survey: Future Trends in Coaching*. Henley Business School: Henley on Thames.

Ribbers, A., and Waringa, A. (2015). *e-Coaching: Theory and Practice for a New Online Approach to Coaching*. Abingdon: Routledge.

# CHAPTER 14

# How can a support team help me in making the most of coaching?

Eliana Gialain

## Introduction

Coaching processes are, in general, individual-centered development processes. But in order to deliver the best value, it can be helpful to think not just about the needs of the coachee, or even the coachee and their line manager, but also their wider system. This systemic approach can help the coachee in achieving their desired goals. In this chapter, we will explore how a professional and personal network of supporters – or a 'support team' – can help a coachee make their change more sustainable and also ensure it adds value to the stakeholder network they serve.

## The importance of the social environment and others' perception and support

While it's easy to think of ourselves and those we work with as individuals, we are all born into and belong in systems: networks of relationships and interconnected activities (Whittington, 2016). In fact, research on the impact of the social environment on emotional and cognitive abilities indicates that one's social environment can support wider competency development (Wheeler, 2008). This can be enhanced when we are able to work on our learning goals across multiple life spheres, allowing the coachee to see how learning in one environment can be applied in many environments. Further, coaching processes can also help us to better understand, and take into account, the views and perspectives of others. While the connection with the coach should be one of those relationships, coachees who have a wider support network are likely to gain most from the support, encouragement and accountability provided by this network (Boyatzis et al., 2019).

Research indicates the importance of considering the relational systems to which we as individuals belong. In the next section we suggest a structured way to involve others in coaching processes and, specifically, how a coachee can identify their support team.

## The support team

A support team is formed of people who have a direct or indirect impact on the coachee's development. It is a network of people who support the coachee in practical and emotional ways – people who can work as 'accountability partners', keeping the coachee on track in their development path. These support-team members can be identified in professional, familial and social environments. Here are a few places a coachee can look to identify potential support-team members:

- Current work environment: manager/supervisor, colleague, peer, internal client, colleague from other functional area that has interface with the coachee's area/activity

- Previous work environment: this could be colleagues the coachee no longer works with, or ex-colleagues; people who have worked with the coachee in the past and have a relevant perception of the coachee's strengths and areas for improvement

- Others within a professional network: particularly those who have been through similar challenges to those the coachee is currently facing, or have experienced further development in the areas they are focusing their coaching process on (for example, if a coaching goal is to change career, a potential supporter could be someone who has been through a similar process, even if this person is not part of the coachee's close network, but is reachable through a mutual connection)

- Family: partners, adult sons and daughters, parents, siblings, other relatives

- Others within a social network: friends, connections from learning programs, therapist, physiotherapist, personal trainer.

Reflecting on this list and identifying a helpful combination of diverse individuals to make a good support team is a great starting place. A coachee should be looking for a complementary group of individuals, maybe three-to-six people in total, who are committed to their success and will make time to discuss the coaching process. Next, we'll explore a practical, structured way for coachees to build their support team.

## Building a support team

Having identified a list of potential supporters, a coachee could follow the steps outlined here to build their own support team.

Step 1: Create a table to evaluate all potential supporters. Table 14.1 provides suggested questions to help a coachee decide who should and shouldn't take part in their support team on this occasion. Please note, the questions are suggestions and should be customized, perhaps with the support of the coach. In addition, support teams should not be considered static; they can change over time, depending on coaching goals and changing needs. It may therefore prove helpful to revisit this table at a midpoint during a longer-term coaching engagement, and each time a new coaching engagement begins.

**Table 14.1: Who should be in your support team?**

|  | Potential supporter 1 | Potential supporter 2 | Potential supporter 3 | etc. |
|---|---|---|---|---|
| Does this person's professional path resonate with mine? |  |  |  |  |
| Will this person be available for feedback sessions at the frequency needed for my development? |  |  |  |  |
| Will this person's strengths help me strengthen mine? |  |  |  |  |
| Do I admire them? |  |  |  |  |
| Have they spontaneously offered me support so far? |  |  |  |  |
| Is there any personal conflict of interests in having their support? |  |  |  |  |

| | Potential supporter 1 | Potential supporter 2 | Potential supporter 3 | etc. |
|---|---|---|---|---|
| Could there be harm in any 'no-compete agreement' at a company level? | | | | |
| Does this person have a good knowledge of my strengths and areas of development? | | | | |
| Can I trust this person to offer me candid challenge and feedback, and will I respond well to it? | | | | |
| Is this person a reference for me in the field area I want to further develop myself in? | | | | |
| SUM OF POINTS | | | | |

Step 2: Evaluate each potential supporter against the questions proposed. In doing so, the Likert scale may be helpful: (1) strongly disagree, (2) disagree, (3) neutral, (4) agree and (5) strongly agree.

Step 3: The individuals with the greatest total points at the end should be more likely to contribute to the coaching process in an effective way. With this in mind, the coachee can go ahead with contacting the individuals, and hopefully building a strong support team for the rest of the coaching process.

As Passmore (2021) puts it, what you are trying to create is your 'A Team', a group of individuals who are more than the sum of their parts when they come together to be supporters, champions, cheerleaders and accountability partners.

## How to get the best out of a support team

By completing the steps above, a coachee will have defined their support team. Considering the coaching goals, coaching session frequency and the whole coaching process duration, the coachee should plan in advance how they will engage their support team in building the conditions for achieving their goals in a sustainable way. They might want to create an engagement map, like the one shown in Table 14.2.

**Table 14.2: Engagement map**

|  | Supporter 1 | Supporter 2 | Supporter 3 | etc. |
|---|---|---|---|---|
| How should you reach out for the first meeting? |  |  |  |  |
| Is someone else's introduction needed? |  |  |  |  |
| Which coaching goal(s) will this individual help out with? |  |  |  |  |
| What indicators/evidence of your behavioral changes or further development will be agreed between you and the supporter? |  |  |  |  |
| What will the engagement's format be? (Phone call, in-person or virtual meeting, etc.) |  |  |  |  |
| What will the engagement's frequency be? |  |  |  |  |
| Will the engagement scheduling happen up front for the whole coaching process or after each coaching session? |  |  |  |  |
| Will this support continue after the coaching process ends? If yes, how? |  |  |  |  |

Particularly in the case of close relationship supporters, it is crucial to define engagement frequency and format, in order not to dilute the important coaching feedback they might provide in other interactions.

## Conclusion

Identifying, building and relying on a support team are key steps to take to get the best out of a coaching process. Supporters can help coachees in keeping the development journey alive outside of the coaching sessions. They also serve as an important motivation along the way, championing the coachee's behavioral change and being there to share their successes and challenges.

## References

Boyatzis, R.E., Smith, M., and Oosten, V.E. (2019). *Helping People Change: Coaching with Compassion for Lifelong Learning and Growth.* Boston, MA: Harvard Business Review Press.

Passmore, J. (2021). *The Coaches' Handbook: The Complete Practitioner Guide for Professional Coaches.* Abingdon: Routledge.

Wheeler, J. (2008). The impact of social environments on emotional, social, and cognitive competency development. *Journal of Management Development* 27(1): 129–45. https://doi.org/10.1108/02621710810840802.

Whittington, J. (2016). *Systemic Coaching and Constellations.* London: Kogan Page.

# CHAPTER 15

# Why should my coach have supervision?

Patrick Rütten

## Introduction

While the coaching industry has seen significant growth over the past decade and coaches have been working hard to support clients to improve both their performance and their wellbeing, a question remains: who is there to support the performance and wellbeing of the coaches? In this chapter, we will provide a review of the role of coaching supervision and why supervision is a critical part of the coaching process, ensuring that coaches have the support structures they need to support and care for their clients.

## What is coaching supervision?

There has been much discussion about supervision in coaching over the past decade, and it is now widely accepted that supervision has an important role to play, but what is supervision? Definitions differ, with professional bodies, practitioners and coaching providers offering their own views on supervision (Tkach and DiGirolamo, 2017; Hawkins et al., 2019); so in Table 15.1 we offer a range of different definitions. What can be seen from a review of these is that, while being there for the coach, supervision is ultimately aimed at the coachee and their individual needs and wellbeing.

**Table 15.1: Definitions of supervision**

Coaching supervision is the interaction that occurs when a coach periodically brings his or her coaching work experience to a coaching supervisor in order to engage in reflective dialogue and collaborative learning for the development and benefit of the coach and his or her clients.

(ICF, 2021)

On a 1:1 or group basis is the formal opportunity for coaches working with clients to share, in confidence, their caseload activity to gain insight, support and direction for themselves… thereby enabling them to better work in the service of their clients.

(Association of Coaching Supervisors [AOCS], 2021)

A non-hierarchical relationship between the supervisor and supervisee, supervision aims to enhance insights and to deepen the understanding of oneself and [one's] own coaching practice.

(Hawkins et al., 2019)

Coaching supervision is a formal and protected time for facilitating a coach's in-depth reflection on their practice with a Coaching Supervisor. Supervision offers a confidential framework within a collaborative working relationship in which the practice, tasks, process and challenges of the coaching work can be explored. The primary aim of supervision is to enable the coach to gain in ethical competency, confidence and creativity so as to ensure best possible service to the coaching client, both coachees and coaching sponsors. Supervision is not a 'policing' role, but rather a trusting and collegial professional relationship.

(Association for Coaching [AC], 2019)

Supervision is a formal, reflective and confidential process used by coaches, working with a qualified supervisor, combining support and challenge, to enhance the coach's confidence, competence and creativity in their practice.

(CoachHub, 2021)

## What are the benefits of supervision?

While organizations might often view the utility of supervision predominantly from a quality control point of view, it is important to point towards the further potential benefits. Hawkins and Smith (2013) propose three functions of coaching supervision: normative, formative and restorative. These functions respectively cover: adherence to ethical guidelines and standards; the maintenance and ongoing development of the quality of coaching work; and the provision of emotional support. Lines (2021) describes the following set of benefits of supervision:

- Protecting coachees (for instance, through case review)
- Offering opportunities for practitioners to reflect and pinpoint room for improvement
- Aiding practitioners in the identification of strengths and areas for development
- Informing practitioners about ethical and professional challenges in their work
- Examining tensions that arise from multiple stakeholders (for example, the company, the client and the profession)
- Evaluating the impact of one's work and how to process effects of the profession on personal aspects of life
- Providing an independent point of view (as the supervisor may be able to see clearly the dynamics that are at play from their third-person perspective)
- Accountability.

Acknowledging the broader spectrum of the value of supervision enables us to see supervision as a quality-control mechanism operating in the short-to-medium term, and furthermore as a developmental cooperation that benefits the parties involved and forms in the long term a basis for a healthy, sustainable industry with a trend of continuous development.

## What's involved in supervision?

Two of the main global professional bodies, EMCC Global and the Association for Coaching, require supervision as a regular development practice. The ICF has a more nuanced approach, but does acknowledge the value of supervision as part of a wider set of professional development activities.

Given the growing evidence of supervision as a force for good in coaching and its growing adoption among seasoned coaches and coaching providers, we believe that coaching supervision is vital to ensuring the highest standards of practice.

## What should you ask your coach about supervision?

Given the benefits for both coach and coachee, it is essential that all coaches are engaged in supervision practice. In Table 15.2, we set out six questions a coach could be asked about their supervision practice.

**Table 15.2: Six questions for a coach**

1. Do you receive regular supervision?

2. How frequently do you receive this supervision?

3. What accreditation does your supervisor hold?

4. What access do you have to your supervision team in an emergency (i.e. can you contact them and how do you do this)?

5. What have you learned from supervision over the past year?

Exploring these questions can give you the detail of a coach's support network, and whether they treat supervision seriously or merely as a tick-box exercise.

A coach should confirm they receive supervision, and depending on the type of coaching they do, they should have around one hour of supervision for every 30–65 hours of coaching practice. The more emotionally challenging the coaching, generally speaking, the more frequent the need for supervision. Roughly, around once a quarter to once a month is a good guideline. We also believe that, just like professional coaching, supervision should be delivered by an accredited coach supervisor. Both the AC and EMCC Global offer supervision accreditation, as do a number of smaller coaching bodies. The ICF does not currently provide accreditation for coaching supervision.

Unplanned events happen, so having a single supervisor who is not part of a team can be a problem. In the best cases, the coach should be able to speak to an emergency supervisor at any time, as urgent coaching issues can always crop up. Every coach will benefit from support and guidance from a more experienced practitioner.

Finally, it can be helpful to explore the insights the coach has acquired from their supervision. If they struggle to think of an example, this raises the question of what benefits they are receiving from it.

These questions can all be included as part of the preliminary discussion with a coach, and can also help ensure the right choice is made around continuing to engage with a coach.

## Conclusion

Supervision is an important element providing the support and developmental space for a professional coach. And supervision is not just for the coach; coachees also benefit from coaches who are actively engaged in supervision, so exploring this during the selection process will benefit the coachee, ensuring their coach has the right support processes in place.

## References

AC (2019). Definition of Coaching Supervision. Retrieved 20 May 2022 from: https://www.associationforcoaching.com/page/WhatisCcachingSupervision.

AOCS (2021). Definition of Coaching Supervision. Retrieved 20 May 2022 from: https://www.associationofcoachingsupervisors.com/supervisors/what-is-supervision.

CoachHub (2021). *Definitions, Processes and Models*. Internal Document. Berlin: CoachHub.

Hawkins, P., and Smith, N. (2013). *Coaching, Mentoring and Organizational Consultancy: Supervision, Skills, and Development* (2nd edition). Maidenhead: Open University Press.

Hawkins, P., Turner, E., and Passmore, J. (2019). *The Manifesto for Supervision*. Henley on Thames: Henley Business School, UK.

ICF (2021). ICF Definition of coaching. Lexington: ICF. Retrieved 3 January 2022 from: https://coachingfederation.org/about.

Lines, S. (2021). Supervision in coaching. In J. Passmore (ed.), *The Coaches' Handbook: The Complete Practitioner Guide for Professional Coaches*. Routledge.

Tkach, J.T., and DiGirolamo, J.A. (2017). The state and future of coaching supervision. *International Coaching Psychology Review* 12(1): 49–63.

# CHAPTER 16

# Where should I meet my coach?

## Jonathan Passmore

## Introduction

While many coaches operate as sole practitioners, others may work for coaching or consulting companies. Each has their preference as to where they offer to meet their coachees. Coachees too have their own preferences, although coaches rarely offer a choice. Yet choosing the meeting spaces is as important as choosing the right coach. Does the coachee want to meet online or in person? In what type of space do they want to meet? In this chapter, we consider the alternatives available for both physical meetings and online options. We will consider the pros and cons of each.

## Where shall I conduct my coaching?

There is widespread agreement that producing the ideal conditions for the relationship to develop involves meeting in a safe, comfortable space, removed from the distractions of everyday life and work. Nancy Kline recommends creating a physical environment that says to people 'you matter' (Kline, 1999: 84). Wider research in the area of environmental psychology also highlights the importance of physical spaces on our thoughts, feelings and behaviors. Coachees need to feel safe and secure if they are to focus and get the most from the session.

The first choice is to consider whether to meet in person or remotely. Each has its advantages. In person may feel more intimate and has been the traditional approach for most workplace coaching. In contrast, online coaching offers a more convenient approach with less travel time, which is reflected in its lower costs. In addition, digital can offer opportunities which physical meetings cannot match, such as links to online learning and global scalability for organizations.

## Physical coaching sessions

*Coachee workspaces*

Coaching frequently takes place in the workplace of the coachee. There are some obvious attractions: it's convenient, because the coach travels to them, and it removes many of the worries of finding a suitable external space. But there are some practical concerns that need to be managed. Coachees can find it difficult to switch off from the demands of the office; emails may be pinging in the background, work colleagues may intrude to talk about a developing issue, and phones may ring if the meeting is in the coachee's private office. There is also the question of keeping a meeting confidential from colleagues, as the coach will need to check in at reception and may need to walk through a shared office space.

For those without a private office, there are other challenges to consider. Many organizations have glass-fronted meeting rooms, making personal and intimate topics more difficult to explore. Further, in many organizations, the simple lack of meeting rooms can also make for an added challenge.

Finally, the need to tidy up afterwards is also an important consideration; wiping down whiteboards and removing flip charts with personal information, while small inconveniences, are factors which need to be managed if the session is to be kept confidential.

*Coffee shop or hotel lobby*

A second option is the coffee shop. It can be convenient for the coachee, as most cities have a wide number of options. The space is cheap, being simply the price of a coffee. Furthermore, most people are not bothered by what's happening at the next table. However, for some, the volume of people coming and going and the nature of the layout, with other people being close by, may mean it's not ideal for private conversations. Moreover, a table can't be guaranteed and the noise, hustle and bustle may be off-putting for a serious, in-depth conversation.

An alternative option is to select a semi-public space in a hotel lobby. This provides more comfortable seating as well as coffee. Many hotels make a feature of creating such spaces. Care, however, needs to be taken in selecting the right hotel, avoiding large TV screens and locations with high footfall, for example close to check-in or baggage storage.

A final alternative under this heading is a private room. Hotels and private members' clubs offer spaces which can be booked by the hour. Such spaces ensure a confidential environment, with less worry about workplace colleagues observing the meeting, but the space comes at a cost and, in addition, there is the inconvenience of travel to the agreed location for both coach and coachee.

### The coach's home

A few coaches offer coaching from their private home or from a consulting space. This option is significantly less well used by coaches compared to therapists, who often use their home as a therapy studio. One downside is that the coachee will need to consider travel time, as well as challenges such as finding parking. A second consideration is whether the space is appropriate for such conversations. If the coach creates a separate space in their home used only for coaching, this can be fine, but for most people it may require either walking through family areas or the management of the space before the coachee arrives, to remove children's toys, an old jumper laid on a chair or a book they're currently reading. Such spaces can also provoke questions about personal photos or other effects, which the coach may be reluctant to discuss with the coachee.

### Coaching outdoors

Coaching outdoors is an option that has grown in popularity in recent years. Coachees benefit from fresh air, open space and the added bonus of exercise. It's also free, and the coach and coachee can vary the location for a different walk for each session, to provide variety and interest. Many coaches who use the outdoors also claim the external environment provides stimuli for their conversation, helping their clients to gain new insights (Burns and Passmore, 2022).

There are, however, a number of downsides. Unless either party lives close to a beautiful location, there will be travel time and cost for the coachee and the coach. Care also needs to be taken to factor in planning routes, parking, health and safety, and weather. For these reasons, outside sessions can offer a nice alternative when the weather is good, rather than a standard approach for every workplace coaching session.

## Digital meeting spaces

Digital coaching has grown significantly since 2015. This has occurred as most coachees have become more familiar with communications technology, such as Zoom, Teams and Google Meet. These technologies offer convenience, reducing the need for travel for the coachee or the coach, thus making coaching more affordable and reducing the carbon footprint incurred by car or plane journeys.

There are three main digital options. The first is a digital meeting room provided by the coach, who may be using one of the commonly used services. The second is a digital meeting room organized by the coachee, using their in-house solution. The third is using a platform provider.

While there are strong upsides in terms of convenience, one potential downside is the perceived reduction in intimacy and a risk that some body-language communication may be missed. In practice, though, there seems to be little evidence for either concern. Such issues can be mitigated by setting up the equipment in the right way, such as having a good-quality sound card, arranging seating with light on the person's face (as opposed to coming from behind them) and ensuring that the camera is eye level and positioned around a meter from the individual, thus enabling both parties to see the whole upper body and not just the face of their interlocutor.

One important consideration which is often overlooked is data protection. If the coach is providing the link for the meeting room or if it's delivered by a company such as a platform provider, it's worth asking where the data from the session is stored. Is it in the EU or US, or does the provider not know? As a bare minimum, the session should be compliant with GDPR, or the data-privacy rules which apply in the countries where both the coach and the coachee are located. For EU citizens, this means the data should be stored within the EU. Many sole traders have not considered these aspects for their business. It's sometimes tempting to think that because the provider is a large company, they will have all these issues covered, but that's not always the case. For example, some larger providers outside of the EU record conversations and expect coachees to explicitly opt out. It's worth asking about these aspects before you start, to ensure both the coachee and the organization are comfortable around compliance with all the privacy and data regulations which apply in their country or state.

## Conclusion

Exploring the issues discussed here upfront during contracting is important, so the needs of both coach and coachee are reflected in the location where coaching takes place. It's easy to neglect this aspect and assume all coaching locations are the same, but the right location can lift one's heart, protect privacy and save hours of travel time in the day.

## References

Burns, A., and Passmore, J. (2022). Outdoor coaching: The role of Attention Restoration Theory as a framework for explaining the experience and benefit of eco-psychology coaching. *International Coaching Psychology Review* 17(1).

Kline, N. (1999). *Time to Think*. London: Cassell.

# SECTION 2

# The coach commissioner's guide to coaching

In this section, we focus upon what should be considered when buying coaching services, such as how to commission coaching provision, the role of team and group coaching, and the role of feedback and assessment.

In Chapter 17: 'How can we build a business case for coaching?' David Tee explores what coaching can provide, the importance of stakeholder engagement, the coaching evidence base and how to build a strategic business case for coaching. In Chapter 18: 'How can we create synergy between the organizational strategy and the coaching program?' Gill Tanner considers how creating synergy between business strategy and a coaching program can ensure successful outcomes, benefiting businesses and stakeholders alike. In Chapter 19: 'What criteria should we use when selecting a coaching provider?' Jonathan Passmore and Yu Dan Shi propose insightful questions to enable organizations to define decision-making criteria when commissioning coaching. IIn Chapter 20: 'How should we select coaches for our coaching pool?' Naila Abdul Karim explores what to consider when selecting coaches for an internal coaching pool, and how to manage the recruitment process. In Chapter 21: 'What are the advantages of using external coaches versus an internal coaching pool?' Laura Chapin explains what is meant by internal and external coaching, as well as the advantages and disadvantages of these options when commissioning coaching.

In Chapter 22: 'How can we design and deploy successful coaching programs in an organization?' Sam Isaacson and Naeema Pasha explore the practical considerations for employers to assess when deploying coaching within their organizations. In Chapter 23: 'How can we generate engagement with a new coaching program?' Valeria Cardillo Piccolino discusses how to communicate with employees about a coaching commission, including what the employee investment is and how this can generate positive outcomes for individuals and organizations alike. In Chapter 24: 'How can we best support coachees in their coaching journey?' Windy Tshepiso Maledu considers the organizational context within which coaching takes place and offers solutions for how to break down barriers. In Chapter 25: 'When should we use coaching rather than mentoring?' Patrick Rütten helps differentiate between coaching and mentoring by offering clear definitions and an explanation for when each intervention may be most appropriate. In Chapter 26: 'When should we use training or appraisals rather than coaching?' Patrick explores how using coaching alongside other HR interventions, including training and appraisals, can create the optimum environment for staff development.

In Chapter 27: 'When should we use counseling or occupational health rather than coaching?' Miriam Schneider-Tettenborn explains how coaching differs from occupational health interventions specifically targeted at employee psychological wellbeing, as well as employer responsibilities in this space. In Chapter 28: 'How can we help our staff to prepare for coaching sessions?' Miriam lays out the organizational context which will support positive coaching outcomes, such as setting meaningful goals and engaging the relevant line manager. In Chapter 29: 'How will we measure the impact of coaching in relation to our strategy?' Liz Pavese explores ways to assess the holistic value of coaching, going beyond a focus upon a single metric. In Chapter 30: 'How can I use coaching to support a change of culture in my organization?' Valeria discusses how coaching can support people as they experience organizational change and specifically focuses on certain groups: the leadership and executive team, ambassadors of change and the workforce. In Chapter 31: 'What are the latest trends in coaching?' Morgan Hyonne identifies and discusses the main trends impacting upon the coaching profession, such as technology-enabled coaching, the democratization of coaching and the professionalization of coaching.

In Chapter 32: 'What is the difference between team and group coaching?' Sam and Qingsong explain that, depending upon the coaching requirements of different individuals/organizations, there are distinct differences between team and group coaching. In Chapter 33: 'When should we use team coaching?' Liz explores more deeply the benefits of team coaching and when it's most appropriately applied to realize its potential value. In Chapter 34: 'When should we use group coaching?' Liz discusses the benefits of group coaching and when best to leverage this approach. In Chapter 35: 'How can psychometrics help a coachee's development in a coaching assignment?' Liz explains what psychometric tools are, how they can help in a coaching engagement and what issues to consider when leveraging psychometric tools. In Chapter 36: 'How can a 360-degree leadership questionnaire help in coaching?' Jonathan Passmore and Laurel McKenzie provide a review of 360s, their role as a development tool, and how they can play a part in 1:1 and team coaching and in evaluation.

In Chapter 37: 'How long should a coaching assignment last?' Gill explores the factors involved, such as individual preferences and needs – offering the thought, however, that coaching assignments should not start without an end in mind. In Chapter 38: 'How long should an individual coaching session last?' Omar Alaoui examines the length of individual coaching sessions based upon the way in which coaching is being delivered and recommends that duration be based upon this – nevertheless, however, encouraging a flexible approach. In Chapter 39: 'What should we expect concerning data protection for our coaching sessions?' Jonathan Passmore and Rui Munakata consider the rules which cover confidentiality and data protection, and how this relates to coachees and organizations who commission coaching.

# CHAPTER 17

# How can we build a business case for coaching?

David Tee

## Introduction

When you are bringing coaching into your organization, it is important to have a very clear rationale as to why. How might coaching create value or help an organization realize additional benefits? There are many considerations when building a business case. This chapter will propose some of the key factors which should help a coaching commissioner develop a business case aligned to their organization.

## Clarity about the offering

Coaching is an international and unregulated industry, meaning anyone can label themselves a coach, resulting in a huge variety of offerings. As Chapter 1 in this book details, coaching is variously defined and practiced, meaning an organization may already have staff that have worked with people labeling themselves as coaches, but have had very different experiences. Therefore, it is important for your business case to be clear as to how you intend coaching to be practiced within your organization. Not only will this highlight what benefits coaching might most likely produce, but it also gives clarity to your staff contemplating signing up for coaching as to what they should experience, and also for any external coaching providers as to how you expect them to work.

## Clarity about when not to use coaching

Coaching is a very powerful and effective developmental intervention, but it is not a cure-all. A business case will be stronger if there is clarity around when not to use coaching just as much as when to use it. Bluckert (2006) warns of the danger of assuming coaching is the optimal tool for every developmental need someone may have, or of imposing it upon entire directorates or layers of management. There will be several reasons for this:

- Some may not be ready or motivated to change

- Some may have a departmental culture or line-management support that does not foster them innovating or implementing the ideas they generate in their coaching sessions

- Some may have a personality or preferred learning style that means alternative developmental interventions will be more optimal for that person at that time.

For these people, reading a book, attending a conference, shadowing a colleague, taking responsibility for a project or some other viable proposition may be a better fit for their particular developmental needs and opportunities. Recognizing the strength in having this variety of methods for developing people, an organization should always add coaching into this repertoire and deploy it purposefully. This should produce a much greater return on investment for the organization from coaching, in turn strengthening the business case.

## Stakeholder mapping

Knowing what the coaching will look like in the organization, and also when people will be signposted towards alternative developmental activities, should already help frame how coaching will be generating benefits. Another useful contextual consideration is to be mindful of the stakeholders who do or could hold an interest or influence regarding a coaching program. It may be particularly important to focus on the latter of these two groups. The individual, team or department that is interested in coaching being introduced into the organization may be clear about its purpose. But there will be other stakeholders that show little interest at present, but whose influence and support may be crucial in the future.

Coaching within organizations is often overseen by specialist functions such as HR or L&D. Professionals within those teams should be mindful of the many possible ways in which coaching will generate value and prove effective and beneficial, and may well set success targets accordingly. An HR professional may track the impact of coaching on talent retention or on employee engagement. However, should the business face a financial downturn leading to a need for a difficult prioritization of spend, it may be senior staff within the finance team, rather than in HR, who determine where the budget is retained. They may not be motivated by changes in scores on an employee engagement survey, instead requiring hard financial data, such as a cost-benefit analysis. A coaching commissioner should be very clear as to the stakeholders that could hold an influence, both now and in the future, and what they would need to see in the business case, so they can anticipate and build this in from the beginning.

## Evidence-based coaching

One of the ways a business case can be compelling is if it is grounded in evidence. The quantity and sophistication of coaching science research is growing year on year and it is therefore worthwhile investigating what is already known about where coaching has been demonstrated to be effective within businesses. For a sophisticated, thorough and contemporary exploration of the evidence, readers are referred to de Haan (2021).

A more concise overview can be obtained from Grant (2016), who summarizes the researched coaching outcomes at that time. Data from workplace coaching studies point to valued changes in stress levels, self-regulation, team working, informed decision making, goal commitment and achievement, resilience, workplace wellbeing and many other desirable employee attributes and behaviors.

A coaching commissioner should not limit the targeted benefits of coaching to those already studied. Being honest in the confidence they can reasonably have that the desired impacts for more novel outcomes will be generated will bolster their business case. In addition, sharing the data generated from coaching within the organization will help to further increase our collective understanding of all the different ways in which coaching does prove effective.

## What matters in the organization?

Much of the best practice literature argues for the importance of aligning coaching to the overall strategic priorities of the organization (see Eldridge and Dembkowski, 2004; Hawkins, 2012; Megginson and Clutterbuck, 2006). The assumption often made is that use of coaching resources should be prioritized around needs and opportunities aligned to particular strategic drivers for your organization. It may be that the organization is looking to increase innovation, broaden diversity or to prioritize expansion in a particular market in the coming years, and wishes to prioritize coaching to these ends. However, it would be simplistic to assume that every organization uses coaching to help it make progress against certain strategic objectives.

There are also businesses that instead provide coaching for their staff because it aligns to their organizational values rather than to their current strategy. An organization may have the value of responsibility or the value of empowerment, and the business case can therefore be made that introducing or increasing a coaching provision is going to demonstrate a willingness to devote resources to helping realize that particular value.

Other organizations see coaching as an end in itself. Members of staff may contract to work with a coach and be given a wide degree of freedom as to how they use those coaching sessions, maybe even for a topic or goal entirely unconnected with their current role in the organization, such as an outside hobby or interest. The mere fact that the business provides staff with coaching opportunities may help the employee feel valued. This may result in the business having a great reputation for investing in its staff, possibly even becoming an employer of choice in the region or sector. However, these are unlooked-for benefits. The coaching is provided to let the employee know the business cares about their growth and wellbeing, regardless of any particular outcomes. For a business case, the coaching commissioner should be clear as to whether the business sees coaching as fulfilling any of these functions, or instead views it as being of innate worth, or maybe has some other motivation, and do then check that this assumption is shared by the key stakeholders.

## Be specific

Whatever the intended function or benefits realization coaching is intended to fulfil, the business case may be more compelling if there is specificity provided. A business case can be thought of almost as an accountability partner. Rather than coaching helping with the organization's people development plan, what specific contribution will it make? Rather than it being proposed to help the organization achieve its objectives, are there one or two particular objectives where the case can be made that coaching will genuinely make a difference? Not only will this level of detail make for a more convincing case for the stakeholders whose agreement is needed, it also shows a confidence and intentionality in how coaching will be targeted, and how the organization can determine in time whether the benefits have been realized.

## Evaluation strategy

As with any business case, a coaching commissioner should devote time to considering what the strategy will be for evaluating the actual benefit of the coaching. Matthewman (2009) encourages us to start by clarifying why the coaching program is being initiated, what it is expected to deliver for the organization, and how (and when) success will be determined. This will point towards which data will need to be collected as the coaching is rolled out, and a defensible timescale for evaluating what actual impact has been created. From that, an organization can then build in its strategy, with numerous evaluation models being suitable for coaching, such as the Passmore SOAP-M model or the Kaufman Model of Learning Evaluation, among others (see Passmore and Tee, 2021 for a discussion of these models).

## Conclusion

Building a business case for coaching involves many decisions. Having clarity regarding what coaching approach the organization will use, when alternative developmental activities may be more optimal, how stakeholders may be determining its worth, what the evidence indicates coaching is able to generate, what the priority needs are for the organization, which of these coaching is specifically targeted towards aiding, and how its success will be determined should all help to produce a compelling business case and a blueprint for success.

## References

Bluckert, P. (2006). *Psychological Dimensions of Executive Coaching*. London: Open University Press.

De Haan, E. (2021). *What Works in Executive Coaching?* Abingdon: Routledge.

Eldridge, F., and Dembkowski, S. (2004). Creating a coaching culture. *Coach the Coach*, Issue 4. Retrieved 10 April 2022 from: https://cdn.ymaws.com/www.associationforcoaching.com/resource/resmgr/Research/CtC4.pdf.

Grant, A. (2016). The efficacy of coaching. In J. Passmore, D.B. Peterson and T. Freire (eds), *The Wiley Blackwell Handbook of the Psychology of Coaching and Mentoring*, pp.15–39. Hove: John Wiley & Sons Ltd.

Hawkins, P. (2012). *Creating a Coaching Culture*. London: Open University Press.

Matthewman, L. (2009). Evaluating coaching effectiveness. *Coaching Psychology International* 2(1): 21–2.

Megginson, D., and Clutterbuck, D. (2006). Creating a coaching culture. *Industrial and Commercial Training* 38(5): 232–7.

Passmore, J., and Tee, D. (2021). Feedback and evaluation in coaching. In J. Passmore (ed.), *The Coaches' Handbook*, pp.355–66. Abingdon: Routledge.

# CHAPTER 18

# How can we create synergy between the organizational strategy and the coaching program?

Gill Tanner

## Introduction

Creating synergy is about the extra energy, power or success that is achieved by two elements working together instead of on their own. The two elements we are concerned with in this chapter are the organizational strategy and the coaching program, the latter of which is in turn part of the wider people-development or HR strategy.

## The organizational strategy

An organizational strategy is a plan, or set of plans, outlining a series of target milestones and how these will be achieved, typically as a cascade from the organizational vision statement. It takes into account the changing external environment such as competitors and PESTLE factors (political, economic, social, technological, legal and environmental), as well as internal circum-stances such as structure, culture, people, finance and systems. Given the dynamic nature of most organizational environments, such plans need to be flexible and able to adapt to changing events.

Traditionally, many organizations have pursued their strategy with limited regard to the role of their people. People have been considered another resource, operated through the lever of command-and-control leadership. The past two decades have changed this notion. In order to survive, organi-zations' perspectives have moved towards seeing people as their key competitive advantage. Skills such as critical thinking, creativity, emotional intelligence, collaboration and the ability to manage change effectively can bring significant added value to the organization and its mission, alongside employee engagement, loyalty and commitment.

Unfortunately, the evidence suggests that the skills needed by organizations and those available do not match; the majority of business leaders believe soft skills to be more important than hard skills (Anderson, 2020), and yet soft skills are underdeveloped in many organizations, predominantly because they are harder to measure. A consensus has emerged that soft skills are no longer 'nice to have' attributes, but rather essential skills to enable organizations to thrive.

A second aspect related to organizational strategy is organizational culture. Culture has a huge impact on organizational success. Peter Drucker is often quoted as saying "culture eats strategy for breakfast," meaning that no matter how good an organizational strategy is, it will fail if the right culture is not in place to support its achievement. In short, "the way we do things around here" (Bower, 1966) is what will either bring a strategy to life or condemn it to failure.

So organizational strategy and people strategies are inextricably linked. But how can coaching help to address these key areas?

## The coaching program

A coaching program is a structured series of coaching interventions aimed at encouraging behavior and mindset change in coachees so that they can become the best version of themselves and the organization can benefit as a result. Coaching is a relatively new discipline and has emerged as a more formalized profession over the last 30 years, but has become an extremely popular development tool for organizations.

Coaching is different from other developmental techniques in that it starts from the premise that the coachee is naturally "creative, resourceful and whole" (Whitworth et al., 1998). The coach uses open questions, active listening, summaries and reflections to stimulate the coachee's self-awareness and sense of personal responsibility, leading to profound learning and behavior change. It can be used in a wide variety of contexts, not least in the business environment.

Businesses have been using coaching in various ways, some tactically (for example, to address a specific issue or develop a particular individual) and some realizing the added value it can bring to an organization by helping to realize strategic objectives. Using coaching tactically is legitimate and is likely to benefit an individual, and maybe even a team, but the real synergy is found when coaching can be used to realize organizational strategy.

## Creating synergy between the organizational strategy and the coaching program

How do you ensure that there is synergy between the organizational strategy and the coaching program? We have already established that people and culture are key elements of the organizational strategy, but it will depend on what the organizational strategy is and the current situation within the organization. The improvement outcomes need to be predetermined by the organization. The achievement of those outcomes and, ultimately, the strategic objectives become the measurement of coaching success.

If we take the example of an organization which cannot compete on a pure cost basis but has a strategy of quality enhancement, it will want to capitalize on the inherent value of its brand to deliver world-class products and services. It will likely need an engaged, high-performing workforce that is empowered and creative.

**Table 18.1: Sample coaching program**

| Coaching Program Objectives | Desired Outcomes |
| --- | --- |
| • Customers as advocates<br>• Increased profitability<br>• Increase in employee retention | • Improvement in leadership skills – emphasis on inclusive leadership<br>• Development of high-performing teams<br>• Improvement in cross-functional working and collaboration<br>• Superior customer service<br>• Improvement in the quality of new ideas and levels of creativity<br>• Enhanced employee engagement |

In Table 18.1, we have illustrated some of the areas where coaching can make a difference, particularly when the program has longevity. Traditionally, organizations focused their coaching deployment towards leaders and senior managers, reflecting the high cost of the intervention and in hope that the benefits would filter through the organization. Whilst this is a worthwhile approach, and there is evidence that the ripple effects of coaching do bring wider benefits beyond the individual, the democratization of leadership suggests a need for the democratization of coaching. Using such a philosophy, spreading coaching to where it is needed can enable a critical mass to gain from the benefits, contributing to a cultural shift.

The introduction of digital coaching makes this possible, with low-cost, scalable solutions; hundreds of coachees across every level can benefit from coaching across an organization, at a fraction of the cost of historic in-person modes of delivery.

As coaching is such an intrinsic part of organizational strategy, it is important to ensure that coaching programs are evaluated. Whilst this can be difficult to do, particularly in terms of producing a return on investment, the program(s) can be assessed holistically through a range of different measures, which reflect the individual program design and key metrics set by the organization, to demonstrate the value of coaching as one of a number of interventions to support the development of the organizational strategy.

## Conclusion

Ensuring that coaching is both an integrated element of the HR strategy and aligned with the organization's strategy optimizes the chances of success. While these can work independently, maximum benefit for the organization and its wider stakeholders is achieved through alignment.

## References

Anderson, B.M. (2020). The most in-demand hard and soft skills of 2020. *LinkedIn Blog*. Retrieved 7 March 2022 from: https://business. linkedin.com/talent-solutions/blog/trends-and-research/2020/ most-in-demand-hardand-soft-skills.

Bower, M. (1966). *The Will to Manage*. New York: McGraw Hill.

Whitworth, L., Kimsey-House, H., and Sandahl, P. (1998). *Co-active Coaching: New Skills for Coaching People Toward Success in Work and Life*. Mountain View, CA: Davies-Black Publishing.

# CHAPTER 19

# What criteria should we use when selecting a coaching provider?

Jonathan Passmore and Yu Dan Shi

## Introduction

Choosing a coaching provider is a little like choosing where to buy your groceries: there is lots of choice. In this chapter, we will help set out some criteria to consider when making a buying decision. Like grocery shoppers, each coaching buyer will place a different emphasis on different criteria: some will be looking for the lowest-cost provider, others will favor value for money, while others still are seeking a premium service and don't mind paying a premium price for it. What's important for a coaching commissioner is that they can secure the right coaching partner for them.

## Coaching for one or many?

A key decision at the start is to be clear whether the buying decision is for one coach or for many coaches – and if so, how many? Coaching providers come in all sizes. Twenty years ago, most coaching practices were sole traders or small consulting companies based in a specific geographical location with a handful of coaches. Over time, coaching has matured. While small providers are still commonly found in every city, there are now medium-sized consulting firms and global coaching providers able to provide coaching in 200+ languages to 100+ countries.

For those seeking one coach, the best option is likely to be a small provider or sole practitioner. For those seeking a consistent approach across a large coachee pool spread across the world, a global provider is likely to be the best option.

The question of which criteria to use can be divided into two parts, the balance of which will depend on the particular organization and its needs:

- Questions about the individual coach or coaches
- Questions about the coaching provider's service.

## Coach criteria

*What qualifications does the coach hold?*

The growth of coaching and the unregulated nature of the market have meant that there are many unqualified coaches offering coaching services. Just like a psychologist, lawyer or an accountant, it's sensible to expect your coach to have undertaken formal training and achieved a qualification in their discipline. In coaching, there are a confusing number of different professional bodies. Germany, for example, has over 30 such bodies. Each has its own standards: some require just a payment to become a member, others ask for a CV to assess an applicant's background, others require completion of an approved training program and an assessment.

There are two main global bodies that coaching commissioners should look out for: EMCC Global and the ICF. You should expect your coach to be accredited (EMCC) or credentialed (ICF) by one of these bodies, or to be a registered psychologist with additional coaching training. It's worth being aware that most bodies also offer 'membership', so be careful not to confuse people who are members with coaches who have completed an extensive program of training and are accredited and/or credentialed. In addition, many universities now offer postgraduate degrees in coaching psychology or business coaching. It's important to note these qualifications are significantly higher in standard than the accredited programs by professional bodies.

*What experience do they have?*

Coaches come with different coaching and work experience. It's worth asking about the coaching hours undertaken. For a professional coach, it's a good idea to look for coaches who have had several hundred hours of coaching practice, working with clients.

In addition to coach experiences, it's a good idea to explore the coaches' business experience. This is harder to categorize, but by reviewing CVs a coaching commissioner could look for people who have worked in management or leadership positions, with teams of 10 people or more as a manager and 100 or more for more senior leadership coaching.

A final factor to explore is sector experience. While the coach will not be providing advice, it is helpful for the coach to understand the technical language, issues and challenges of the sector in which the coaching program will be taking place. This may come either from having worked in the sector or from experience of coaching clients. This can be taken at face value or, when interviewing the coach, a coaching commissioner could ask some technical questions to explore the depth of their understanding about the current issues in the sector.

*Does the coach receive supervision?*

Supervision is an essential ingredient for high-quality coach practice and is now widely accepted by professional bodies. Supervision provides a space for coaches to reflect, be challenged, and learn about themselves and their practice. It's a good idea to expect all coaches to be in supervision with a qualified supervisor. One way to check this is to ask for the name of the supervisor and which body they are accredited by, and then to check them out online, as most professional bodies hold a public register.

*Chemistry and cost*

The price offered needs to fit the budget you have available. Costs vary widely in the industry, with in-person coaching, needing to cover their travel time and cost, generally more expensive than online providers. Given a coaching session could involve, say, two hours travel time for the coach, coaching delivered in person may be several times more expensive than online coaching.

Secondly, in terms of chemistry for a one-off coach, a chemistry meeting for 30–40 minutes allows both parties to explore how they would work together, with the option of a 'no-fault divorce' clause, so either party has the right to say no, without it appearing as a criticism of the other person; some online providers are now using advanced technology tools to improve matching even further.

*Approach*

The final aspect to consider is to explore the approaches used by the coach. Selecting a coach who uses a single model or tool is likely to be less effective than using a coach who has been trained in a wide range of approaches (Wang et al., 2021). What's also important is understanding when the coach believes different approaches should be used and why. This involves an exploration of the science and research underpinning the frameworks they use (Passmore, 2021). The best coaches should be able to provide specific evidence from individually named research studies as to the evidence that underpins their approach.

**Table 19.1: Seven key questions for coaches**

| | |
|---|---|
| 1. | Which professional body accreditation (qualifications) do you hold? |
| 2. | How many hours of coaching practice do you have? |
| 3. | What experience do you have of working in this sector? |
| 4. | Are you in supervision, and with whom? |
| 5. | What's the cost of the program? |
| 6. | Can I withdraw or swap coaches at any stage? |
| 7. | What models are you trained in and do you use, and what's the evidence for their efficacy for this type of presenting problem? |

Let's turn now to the criteria for organizations. As well as getting the right coach, it's a good idea to select the right organization, as added-value services range widely between providers.

## Large-program criteria – coaching-provider criteria

In addition to asking the specific questions about the coach community, for coaching at scale, a number of coach-provider questions are worth exploring when considering coaching for a large community or a global employee population.

*In what time zones are coaches available?*

In large programs, having coaches in the same time zone as the workforce helps to ensure that coaches are available when they are needed during a standard working day. With global workforces, and more people working remotely and in diverse locations, this can be more important than it was a decade ago.

*In what languages is coaching available?*

With over 7,000 languages in use across the world, this can be tricky, but expecting the coaching provider to provide coaching in 50–100 of the most popular languages is reasonable. When asked, most coachees express a preference for receiving coaching in their native language. Asking about the range of languages available, with a particular focus on any large communities with particular language preferences, can help in ensuring that a sufficient number of coaches are available in the coaching pool.

While many providers offer a range of languages for their coaching conversations, it may be useful to ask if the website or app is available in multiple languages. In addition, many large providers also offer learning content through a learning library within their platform; if this supplementary learning material is available in multiple languages, ask how much is available and in which other languages?

*Scale*

On larger assignments, a key factor is scale: how many coaches can the provider make available? Secondly, how diverse is their pool in terms of gender, ethnicity and racial characteristics? The exact scale and mix of the coaching pool a coaching commissioner is seeking will depend on their organizational needs, but as a general guide a coaching pool five times larger than the coachee population should give sufficient choice and diversity.

*Evaluation*

Most organizations are concerned about evaluation. There has been an obsession in coaching with seeking to measure return on investment (ROI), but while quick and easy, it is not the best way to measure individual behavioral change or organization impact accurately. Instead, for organizations that are serious about assessment, it may be better to link the coaching program to the organization's competency framework, or use an internal behavioral 360 questionnaire. Experience suggests that team-member ratings are actually the most accurate assessment of a coachee's behavior. Coachees could undertake the assessment before the coaching starts and after the program has been completed. To really assess the value of a program, the coachee population should be compared with a similar group of employees who did not benefit from the coaching program. Of course, as well as short-term effects, coaching is like other L&D interventions in that it builds the overall leadership muscle of the organization, producing longer-term benefits which may be difficult to measure in the short term.

*Data security and personal data management*

For coaches or for employees based in the EU, as well as in a number of other territories, such as Australia and China, there are rules regarding the management of personal data. The assumption is that this only relates to where the organization is based, but most laws also cover the coach, as well as the storage of data. Seeking advice from the organization's compliance team will help to ensure the provider is fully compliant with GDPR and other relevant data security and privacy laws.

**Table 19.2: Key questions for larger coaching providers and platforms**

1. Do you have coaches in a range of time zones and, if so, which ones and how many?

2. Do you provide your coaching in the following languages...?

   2a. Is your app/website available in these languages?

   2b. Is your additional learning content available in these languages?

3. How many coaches do you have available for this assignment?

4. How will you help us evaluate the impact of this program?

5. How do you comply with GDPR?

   5a. Are you ISO 27001 compliant (and compliant with other national requirements for work in these territories)?

   5b. 5b. Are you Schrems II compliant?

   5c. Are you SOC2 certificated? (Please supply a copy of your certificate.)

## Conclusion

In this chapter, we have suggested a range of questions to consider for those looking to identify a personal coach or a large coaching provider. By taking control of the process, establishing clear criteria and exploring the offer from three or four providers, a coaching commissioner can ensure that the best-value decision is made, contributing value both to the individuals who receive coaching and to the organization.

## References

Passmore, J. (2021). *The Coaches' Handbook*. Abingdon: Routledge.

Wang, Q., Lai, Y.L., Xu, X., and McDowall, A. (2021). The effectiveness of workplace coaching: A meta-analysis of contemporary psychologically informed coaching approaches. *Journal of Work Applied Management* 14(1). Retrieved 20 April 2022 from: https://www.emerald.com/insight/content/doi/10.1108/JWAM-04-2021-0030/full/pdf?title=the-effectiveness-of-workplace-coaching-a-meta-analysis-of-contemporary-psychologically-informed-coaching-approaches.

# CHAPTER 20

# How should we select coaches for our coaching pool?

Naila Abdul Karim

## Introduction

In recent years, there has been an influx of service professionals marketing themselves as 'coaches', making the task of identifying coaches suitable to meet organizational needs difficult for coaching commissioners. Unlike psychotherapy or medicine, there is no single governing body for the coaching profession, and coaches tend to come from varied experience and coach-training programs. It's possible to come across a coach with great references and a wealth of experience who isn't necessarily the right fit to a given organization's or individual coachee's needs. So how should a coaching commissioner go about selecting the coaches for a coaching pool once they have selected their coach provider? In this chapter, we look to further explore the areas one should consider while building a coaching pool.

## Where to start when selecting coaches for a coaching pool

Some providers offer their whole pool, allowing the coachee to choose. This works well, as it allows the coachee to be in the driving seat. However, other coaching providers offer access to a select or reduced pool, inviting the coach commission to pick their favored 10, 20 or 50 coaches, who then become the coach pool for that organization.

As a starter when building a coaching pool, any coaching commissioner should be clear about what organizational purpose the pool has and what intervention they have in mind. This book has covered elsewhere the differences between coaching and other disciplines (see chapters 25, 26 and 27 on mentoring, appraisals and occupational health), and clarity around this will help inform the sort of criteria one might use when identifying appropriate coaches. The next step, described in more detail in Chapter 22, is to define the specific objectives that coaches will have in terms of supporting coachees in achieving the desired outcomes from a program-wide perspective. This brings clarity to the coaches in the pool and enables the coaching commissioner to select coaches who are well-equipped to use strategies that will help to achieve these outcomes.

For instance, if coaching is being used to roll out a global women's leadership development program, and given research which suggests that women typically choose women coaches, having 80–85% women in the pool would be a wise choice.

## Key criteria to consider while selecting coaches

The criteria below can help a coaching commissioner navigate the process of selecting coaches if required to do so. But it is helpful to bear in mind that only focusing on one or two criteria alone may not necessarily guarantee the 'right fit'. We always advocate giving as much choice as possible to the individual coachee, as the evidence suggests this increases the chances of a successful match.

### Affiliation and accreditation

Coaching is currently a largely self-regulated profession, with coaches coming from various disciplines. It is important to understand the coach's qualification(s) in order to ensure the quality and impact they bring to the coaching relationship. Therefore, consider choosing coaches who are members of one of the two global coaching professional bodies (ICF and EMCC). Coaches who are accredited by one of these two professional associations will provide a common standard in coach quality.

### Coaching and industry experience

It is helpful to define the type of coaches you are looking for in your coaching pool. This could be someone with industry-specific knowledge or experience. Such knowledge means they are more likely to understand the technical language used in your industry and also have some understanding of the challenges faced by the coachees. This background also provides instant credibility in the eyes of coachees, further helping the formation of the coach–coachee relationship.

*Coaching philosophy/approach*

There are a wide range of coaching philosophies, approaches, models and techniques out there, and so an identical coaching issue presented to two coaches will lead to two quite different coaching sessions. Finding out how a coach thinks about coaching will help inform the judgment both about the provider and the coach. Apart from understanding the coach's experiences, skills and qualifications, a coaching commissioner may want to seek references for each coach, to get a sense of their style, or observe them in a live coaching session. This can work when the organization is selecting coaches for 10 or 20 managers but is much harder when it is selecting coaches for 50 or 100.

*Diversity*

When choosing coaches, diversity should be considered to ensure the coaches selected reflect the diversity in the organization, including gender, race, ethnicity, language preferences and time zones. Uniformity among coaches increases the risk of a coachee not fully engaging, thus reducing the impact of the program. Secondly, the best coaches to include in a coaching pool are those with experience of having engaged with a diverse range of coachees. It's important that coaches are equipped with the necessary tools to support their coachees, creating a space that is safe for them to share their true perspectives without judgment.

*Chemistry*

As coaching is an important relationship, coachees should be empowered to select which coach they want to begin with. When a coachee feels that they have good chemistry with their coach, it gives them a greater sense of buy-in and ownership of their learning journey. The same is true from the perspective of the coach; the two-way trust relationship is the best foundation to build a coaching assignment from. Research tells us that the best coach for any given coachee and the one they will trust the most, regardless of skill, knowledge and experience, is the coach they select (Wilson, 2011).

*Continuous professional development (CPD)*

Coaching is not a static process. Instead, like any profession, coaches should be engaged in continuous professional development (Passmore and Sinclair, 2021). CPD provides personal and professional development for the coaches to maintain their accreditations while at the same time continuing to improve their practice. As a part of the selection process, validating that the coach community benefits from CPD can be useful.

*Coaching supervision*

Coaching supervision is an important element in a coach's practice, as this collaborative learning process continually builds the coach's capacity through reflective dialogue that benefits both the coach and their coachees. A coach having coaching supervision means that they have a safe environment where they can clarify sensitive topics with their supervisor before making important decisions.

*Accessibility*

Understanding the format in which the coaching program is intended to be delivered, and ensuring the coach is able to deliver in that particular format, is important. Most large organizations have now switched since 2019 to online provision for most if not all of their coaching. This gives greater flexibility, but it is best to check if the coaches being selected have the technology and skills to work in online formats. With this final point particularly in mind, a coaching commissioner should also verify that the coach provider has the necessary infrastructure and IT control environment to support secure and reliable delivery online. This is also the case for face-to-face sessions: if the organization is not providing the venue, where will coaching take place? And how will the provider ensure it is confidential and that the venue is appropriate?

*Availability*

Lastly, the coaches provided should have sufficient time in their calendar to cater to the timelines and time zones of the coachees in the program. Hiring an excellent and popular coach with limited availability is likely simply to lead to frustration. Having more coaches than necessary in a coaching pool is good practice, so even if the provider offers a reduced pool in this way, this should include around twice the number of coaches as coachees within the program, thus ensuring choice and availability.

## Conclusion

Coaches play a key role in making a coaching program a success, as they have the capacity to drive and attain the desired goals and objectives. The criteria discussed in this chapter are a guide that will help narrow a coaching pool to become more relevant and qualified. Thus, understanding a coach's background, philosophy and approach will ensure the most appropriate selection of coaches to best fit the needs of an organization.

## References

Passmore, J., and Sinclair, T. (2021). *Becoming a Coach: The Essential ICF Guide*. Berlin: Springer.

Wilson, C. (2011). Developing a coaching culture. *Industrial and Commercial Training* 43(7): 407–14. doi:10.1108/00197851111171827.

# CHAPTER 21

# What are the advantages of using external coaches versus an internal coaching pool?

Laura Chapin

## Introduction

As more organizations recognize the effectiveness and impact of coaching for individuals, teams and the organization as a whole, those leading the design and implementation of coaching practices and programs are faced with deciding if they will use external coaches, an internal coach pool or a combination of both. In this chapter, we'll define what we mean by internal and external coaching, and offer a summary of the advantages and disadvantages of each. It's worth saying at the start that there is no single right answer, and each answer needs to reflect the unique characteristics of an organization and its history to date in developing their coaching offer.

## What is external coaching?

External coaching is coaching delivered by someone outside the coachee's organization. The external coach is typically accredited and brings significant coaching experience and coaching hours. Most external coaches are contracted for services by the organization for a specific scope of work and for a specific period. This may be for a particular individual, say a senior leader, or it may be connected to a program, for example a women's leadership development program. These coaches may be working with many people at any time and while a significant portion of their working time is devoted to coaching, they may deliver other services such as coaching supervision, mentoring and/or training.

## What is internal coaching?

Internal coaching is coaching delivered by a person who works in the same organization as the coachee. In the context of this chapter, an internal coach refers to a coach who has received some training, maybe by having undertaken a certified program or possibly having secured accreditation. In most instances these coaches are undertaking coaching in addition to their day-to-day role, and thus may have a few coachees who they work with in any given period. In a few instances, organizations have their own professional, accredited, full-time coaches, but this is the exception rather than the norm (St John-Brooks and Isaacson, 2023).

What are the advantages and disadvantages for using external coaches versus an internal coaching pool?

**Table 20.1: External versus internal coaches**

| | Advantages | Disadvantages |
|---|---|---|
| **External Coaches** | • Specific expertise/specialty (e.g. executive level, leadership, wellbeing, sales, industry, etc.) | • May lack full understanding of complex organizational dynamics and/or cultural nuances; may not fit organizational culture |
| | • May have higher level of credentialing and/or deeper and broader coaching experience | • Needs orientation about the organization (e.g. mission, vision, values, strategy and culture) and context of the coaching (e.g. independent engagement, part of a leadership program or organizational initiative) |
| | • Larger pool of coaches offers increased opportunity for matching, fit, diversity and scaling coaching to a wider coachee population | • Typically costs more than internal coaching, with direct cost for engagements or digital coaching licenses |
| | • Coachee perception of increased objectivity; coach can offer unbiased perspective as they are not involved in organizational politics or relationships | |
| | • Coachee perception of increased confidentiality may enable greater transparency and candor | |
| | • External view can offer a fresh perspective from a wide range of organizational experiences | |
| | • Senior executives in particular may be more comfortable with external coaching for personal reasons or in light of organizational politics | |

| | Advantages | Disadvantages |
|---|---|---|
| **Internal Coaches** | • Cost may be less when the coach does coaching as part of their role (e.g. coaching may not be 'charged back' to the coachee's business area/function)<br><br>• Increased awareness of organizational dynamics and/or cultural nuances<br><br>• Organization can have more control over specific coaching approaches | • May not have the same credentials and/or depth and breadth of coaching experience as external coaches<br><br>• Limited coach pool size may hinder effective matching and/or ability to scale, particularly as coach–coachee relationships should not be in the same chain of leadership and should ideally be in a different part of the organization<br><br>• Concerns about confidentiality may cause coachee to hold back and be less candid about challenges, concerns, fears, emotions and professional relationship issues<br><br>• May have limited availability for coaching sessions when coaching is only part of their role and they are managing multiple priorities<br><br>• May experience role confusion or blurring (e.g. coach needs to be explicit about what their role is as a coach and set boundaries between this and the other roles they play in the organization)<br><br>• Personal bias may color objectivity, inhibit transparency and/or limit the coach's perspective<br><br>• If coaches do not have the credibility and experience associated with high standards of professional coaching, the perception of coaching effectiveness and adoption of coaching more generally may be impacted |

Both internal and external coaching offer advantages and disadvantages. The decision as to which to select will depend on the situation. Factors might include the history of coach development in the organization, coachee locations and languages, available budget and the perception of coaching as an important and effective tool for improving performance.

In some instances, organizations keen to build a coaching culture may do both, leveraging external coaches for specific needs while also using internal coaches.

The following questions might help a coaching commissioner when evaluating which option to use in their organization:

- Who is in the coachee population?

- What are their needs?

- Do the internal coaches have the experience, expertise and capacity to support these coaching needs? Or would the needs be better met through external coaching, or a combination of both internal and external coaching?

- What is the organization's level of trust in coaching as an effective approach to development?

- What resources and staffing does the organization have in place to manage coaching programs?

- What role does organizational politics play?

## Does external digital coaching offer specific advantages?

In addition to the advantages previously discussed for external coaching, external digital coaching may offer further benefits that enhance the appropriateness of using external coaches. Depending on the provider, digital coaching may offer:

- Cost-effective delivery with the ability to scale to all levels in the organization, across time zones and multiple languages

- Access to a larger and more diverse pool of coaches

- Opportunities to use integrated assessments

- Access to unique learning content

- More flexibility around access to coaches

- Efficient matching of coaches to coachees' individual needs

- Metrics and data insights to measure the impact of coaching, while maintaining coachee confidentiality.

Digital coaching providers are maximizing the benefits of both internal and traditional external coaching, while mitigating many of the potential drawbacks formerly associated with external coaching.

## Mixed provision

For some organizations, a mixed provision model is the best option for their needs. Many of these started out building their own internal coaching pool when the costs of external coaches were high, but with the introduction of online digital coaching, costs have fallen. Having already invested in building an internal pool of coaches, each of whom has a qualification or even accreditation, it seems sensible to optimize use of that internal resource. The challenge for these organizations often becomes how to maintain the pool on a continuous basis as people leave and how to keep members of the internal coach community up to date by providing professional development and coaching supervision opportunities.

For these organizations, a mixed approach of leveraging a small pool of internal coaches (who receive ongoing professional development and coaching supervision opportunities) supplemented by a pool of external coaches may be the best option.

## Conclusion

External and internal coaches offer different benefits and drawbacks, dependent on the organizational context and coaching needs. By consciously reflecting, the organization can make informed decisions about when to use external or internal coaching, or a combination of both, to best meet the desired objectives.

## References

St John-Brooks, K., and Isaacson, S. (2023). Internal Coaching. In T. Bachkirova, E. Cox and D. Clutterbuck (eds), *The Complete Handbook of Coaching*. London: Sage Publishing.

# CHAPTER 22

# How can we design and deploy successful coaching programs in an organization?

Sam Isaacson and Naeema Pasha

## Introduction

The dynamic nature of the modern world is piling pressure on organizations to offer increasingly more individualized formats of L&D. Several sources report an increasing trend in demand for coaching to support employees in increasingly complex work environments (ICF Global, 2020). Coaching inherently lends itself to solving this problem, and yet the challenge of how to design and deploy a successful coaching program is real. This chapter will outline practical considerations aimed at enabling an organization to assess, with confidence, approaches to designing and deploying a coaching program.

## Design cascading from purpose

There are many factors to consider when designing a coaching program, and we'll cover these in the coming pages. The biggest question to answer, however, is more fundamental and strategic, and leads to a natural cascade of decision making. Let me explain what I mean by that: the more tactical questions that need answering, such as whether an internal or external coaching pool is a better fit (see Chapter 21: 'What are the advantages of using external coaches versus an internal coaching pool?'), will become easier to answer, and in some cases obvious, if this first-order question has an answer. And that question is: what is the purpose of the coaching program?

In some organizations, a coaching program will be essentially an employee benefit. In others, it might be a precision tool used to promote a specified desirable behavior. Or it might have a longer-term, more-strategic purpose to fundamentally shift the leadership culture. Coaching is not a one-size-fits-all intervention and it's too easy to fall into the trap of imitating what seems to have worked elsewhere, when something different is needed.

*Case study: Coaching as a culture-change tool*

> *Susan, the new Head of L&D at a large charity, had a good experience of coaching from her previous employer. There, employees returning to work after long-term absence had the option of six sessions from an internal coach to get them back up to speed on organizational changes and to give them a listening ear.*
>
> *Susan introduced the same offer as part of a leadership program that was intended to fundamentally transform the organizational mindset to that of a coaching mindset, away from some systemic issues. Several leaders did not opt for the coaching, saying they did not see how it would help, and those that did take up the offer fed back that, while the conversations felt helpful at the time, they did not have a significant or long-term impact.*
>
> *Two years later, Susan left the organization, concluding that she should have:*
>
> - *Used external coaches, as the internal coaching pool was not experienced enough*
>
> - *Made the coaching mandatory, as the coaching culture change was a decision coming from the CEO, intended to meet the needs of the required mindset change.*

## The look and feel of a coaching relationship

How many sessions are the right number to have in a coaching relationship? Many coaches would claim the number is six, stemming from the number of counseling sessions NHS budgets allowed when talking therapies were first introduced. But six is by no means universal; analysis on internal coaching from ten years ago (St John-Brooks, 2014) concluded that the average number of sessions for internal coaches was four, and updated analysis from coaching.com in 2021 concluded that internal and external coaches delivered an average of seven and eleven sessions respectively. Some coaching providers prioritize speed of access over the relationship, leading to single, standalone sessions without a longer-term relationship being the norm. Others believe in coaching as part of an 'infinite game' (Carse, 1987), where coaching sessions should be available indefinitely. What is the right number for your organization? If the purpose has been stated clearly, this question is likely to have already been answered.

The same is true for the question of what approval steps ought to be required before initiating a coaching engagement. Various constraints will naturally be in place, an important one of which will be budget, and so it might not be appropriate to allow anyone to access coaching at the drop of a hat. That said, of course, depending on the purpose of the coaching, it might be entirely appropriate, and in some cases restricting access might only serve to frustrate the goals the coaching program is specifically there to achieve. In a practical sense, approvals should be limited to the lowest level possible, to maximize ease of access, while ensuring preventative measures are in place to stop inappropriate misuse of the service.

Other aspects of a coaching program that should be considered include the length of coaching sessions, and any psychometrics, competency frameworks and coaching models that should be insisted on as part of the experience. In all of these cases, a clearly stated purpose will make those decisions natural conclusions to draw.

As a general rule of thumb, always favor agility over artificial constraints. The value of coaching comes from the fact that it is personalized for the coachee, and the coach adds value through their unique, personal approach. To enforce a particular session length, number of sessions or element of content will, in many cases, undermine the coaching itself through an unconscious parent–child relationship between the coaching program leader and the coach–coachee partnership, where an adult–adult relationship would be much more consistent. Naturally, there is a need for pragmatism to ensure the coaching will be used and have its desired impact, but leaning towards flexibility of the service will prove a good stance in most cases.

## From design to deployment

Having designed a high-quality coaching program, how do we go about making it available to a population of coachees? There are three big concepts to consider when moving from design to deployment, and we'll look at each here.

*Key stakeholders*

Coaching is all about people; that's true of coaches and coachees, and it's true of coaching programs as a whole. If the key stakeholders are brought into a coaching program in an organization, it will be successful more often than not. One of the biggest criticisms aimed at people professionals in organizations is that the tail ends up wagging the dog, and people 'in the business' feel that leadership and culture interventions are 'done to them', rather than supporting them in achieving their objectives. And coaching certainly ought to be seen as support rather than a forced waste of time!

Engaging key stakeholders from the outset, therefore, is a good investment of energy. Building a small, cross-discipline committee will help to increase buy-in and generate a natural population of champions. This ought to include one representative of the coaches, one representative of the coachees, one representative of the organization itself (ideally someone in a role such as CFO), perhaps one representative of the people team, and the coaching commissioner themself. This combination will bring together the key voices to shape the program and ensure all needs will be met through its deployment.

Project documentation and activities will emerge from this, and plenty has been written elsewhere around how to manage that well, but the truth is that if a committee such as the one described above is active and fully signed up, with enough transparency over the detail, the outcomes will almost certainly be realized.

*Communications*

The natural next step from identifying and involving the key stakeholders above is getting the word out more widely (see also Chapter 23: 'How can we generate engagement with a new coaching program?'). It's a pleasant thought that an inspired coachee might tell all of their colleagues about the plans for an upcoming coaching program, and yet in reality there are certain details that should be communicated clearly and several times, in order to ensure that the end results are as planned.

Coaching is one of those topics that can contain a lot of assumptions – what does the word 'coaching' mean, anyway? It's important to say everything that needs saying, without overwhelming people with the equivalent of internal sponsored ads. Coaching should be exciting, not annoying. Limiting communications to a complete and succinct brief, accessible in multiple formats, and ensuring that it's appropriate for each audience, will increase interest and decrease frustration.

Think about a coaching program designed with the purposes of broadening the perspective of its coachees. A reasonable lens to put on the coaching would be a systemic coaching framework, so coaches will therefore need to know that they are required to draw on this specialism. At the same time, it will be equally important not to tell coachees about that level of detail if they don't ask; it's likely that they won't hold sufficient foundational knowledge to fully understand what 'systemic coaching' means, and whether or not they do, it's not necessary for their engagement. A simple phrase such as "In advance of your first session, consider the people and communities who are affected by your role" would be more than sufficient.

*Velocity of deployment*

Finally, when it comes to the practicalities of deploying the program, the pace must be right. Make it too fast, particularly if the time demands are greater than under normal circumstances, and even those who want to be a part of it will lose interest among the challenges of the day-to-day. Too slow, and frustration and cynicism will tar it with negativity, bringing a curse on its future. As discussed above, if the key stakeholders can agree unanimously on the 'Goldilocks' pace, its deployment is much more likely to be successful.

If in doubt, err on the side of speed, particularly for coachees. A safe assumption is that people are likely to be impatient, so giving them access to the program at the point that they find out about it might generate a flurry of activity that puts high demand on the program team, but will also produce a wave of positivity if done well.

One way to almost guarantee that it is done well is through a pilot, in which one select group gets faster access to the experience in order to validate it and rapidly learn lessons before scaling up. Building this in as an important part of the deployment should prove its effectiveness and produce an important population of champions in order to increase adoption when the population is expanded. And at that point, don't hold back!

## Conclusion

Coaching programs can take many forms and don't work in a one-size-fits-all capacity. Identifying a clear purpose for a program will inform many of the more tactical decisions that need to be made, and incorporating the key stakeholders into design of the deployment plan will prove beneficial in its uptake.

## References

Carse, J.P. (1987). *Finite and Infinite Games.* New York: Ballantine Books.

ICF Global (2020). *2020 ICF Coaching Study: Executive Summary.* https://coachingfederation.org/app/uploads/2020/09/FINAL_ICF_GCS2020_ExecutiveSummary.pdf.

St John-Brooks, K. (2014). *Internal Coaching: The Inside Story.* London: Karnac Books.

# CHAPTER 23

# How can we generate engagement with a new coaching program?

Valeria Cardillo Piccolino

## Introduction

One of the most asked questions in a conversation between coaching commissioner and coaching provider is how to generate engagement with a new coaching program. What are the key drivers to generate buy-in? In this chapter, we will explore how organizations can secure strong engagement with a new coaching program.

## Employee engagement in an initiative: main drivers

By understanding how overall employee engagement works and the main elements needed to generate it, we can identify interesting insights on how to engage employees (i.e. coachees) and the wider stakeholder system in a coaching initiative.

Employee engagement is a critical factor in driving results and implementing changes. In every coaching initiative, there are a number of key stakeholders to consider:

- The employees who will be invited to undertake coaching (coachees)
- The line managers of the coachees
- The main sponsor of the program (i.e. the director or C-suite executive)
- The leadership team
- The program manager
- The coaching commissioner (if not already included above)

- The coaches

- Other key individuals involved in the delivery of the program, such as coaching supervisors.

Regardless of stakeholder group, there are six steps we can follow to engage them all in a coaching initiative.

## How to engage in a coaching initiative

*Step 1: Be clear about the reasons for the program*
*(personal, team and organizational level)*

The first step for all levels is to clarify the purpose of the initiative and the specific benefits they may get. In essence, what's in it for each of these stakeholders? Articulating the advantages at the levels of the personal, the team and the organization in specific ways for each stakeholder will increase engagement.

For example, we may want to communicate to the coachee that coaching will help them improve their leadership skills, positioning them for more rapid career development. We may want to position the same initiative for their managers as a way to engage the coachees: coaching improves retention, helps improve team performance and will be seen as a perk. And the sponsor and executive team will be energized by how the program connects to the overall talent-development strategy, with a stated aim such as improving retention, addressing inclusion or improving leadership capability.

The questions that we need to provide an answer to before communicating the idea of starting a coaching program are, therefore:

1.   What's in it for each key stakeholder group?

2.   What are the benefits for their team(s)?

3.   How is this initiative linked to the overall organization's strategic goals?

4.   What is the organization aiming to achieve through the program? (I.e. how will we measure this over time and what will we compare it with?)

*Step 2: Set correct expectations on coaching*

As a second step, we need to set proper expectations about coaching itself. The questions that you might want answered are:

- How does coaching work?

- What are the differences between coaching and other forms of personal/professional development (training, mentoring, consulting, psychotherapy)?

Since coaching is very often confused with mentoring or training, a coachee might expect to play a more passive role and receive advice from an expert in the field. The impact of a coach asking self-reflective questions, if it's the first time they've engaged in this way, could generate a feeling of being lost in the process, or confused about its value or purpose. This is especially likely to be the case in organizational cultures used to more autocratic leadership styles. At the same time, a line manager could expect the coach to share a lot of information on the coachee's development. It is therefore crucial to clarify the roles, responsibilities, limits and boundaries of the relationship.

*Step 3: Craft proper messages and storytelling*

Finally, once these messages are clearly articulated, it's important to engage leaders and executives in communicating them across the organization. Different organizations have different processes. Confusion around a coaching program can quickly lead to frustration and disengagement with the initiative. On the other hand, the strong involvement of managers and executives can boost engagement.

*Step 4: Privilege positive goals connected to professional development*

As mentioned above, a sense of personal growth and professional development connected to the participation in the initiative can drastically improve the level of engagement and motivation of the coachees. One of the ways to do that is to connect the program to a personal development plan based on the company's performance management system. Employees will feel that the organization is investing in their growth in a personalized way. Coaching in this case is positioned not as a remedial tool but as a privilege and development booster for those with potential for the future, creating a feeling of recognition and appreciation.

It is also advisable to promote goals and development plans in a positive way, associating them with strengths, talents and what people can improve further, rather than with what is missing or lacking. Insights from positive psychology suggest that identifying our strengths and using them are associated with higher levels of happiness (Seligman et al., 2005). In order to engage the employees in a coaching program focused on their development, make it clear they will benefit from making it a priority and focusing on key topics. They will need to consider what works, what they can improve, and what opportunities and resources they can leverage in order to generate their plan of action.

*Step 5: Engage coachees by fostering their autonomy*

In order to foster intrinsic motivation towards the coaching program and therefore increase the potential outcomes, a high degree of freedom and responsibility is critical; coaching is a tool which seeks to promote greater personal responsibility and choice. A successful coaching program allows coachees the freedom and space to personalize their development path, whilst being in alignment with the corporate goals and strategy. Autonomy, mastery and purpose are therefore intrinsic components of any program design, with the benefit of increased employee motivation (Pink, 2010).

This happens in coaching by choosing the coach, the goals to work on and, during the process itself, by developing awareness and a sense of responsibility towards finding new, creative solutions or perspectives. One of the deepest transformative effects of coaching is the possibility to create a 'personal development path', leveraging the coachee's unique strengths and connecting with their values and aspirations.

*Step 6: Recognize results (measured)*

As much as it is important to craft clear messages to draw engagement, it is also important to celebrate results and set appropriate organization measures for success (Grant, 2012).

Among the messages to spread are the concrete results achieved and storytelling, particularly from well-respected characters in the organization and senior leaders, who can be invited to share their experiences of coaching. The more people can be inspired by listening to coachee testimonials, the stronger the level of engagement. Such stories can cover the following questions:

- What are the benefits that coachees have achieved in their life?

- How did coaching facilitate a certain change or the development of awareness?

- How are they using the new learnings in their day-to-day activities and roles?

- What limiting beliefs have they dismantled, gaining more freedom, creativity and perspective?

## Conclusion

Coaching ignites deep change and growth in people. As with any other program, it needs to be coherent with a larger strategy. It should be communicated effectively and people should be properly engaged from the beginning. Mandating it as a top-down program, without proper framing and without involving all the people who will be impacted by it, risks reducing its efficacy and potential.

## References

Grant, A.M. (2012). ROI is a poor measure of coaching success: Towards a more holistic approach using a well-being and engagement framework. *Coaching: An International Journal of Theory, Research and Practice* 5(2): 74–85. DOI: 10.1080/17521882.2012.672438.

Pink, D. (2010). *Drive: The Surprising Truth About What Motivates Us*. Canongate Books: Edinburgh.

Seligman, M.E.P., Steen, T.A., Park, N., and Peterson, C. (2005). Positive psychology progress: Empirical validation of interventions. *American Psychologist* 60(5): 410–21. https://doi.org/10.1037/0003-066X.60.5.410.

CHAPTER 24

# How can we best support coachees in their coaching journey?

Windy Tshepiso Maledu

## Introduction

Coaching can at times feel like a journey embarked on by the coachee alone, with touchpoints with a coach but in effect experienced in isolation. And yet coaching in an organizational context inherently includes different stakeholders, who may either be allies or barriers to the benefits of coaching. When these networks come together in a positive way to support a coachee, they can make a significant contribution towards an increased likelihood of success. The coaching commissioner, coach, line manager and others all have an important contribution to the coaching journey. In this chapter, we will explore how to set up an environment to provide the maximum level of support to a coachee's coaching journey.

## Who is in the employee's system?

A foundation of coaching is empowerment, so a good place to begin is in encouraging the coachee to take ownership of identifying their own support network. As they prepare for coaching, one useful activity to encourage them to undertake is to spend a few minutes thinking about who is in their personal network. They might find it tempting to restrict the thinking to the organization, but it's also important to recognize that everyone has a broader network of friends, family and others for insight, ideas and support.

By mapping their system and the key stakeholders, they can begin to think about the ways they can invite these others to support their coaching journey. In some cases, this might be more formal support, such as a line manager connecting the coachee's coaching to their 1:1 conversations, joining an early coaching session or a review meeting. But it can also be informal support from colleagues and the wider network; activities identified and implemented by the coachee are very likely to be the most effective.

## How can organizations support coaches in their coaching journey?

We know from research how important a supportive organizational culture is to coaching success (Carter et al., 2014). It is critical for organizations in general, and line managers in particular, to support their employees during a coaching program.

### 1. Organizational support

The organization can firstly create a climate of support, linking coaching to wider HR policies and practices. Examples of this might include objective setting, relevant organizational policies and program sponsorship:

*Set broad objectives and frame them positively*

Establishing organizational objectives helps to provide a framework for the coaching. By using positive, simple and direct language in these objectives, employee engagement and understanding of these goals can be enhanced.

*Modify policies and processes to enable coaching*

HR has a part to play to ensure that the right organizational policies and processes are in place to support coaching. This can involve everything from encouraging managers to integrate coaching conversations into 1:1 conversations, to informing performance management processes and creating a culture which supports managers using a coaching style to engage their teams.

*Identify coaching champions or sponsors*

Having a strong, well-prepared and adequately supported network of coaching champions has proven to be one of the most effective success factors in the roll-out of various coaching initiatives. Champions also play an important role in sustaining coaching culture within the organization, sharing their stories alongside supporting the sponsor to secure wider corporate support.

The role of an executive sponsor is also important. A sponsor who has personal experience of coaching and can share this with the board helps, as does a sponsor who understands the connection between the HR strategy and the role coaching will play as part of this strategy.

### 2. Line-manager support

When coaching is viewed as a strategic priority in the organization, line managers are more likely to see the need to participate in the process. There are several steps line managers can be encouraged by coaching commissioners to take, to support the coaching process.

### Tripartite meeting

We have discussed the value of tripartite meetings. The tripartite meeting is an opportunity for the coach, coachee and line manager to align at the contracting stage of a coaching program. This can ensure the coaching goals are aligned, give the line manager a stronger stake in the process and ensure they have agreed the coaching agenda. This initial meeting might be complemented by midpoint and closing review meetings, to ensure the coaching is perceived by both the coachee and line manager to be having a positive effect, with opportunities for realignment or adjustment to the goals.

### Goal-setting

Once agreed, the line manager also has an important part to play in supporting the coachee's journey towards their goals. They can do this through the 1:1 process, as well as through wider performance evaluation and development opportunities. Simply including some time during each 1:1 to check on how coaching is progressing would be helpful, communicating both the line manager's interest and also providing space for the coachee to talk about any issues, hurdles or barriers they are facing, to thus leverage the support of their line manager to help them overcome these barriers.

### Feedback and support

Finally, offering development feedback is an important part of any line manager's role. During the coachee journey, the line manager can give feedback on positive behavior or performance changes that they notice, to encourage the coachee on their journey, and also allow them opportunities to explore the feedback and develop new insights or actions with their coach.

### 3. Wider network

The role of the coachee's wider network should also be considered. This might be informal relationships inside the organization, as well as friends, family and others outside of work. There are three specific roles that a coachee could categorize a trusted colleague under; the coaching commissioner's job here is to provide appropriate support and guidance to those individuals within existing processes. The three categories are accountability partner, champion and listener.

### Accountability partner

This informal role is arguably the most important, and is best done by someone selected by the coachee, as there is a need for trust and respect. The role is one of holding the person to account for their commitments; challenges and busyness can take priority when under pressure, and things can slip. The role of the accountability partner is to gently remind, encourage and nudge the coachee back onto the right path.

### Listener

The listener role, or thinking partner, is someone who is willing to make time to listen while the coachee processes, verbally, the coaching conversation. While some people like to do this internally and privately, others prefer to verbalize their thinking. This provides the opportunity for them to process and make sense of what they explored during the session.

This role appears easy but is difficult, so selecting the right person, who can pay the sort of generative attention that good listeners do, without wanting to jump in and offer advice, is important.

### Champion

Most people need someone who prizes or champions them. The champion is a partner who will affirm, praise and encourage the person, cheering them on, whatever goal the coachee has picked. Whoever steps into this role, it's not their task to be a critical thinker or offer challenges, but to regularly affirm and encourage the person to keep going, even when the going gets tough.

## Conclusion

In this chapter, we have discussed how the culture of the organization could be a potential tool to help coachees make the most of their coaching journey. Ensuring the right support structures are in place, such as support from senior leaders, alignment with organizational processes and gaining buy-in from key stakeholders through first-hand coaching experience, makes a big difference.

## References

Carter, A., Blackman, A., and Hicks, B. (2014). Barriers to successful coaching outcomes. In P. Lindall and D. Megginson (eds), *Book of Conference Proceedings from the 4th EMCC Research Conference*. Luxemburg: EMCC. Retrieved 10 April 2022 from: https://www.employment-studies.co.uk/system/files/resources/files/barriers_to_successful_coaching.pdf.

# When should we use coaching rather than mentoring?

Patrick Rütten

## Introduction

The ability to differentiate and assess the suitability of different organizational interventions is critical to the value that they can bring to organizations and individual employees. In this chapter, we aim to help differentiate between coaching and mentoring by offering clear definitions for each, as well as greater clarity about when each might be the best, or most appropriate, intervention.

## Differentiating between mentoring and coaching

In order to helpfully differentiate between different organizational interventions, we can approach from two perspectives. The first of these is to consider the theory – the differences in academic definitions, as well as research insights. A second angle is a more practical one: considering how different organizations are using coaching and mentoring in the workplace in practice.

Some scholars remain unconvinced that coaching and mentoring are different in nature (such as Koopman et al., 2021), but most writers acknowledge that coaching and mentoring have matured from abstract beginnings over the past 30 years, and while similar are importantly different interventions, each with distinctive benefits.

The EMCC defines coaching as: "an art: that of helping a person or a group to develop and enhance their professional, relational and personal potential in the realization of their projects and to take their rightful place in the relationship they have with themselves, others and their environment" (EMCC,

2022a). In contrast, mentoring is defined as: "a learning relationship, involving the sharing of skills, knowledge, and expertise between a mentor and mentee through developmental conversations, experience sharing, and role modeling. The relationship may cover a wide variety of contexts and is an inclusive two-way partnership for mutual learning that values differences" (EMCC, 2022b). Many other writers have also offered definitions of each (for a fuller discussion about definitions, see Passmore and Lai, 2019).

Coaching has long been described as more egalitarian than other 'helping relationships' such as mentoring (Grant and Cavanagh, 2004). A mentor is usually assumed to carry expertise and experience in the specific discipline or domain in which the mentee is working or aims to develop. In the workplace, mentors typically provide guidance on career development and networking (Eby et al., 2013), providing job-related (content) guidance to their mentees. In contrast, a coach is generally not expected to have expertise in the client's discipline or domain of work, and the directions taken across this form of cooperation are guided by specific objectives.

More generally, the evidence suggests the level of experience held by the coach is not a significant factor in coaching outcome (Graßmann and Schermuly, 2020). This differs from the inherent nature that experience and expertise play in the mentoring relationship, where the very role of the mentor is that of a 'wise sage'. As a result of the expertise, experience and reputation of the mentor, it is inevitable that the dynamics of many mentorship relationships will carry some degree of hierarchy or power which will impact on the nature of the helping relationship.

So, at least at a conceptual level, there are important differences between coaching and mentoring. What does that mean in practice? There are several factors of difference that emerge; I'll highlight three.

Firstly, contracting often adopts a more formal approach in coaching than in mentoring. Contracting is generally accepted to be a starting point for coaching, to the extent that associations such as the ICF include explicit references to contracting in their Professional Coaching Core Competencies. In contrast, few mentoring relationships are bounded by a documented contract or formal terms of engagement.

Secondly, the length of the relationship is different for each. Coaching tends towards a more targeted relationship, as short as four meetings, while in comparison mentoring relationships often flow over many years, with a more frequent and informal approach to scheduling meetings.

Thirdly, the approach used will differ. A mentor's inclination may be to use an instructional approach, sharing their wisdom and experience – after all, that is why the mentee has selected them. In comparison, the coach will adopt a facilitative style, inviting the coachee to think about their strengths and inner resources to gain insight and plan actions.

Jonathan Passmore (2021) provided a useful summary of the two different intentions at a practical level across a range of different dimensions (see Table 24.1).

**Table 24.1: Mentoring versus coaching – a practical guide**

| Criteria | Coaching | Mentoring |
|---|---|---|
| *Level of formality* | More formal: Typically involving a written contract or agreement | Less formal: Typically, word-of-mouth agreement |
| *Who's involved in contracting?* | Two or three parties: Can often involve a sponsor or line manager in an initial tripartite meeting at the start and at the end | Two parties: Mentor and mentee |
| *Length of contract* | Shorter: Typically, 4–12 meetings agreed over 12 months or less | Longer: Typically, unspecified number of meetings; often runs over 3–5 years (and beyond) |
| *Focus* | More performance focus: Typically concerned with development of skills for current role and performance | More career-focused: Typically concerned with long-term career development |
| *Level of sector knowledge* | More generalist: Typically, coaches have limited sector knowledge | More sector knowledge: Typically, mentors are a respected person in the organization or sector |
| *Training* | More training: Typically, coaches are trained and accredited | Less training: Typically, are untrained or may have a single day's worth of training as mentors, but bring formal qualifications from their sector role |

## When is it best to use which intervention?

Organizations thus have the chance to deploy two organizational interventions with a high degree of individual focus and personalization. So, when should organizations employ coaching instead of mentoring, and vice versa? The answer might not always point clearly in one direction. In fact, organizations should use both and see them as complementary, in the same way training and lectures can serve different purposes. Depending on the desired outcome, such as which skills and knowledge are being developed, a decision should be made about whether coaching or mentoring is the right choice.

Of course, there are significant intersections between the two, in both theory and practice. However, it may be helpful to think about the following aspects to establish which might be the most suitable approach given your specific circumstances:

- Is the focus area of development related to the employee's current short- or medium-term personal growth and current role performance (coaching), or is it about long-term career management (mentoring)?

- Is the focus about developing a personal plan (coaching) or being developed by someone else (mentoring)?

- Is the focus about managing the self (coaching) or about leveraging connections and relationships from another (mentoring)?

- Is it about exploration and greater self-awareness (coaching) or the acquisition of domain-specific knowledge (mentoring)?

Naturally, the reality is that many coaching conversations stray into some areas of mentoring, and some mentoring conversations are delivered most effectively through (elements of) coaching. Having the best of both worlds is an ideal, and many leaders during the course of their career use both. Every employee at one time or another will need both to enhance their role performance and to think through current role challenges and issues with a coach, and also learn from a mentor who has been able to act as a role model.

## Conclusion

As individualized learning formats gain popularity, organizations are moving away from the 'sheep dip' approach to development, increasing the demand for both coaching and mentoring. By widening and deepening its toolkit for development, an organization is better placed to meet the unique needs of its people. Coaching and mentoring are sisters, and each has a place in every organization's suite of development interventions.

## References

Grant, A.M., and Cavanagh, M.J. (2004). Toward a profession of coaching: Sixty-five years of progress and challenges for the future. *International Journal of Evidence Based Coaching and Mentoring* 2(1): 1–16.

Graßmann, C., and Schermuly, C.C. (2020). Understanding what drives the coaching working alliance: A systematic literature review and meta-analytic examination. *International Coaching Psychology Review* 15(2): 99–118.

Eby, L.T.d.T., Allen, T.D., Hoffman, B.J., Baranik, L.E., Sauer, J.B., Baldwin, S., Morrison, M.A., Kinkade, K.M., Maher, C.P., Curtis, S., and Evans, S.C. (2013). An interdisciplinary meta-analysis of the potential antecedents, correlates, and consequences of protégé perceptions of mentoring. *Psychological Bulletin* 139(2): 441–76. https://doi.org/10.1037/a0029279.

EMCC (2022a) *Definition of Coaching*. Retrieved 5 March 2022 from: https://www.emccbelgium.org/en/find-a-coach/about-coaching.

EMCC (2022b) *Definition of Mentoring*. Retrieved 5 March 2022 from: https://www.emccglobal.org/leadership-development/leadership-development-mentoring.

Koopman, R., English, P.D., Ehgrenhard, M.L., and Groen, A. (2021). The chrono-logical development of coaching and mentoring: Side by side disciplines. *International Journal of Evidence Based Coaching & Mentoring* 19(1).

Passmore, J. (2021). Coaching defined and explored. In J. Passmore (ed.), *The Coaches' Handbook: The Complete Practitioner Guide for Professional Coaches*. Abingdon: Routledge.

Passmore, J., and Lai, Y.-L. (2019). Coaching psychology: Exploring definitions and research contribution to practice? *International Coaching Psychology Review* 14(2): 69–83.

# CHAPTER 26

# When should we use training or appraisals rather than coaching?

Patrick Rütten

## Introduction

Interest in workplace learning has increased during the last decades. Literature reviews attribute this partially to how our workplace characteristics have changed (see, for example, Mikkonen et al., 2017) and a shift in many national economies to knowledge-based work (see Manuti et al., 2015). Alongside this has come a more dynamic work environment, which has created a desire to move beyond preparing people for today's challenges, and to resource employees for tomorrow. In this chapter, we will discuss the unique characteristics and benefits of training, appraisals and coaching, to understand why these are not replacements for one another, and how each has an important and complementary part to play in organizational L&D strategy.

## Training, appraisals and coaching

Just as the nature of work has changed over the last 30 years, workforces also need to constantly adapt to the evolving organizational, societal and economic environment. Many organizations seek to meet these changes through their L&D strategy. This strategy should bring together an analysis of the environment with the skills, knowledge and attitudes needed for the organization to thrive, while answering the question of how the multiple levers available for developing their talent can be used to achieve these ends.

## Training

Training usually involves a predefined syllabus based on learning objectives, shaped to provide learning experiences through the use of various media. Training can be used as an anticipatory instrument to develop new knowledge, skills and attitudes that are required now, such as the use of a new software package being introduced or how to follow a new organizational process. In essence, training is good for supplying the knowledge required to meet a new task or for compliance. In practice, however, there is a temptation for training also to be used to address virtually any perceived gap in current needs that are identified across operations.

Training is an excellent intervention that enables new knowledge to be shared at scale with a standardized set of content, producing, at least in theory, uniform knowledge and competence. This structured approach allows for control over the content, standardized evaluation of trainers, and assessment. However, the true effectiveness of training relies on multiple aspects, many outside of the training designers' control. These include the prior knowledge of the learners, the learners' motivation, interpersonal relationships between participants and the trainer, as well as the quality of content and the ability to transfer from the theory of the classroom to the practice of the office.

While an essential component in almost all L&D strategies, research studies have highlighted the challenges of optimizing the value of training (see, for example, Hughes et al., 2020). Apart from the challenges of training design and delivery, the greatest challenge is that transfer of knowledge from the classroom to skills at the desk. This is where coaching can make a significant contribution, complementing training by helping employees reflect on the knowledge, integrate it with their existing skills, knowledge and experience, develop plans for testing out the new insights, and practicing in an environment where support is balanced with challenge. Studies (such as Passmore and Rehman, 2012) have shown that combining coaching with training wields significantly greater power than a simple instruction-only approach.

## Appraisals

Appraisals in recent years have become a tool which is often derided at work as being little more than box ticking. However, when done well, appraisals can make employees feel valued, increase organizational commitment, and provide personal and career development (Strebler et al., 2001).

One of the main problems with the appraisal is that it is seen as a highly structured, one-off (often annual) event. This lack of personalization and the infrequent nature of the conversation make it stand out as unusual. But good managers can make feedback and performance conversations a valuable part of everyday interactions.

Rudman (2020) offered guidance on how to manage performance conversations. He suggested that most appraisees have a set of questions for which they are seeking answers, which include:

- What do you want me to do?

- To what standard do you want me to do it?

- How am I doing now?

- How will I be rewarded?

For an appraiser to be able to articulate answers to these questions, the organization needs to be able to define:

- What work it needs people to do

- Which performance standards it will set

- What feedback it will provide

- What rewards it will offer.

What matters most is to make feedback a regular event, with a greater focus on the positive, and, when providing developmental feedback, to make good use of specific evidence. But just providing feedback is not enough: performance improvement comes not just from what we have done well or need to do better, but from the ongoing conversations about how we can do better by doing things differently. This is the added value that coaching can bring to the appraisal process:

- Helping to set goals

- Establishing measures of success

- Discussing options and plans

- Identifying consequences and required resources

- Implementing through experimentation

- Providing space for reflection and further feedback.

In summary, appraisals are most useful when they are part of a wider system of regular feedback and developmental conversations to support behavioral change.

## Coaching

Given this overview of appraisals and training, and how coaching can be used to support both, it can feel tempting to introduce coaching only in these roles, thanks to the immediate applicability in L&D strategies. But coaching has other roles to play. By using an independent coach, the coachee can reflect on their purpose within their role, explore their strengths, consider the system in which they work and how they leverage their network to deliver value, and finally explore in an open and authentic way their weaknesses, worries and fears. Through this support, the coachee can harness self-awareness and personal power to become more impactful in their role. Such assets may be difficult to measure, but research has shown over and over again that the impact of coaching transcends today's job roles, and creates employees fit for tomorrow.

## Conclusion

While coaching, appraisals and training do not always offer perfect results when used in isolation to build new knowledge, skills and capabilities, they are essential ingredients in any L&D strategy and can be intelligently combined to maximize effectiveness. The best organizations make use of a range of approaches, including training and appraisals alongside coaching, to optimize people development, wellbeing and performance.

## References

Hughes, A.M., Zajac, S., Woods, A.L., and Salas, E. (2020). The role of work environment in training sustainment: A meta-analysis. *Human factors* 62(1): 166–83.

Manuti, A., Pastore, S., Scardigno, A.F., Giancaspro, M.L., and Morciano, D. (2015). Formal and informal learning in the workplace: A research review. *International Journal of Training and Development* 19(1): 1–17.

Mikkonen, S., Pylväs, L., Rintala, H., Nokelainen, P., and Postareff, L. (2017). Guiding workplace learning in vocational education and training: A literature review. *Empirical Research in Vocational Education and Training* 9(1): 1–22.

Passmore, J., and Rehman, H. (2012). Coaching as a learning methodology – a mixed methods study in driver development using a randomized controlled trial and thematic analysis. *International Coaching Psychology Review* 7(2): 166–84.

Rudman, R. (2020). *Performance Planning and Review: Making Employee Appraisals Work.* Abingdon: Routledge.

Strebler, M., Robinson, D., and Bevan, S. (2001). *Performance Review: Balancing objectives and content. London: Institute for Employment Studies.*

# CHAPTER 27

# When should we use counseling or occupational health rather than coaching?

Miriam Schneider-Tettenborn

## Introduction

As mentioned, coaching is not the solution for every problem. When it comes to health and wellbeing, there is a limit as to when coaching should be used and when the coach should refer the coachee to a professional counselor or occupational-health professional. Occupational health can be understood as the physical and mental wellbeing caretaker in an organization. This ranges from traditional health-and-safety measures, such as ensuring the accessibility of fire escape routes, to ensuring employees' psychological wellbeing. In this chapter, we will focus on the mental-health aspects of occupational health, firstly through exploring three approaches of occupational-health interventions and how coaching fits into those levels, and secondly by proposing a clear differentiation between coaching and counseling, and when each should be used.

## Occupational mental health at three levels

LaMontagne and colleagues (2014) advocate for an integrative approach to occupational-mental-health interventions. They outline three levels of measures – the primary (preventative), the secondary (ameliorative) and the tertiary (reactive) – as can be seen in Figure 27.1.

**Figure 27.1: Wellbeing at work – three stages of intervention**

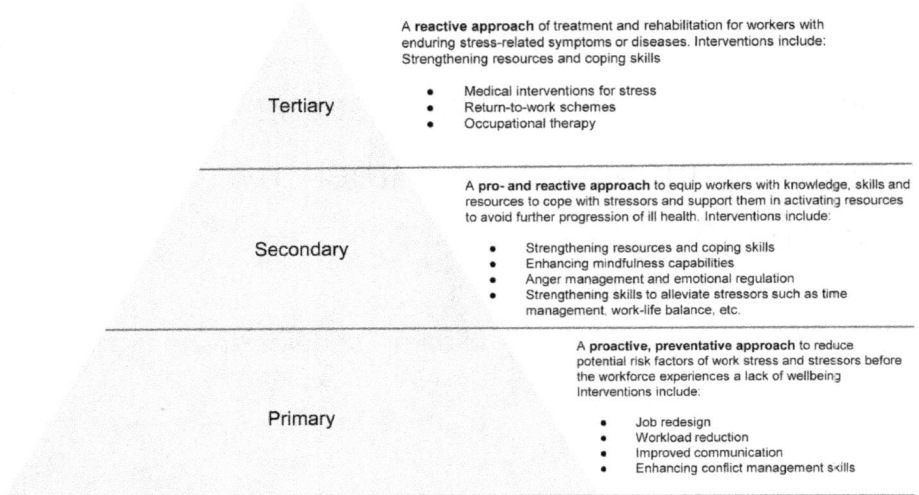

A **reactive approach** of treatment and rehabilitation for workers with enduring stress-related symptoms or diseases. Interventions include: Strengthening resources and coping skills

**Tertiary**

- Medical interventions for stress
- Return-to-work schemes
- Occupational therapy

A **pro- and reactive approach** to equip workers with knowledge, skills and resources to cope with stressors and support them in activating resources to avoid further progression of ill health. Interventions include:

**Secondary**

- Strengthening resources and coping skills
- Enhancing mindfulness capabilities
- Anger management and emotional regulation
- Strengthening skills to alleviate stressors such as time management, work-life balance, etc.

A **proactive, preventative approach** to reduce potential risk factors of work stress and stressors before the workforce experiences a lack of wellbeing Interventions include:

**Primary**

- Job redesign
- Workload reduction
- Improved communication
- Enhancing conflict management skills

(Adapted from LaMontagne et al., 2014)

*Primary level*

At the bottom of the intervention pyramid lie primary approaches. These are the foundation of a healthy workplace: proactive measures to enhance the wellbeing of the workforce. These approaches strive to reduce extreme stressors (Quick, 1998) and set up the environment to be as healthy as possible. Examples are workload management and job design, as well as preventative upskilling of the workforce. Such upskilling may be training and development offers to, for example, improve communication skills, which may lead to better communication, improved collaboration and help prevent conflict. The goal of this primary level is for risk factors to be mitigated as much as possible.

Coaching at this level can support the preventative approach. It can help coachees gain increased self-awareness, clarity on values, resources and clients, and enhance skill-based learnings such as communication or collaboration skills (Jones et al., 2016). Even further, coaching at the primary level can help coachees develop psychological resources (mindsets) and stress-management skills ahead of time, as well as support the process of job crafting so that extreme stressors are averted. For leaders specifically, it has been found that coaching can in fact have a preventative effect on poor psychological health (Weinberg, 2016).

*Secondary level*

In organizations, stressors can hardly ever be fully avoided and some are even argued to be useful, such as 'eustress', a positive kind of stress, inducing challenge and motivation (Hargrove et al., 2011). At this level, occupational health for workplace wellbeing aims for three outcomes:

1. To support employees in dealing with stressors that cannot be averted

2. To equip employees with knowledge, skills and resources to cope with stressors

3. To support employees in activating resources to avoid a potential progression towards ill health (LaMontagne et al., 2014).

In short, interventions at this level "focus on providing individuals with a toolbox of coping methods for dealing with stressors" (Quick, 1999: 189). This toolbox may entail interventions on mindfulness or cognitive behavioral therapy, as well as training on self-leadership, such as time management and work–life balance skills.

Coaching at this secondary level can help to equip this toolbox. It has been shown to enhance coping skills such as resilience (Grant et al., 2009), as well as strengthening resources such as self-enhancing attributions (Moen and Skaalvik, 2009), confidence and self-acceptance. These, in turn, positively impact wellbeing (Donaldson-Feilder and Bond, 2004). Coaching, especially positive psychology coaching, can develop the mindfulness capabilities of employees (Spence et al., 2008) which facilitate coping with a stressful environment. Finally, coaching can also help to improve cognitive skills such as self-efficacy (Baron and Morin, 2010) and problem-solving skills (Jones et al., 2016), which enhance an individual's ability to tackle stressors.

*Tertiary level and the need for counseling*

At the third level, occupational-health approaches are reactive. Quick (1998: 189) has termed this "the last line of defense for stress management", but indeed at this level the last line of defense may have already fallen. Tertiary occupational-health interventions aim to treat and rehabilitate workers with enduring stress-related symptoms or diseases. Approaches here are 'return to work' schemes after a long absence of illness, and occupational therapy or medical treatment for stress (LaMontagne et al., 2014). Treatment that is needed at this level often addresses clinical expressions of mental ill-health such as burnout or even depression.

This is the level where coaching is no longer an appropriate offering to the workforce. Once employees have reached this level of distress and suffer from a clinical level of expression, appropriately trained counselors or psycho-therapists are needed. One of the challenges here for coaches is that there is no expectation that they would be trained to recognize signs of clinical distress; some research argues that coaches who are better trained are actually more unlikely to refer clients on to appropriate treatment (Schermuly and Graßmann, 2019).

## 27.2: Application of coaching within the occupational health pyramid

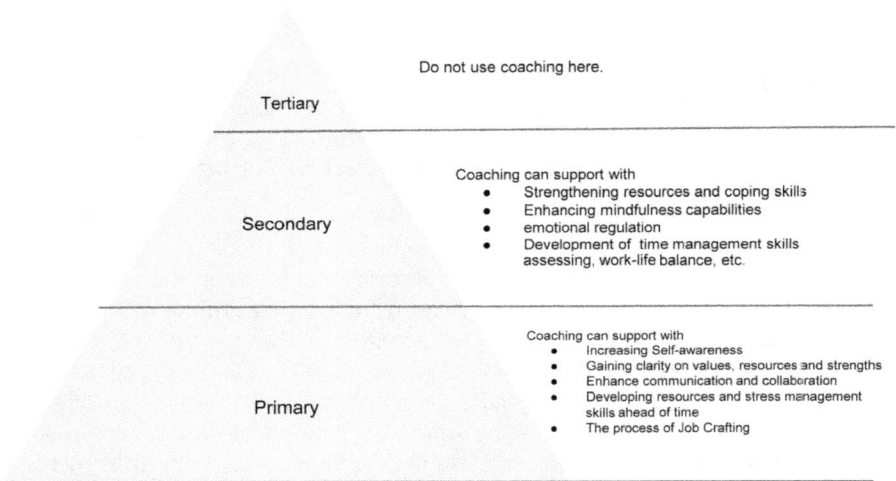

Do not use coaching here.

Tertiary

Coaching can support with
- Strengthening resources and coping skills
- Enhancing mindfulness capabilities
- emotional regulation
- Development of time management skills assessing, work-life balance, etc.

Secondary

Coaching can support with
- Increasing Self-awareness
- Gaining clarity on values, resources and strengths
- Enhance communication and collaboration
- Developing resources and stress management skills ahead of time
- The process of Job Crafting

Primary

Application of coaching in the occupational health pyramid

One helpful model to determine the suitability of coaching is the 'flourishing at work' model for wellbeing coaching, originally developed by Grant and colleagues (2009; see Figure 27.3). The bottom-left quartile ('Burnout') represents the area of low engagement and low wellbeing, the distressed and dysfunctional zone. This is where employees find themselves nearing burnout, possibly with additional mental-health issues such as clinical depression or anxiety. This area, especially when nearing further mental-health problems, is not an area where coaching should be the (main) source of support for employees. Instead, counseling needs to be offered. If made available from the organization, ideally this should be available anonymously and easily accessible.

The 'Distressed but functional' zone may be a trickier area in which to distinguish between the need for counseling and the appropriateness of coaching. Employees in this area may seem like high performers whilst actually suffering silently from anxiety, extensive stress or other negative mental-health symptoms. Well-trained coaches should be able to spot these and either support clients in dealing with their symptoms or recommend counseling as a better option.

In the 'Acquiescent' zone of the model, clients may be well, but not engaged in their day-to-day work. Coaching is useful here to help them identify their motivations and align with organizational values and goals. Finally, when people are in the 'Flourishing at work' zone, coaching can support them in furthering their strengths and resources, the things that got them there, in order to accelerate clients' goal achievement and maximize their positive impact in the organization.

**Figure 27.3: Mental wellbeing and engagement**

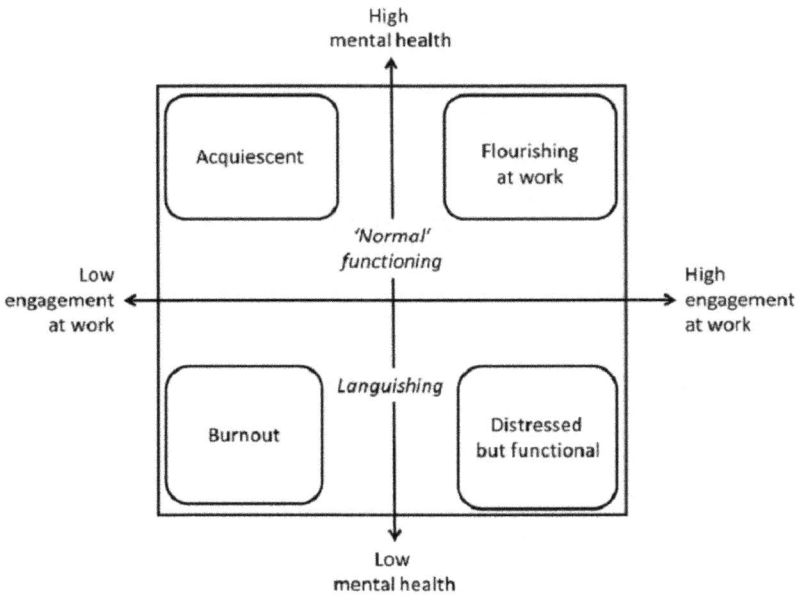

(Adapted from Grant et al., 2010)

## Conclusion

Occupational health can encompass many approaches to support an employee workforce. Coaching is an ideal solution to support employees, but it is not a clinical intervention. Coaches, even accredited coaches, are not trained or skilled to manage such issues. Instead, individuals with clinical issues should be referred to a doctor or clinical psychologist. The best option is always for organizations to have a range of different pathways to support their employees, from training and appraisal and from coaching to providing EAP schemes for clinical issues. Pretending these are all the same risks or that coaches can cope with mental-health problems risks not only confusion but also putting both coach and client at risk.

## References

Anstiss, T., and Passmore, J. (2017). Wellbeing coaching. In C. Cooper and M.P. Leiter (eds), *The Routledge companion to wellbeing at work*, pp.237–48. Abingdon: Routledge.

Baron, L., and Morin, L. (2010). The impact of executive coaching on self-efficacy related to management soft-skills. *Leadership & Organization Development Journal* 31(1): 18–38.

Donaldson-Feilder, E.J., and Bond, F.W. (2004). The relative importance of psychological acceptance and emotional intelligence to workplace well-being. *British Journal of Guidance & Counselling* 32(2): 187–203. https://doi.org/10.1080/08069880410001692210.

Grant, A.M., Curtayne, L., and Burton, G. (2009). Executive coaching enhances goal attainment, resilience and workplace well-being: A randomized controlled study. *Journal of Positive Psychology* 4(5): 396–407.

Hargrove, M.B., Quick, J.C., Nelson, D.L., and Quick, J.D. (2011). The theory of preventive stress management: A 33-year review and evaluation. *Stress and Health* 27(3): 182–93.

Jones, R.J., Woods, S.A., and Guillaume, Y.R. (2016). The effectiveness of workplace coaching: A meta-analysis of learning and performance outcomes from coaching. *Journal of Occupational and Organizational Psychology* 89(2): 249–77.

LaMontagne, A.D., Martin, A., Page, K.M., Reavley, N.J., Noblet, A.J., Milner, A.J., and Smith, P.M. (2014). Workplace mental health: Developing an integrated intervention approach. *BMC Psychiatry* 14(1): 1–11.

Moen, F., and Skaalvik, E. (2009). The effect from executive coaching on performance psychology. International Journal of Evidence Based Coaching and Mentoring 7(2): 31–49.

Quick, J.C. (1998). Introduction to the measurement of stress at work. *Journal of Occupational Health Psychology* 3(4): 291–3.

Quick, J.C. (1999). Occupational health psychology: The convergence of health and clinical psychology with public health and preventive medicine in an organizational context. *Professional Psychology, Research and Practice* 30(2): 123–8.

Schermuly, C.C., and Graßmann, C. (2019). A literature review on negative effects of coaching – what we know and what we need to know. *Coaching: An International Journal of Theory, Research and Practice* 12(1): 39–66.

Spence, G.B., Cavanagh, M.J., and Grant, A.M. (2008). The integration of mindfulness training and health coaching: An exploratory study. *Coaching: An International Journal of Theory, Research and Practice* 1(2): 145–63. https://doi.org/10.1080/17521880802328178.

Weinberg, A. (2016). The preventative impact of management coaching on psychological strain. *International Coaching Psychology Review* 11(1): 93–105.

# CHAPTER 28

# How can we help our staff to prepare for coaching sessions?

Miriam Schneider-Tettenborn

## Introduction

Client readiness is a significant predictor of enhanced leadership effectiveness after coaching (MacKie, 2015) and coaching success in general (Athanasopoulou and Dopson, 2018). When commissioning coaching for staff, supporting them in their preparation will ensure they get the most out of their engagement. Many factors can support in setting up coaching for success, and we will discuss a key selection of these in this chapter.

## Preparing the mindset

Preparation for coaching can be as pragmatic as thinking about goals and topics. Setting up coaching participants for success is also related to the person's mindset and how they are about to engage with the coaching journey. Motivation and readiness for change are key factors in the success of coaching (de Haan et al., 2013), so emphasizing the importance of a psychological commitment to the process can be a big enabler for effectiveness (Bozer and Jones, 2018). In addition, coaching participants' expectation as to how much the coach and the coaching process are going to be able to help them can impact both their involvement and coaching success.

Of course, an organization cannot simply tell its employees to be hopeful or to expect coaching to act as a magic spell. Communication around coaching is key in setting the stage and preparing the mindset for coaching; explaining how coaching works and what to expect from the process is always helpful. Positioning it as a carrot rather than a stick provides a good starting point to then hand over the mantle to the coaching participant to manage the coaching journey, empowering them from the get-go.

## Highlighting the importance of the relationship

Educating coaching participants on the importance of trust and the working relationship with their coach can also be helpful. Both are key ingredients for a successful coaching process (Graßmann et al., 2020); trusting the coach and their capability to support the coaching participant along the process increases the likelihood of the coaching participant opening up and discussing important goals. The so-called 'working alliance' is one of the key ingredients for a successful coaching process, incorporating rapport, agreement on goals and agreement on actions. If there is strong disagreement on any of these points, the coaching participant should know that they are able to change their coach at any point in time, even if they have already started the coaching sessions. The ability to choose the right coach should also be raised by the coach in the initial contracting session. An organization can support its people by emphasizing the importance of the working alliance and their choice about whom to work with.

## Encouraging meaningful goals

One of the key benefits of coaching is that it helps participants to strive for and achieve their goals, and goal-setting can serve as a powerful motivator (Locke and Latham, 2002). An organization can set up coaching participants for success by encouraging them to find goals that are meaningful to both them and the organization, and by setting SMART goals (specific, measurable, aligned, realistic, time-bound). This is important as it has been found that unrealistic or excessively difficult goals can in turn be demotivating (Athanasopoulou and Dopson, 2018), while goals that are meaningful can accelerate motivation towards achieving them. As a result, coaching can act as a slingshot for staff on their way towards goal attainment, and if they are truly aligned to organizational objectives the positive contribution to the organization as a whole will be tangible.

## Engaging the line manager

Line-manager support has been found to enhance successful coaching journeys (Bozer and Jones, 2018). Thus, it is in the interest of a coaching commissioner to ensure the support of line managers, and in the interest of coaching participants to engage their line managers with regards to goal-setting and asking for feedback. Participants may find it helpful to ask for feedback from their line managers as to what they would suggest as relevant coaching topics; this may be relevant goals or development areas (see also Chapter 48: 'How should the line manager give feedback to support the coaching assignment?').

Line managers should be clear that coaching is not a performance-management tool. It continues to be the responsibility of the line manager to address performance-management issues. Coaching can support the individual integration of possible performance development feedback for the coaching participant. But coaching is a solution-, strength- and future-focused intervention, and thus will go much beyond performance challenges. Engaging the line manager in goal-setting may catalyze the line manager's support throughout the journey by checking in on coaching progress, giving feedback on observed changes and, perhaps most importantly, respecting the time their staff spend receiving coaching.

## Allowing for space – through time and space

Another key enabler for coaching participants is to empower them to spend time on their coaching. Clear communication about prioritizing coaching engagements in the working week and during work hours can allow for the space and for coachees to engage with coaching regularly. Highlighting the importance of spending time beforehand to prepare for coaching, and afterwards to reflect upon it, will also help them to get the most out of coaching. In addition, providing a safe space, such as closed-off meeting rooms or encouraging staff to do coaching from their home office, may allow them to fully immerse themselves in the coaching process.

## Conclusion

In summary, it is important to recognize that factors generated by the coaching participant as well as the organizational context will set up a coaching engagement for success – or hinder it. Honoring the points laid out in this chapter will help an organization set up its people for success for their coaching sessions.

# References

Athanasopoulou, A., and Dopson, S. (2018). A systematic review of executive coaching outcomes: Is it the journey or the destination that matters the most? *Leadership Quarterly* 29(1): 70–88.

Bozer, G., and Jones, R.J. (2018). Understanding the factors that determine workplace coaching effectiveness: A systematic literature review. *European Journal of Work and Organizational Psychology* 27(3): 342–61.

de Haan, E., Duckworth, A., Birch, D., and Jones, C. (2013). Executive coaching outcome research: The contribution of common factors such as relationship, personality match, and self-efficacy. *Consulting Psychology Journal: Practice and Research* 65(1): 40.

Graßmann, C., Schölmerich, F., and Schermuly, C.C. (2020). The relationship between working alliance and client outcomes in coaching: A meta-analysis. *Human Relations* 73(1): 35–58.

Locke, E.A., and Latham, G.P. (2002). Building a practically useful theory of goal setting and task motivation: A 35-year odyssey. *American Psychologist* 57(9): 705.

MacKie, D. (2015). The effects of coachee readiness and core self-evaluations on leadership coaching outcomes: A controlled trial. *Coaching: An International Journal of Theory, Research and Practice* 8(2): 120–36.

CHAPTER 29

# How will we measure the impact of coaching in relation to our strategy?

Elizabeth Pavese, PhD

## Introduction

With coaching's rising profile, it is important to understand how the quality of coaching and the outcomes of coaching can be evaluated and thus ensured in any coaching program. How can we know that coaching worked and measure the coaching outcomes of our workforce and organization? While return on investment (ROI) is a popular metric and well known to business leaders, it can be misleading if used as the one metric of focus, especially for coaching. In this chapter, we will explore ways to assess the holistic value of coaching, going beyond a focus on a single metric.

## The issue with ROI alone

ROI is often the first metric that comes to mind when business leaders are advocating for specific programs or initiatives and want to be able to connect the value back to the economic engine of business. And while ROI has been a focus in much coaching literature (McGovern et al., 2001), it has received considerable scrutiny (for example, De Meuse et al., 2009; de Haan, 2016; Grant, 2012) for a variety of reasons.

Firstly, coaching is a highly personalized and individual process, where no one coaching engagement looks the same as another. Further, coaching success is predicated in large part on the relationship between the coach and the coachee. It's a powerful intervention because it provides a safe space to learn, be vulnerable and deeply reflect on the premise that ethics and confidentiality are at the center of this engagement. This impacts our measurement abilities as we need to ensure that the practice adheres to coaching ethics and retains confidentiality. Because it is so individual, it is really hard to compare coaching, as no one session is the same as any other.

Secondly, while the individuality of coaching is a core strength of the intervention, this too presents its own measurement challenges. Specifically, the reliance on self-ratings may cause bias and present a timing issue with measurement, since behavior change is a long-term process and the result of many factors that cannot be isolated to coaching alone.

It's not that we cannot assess and measure the impact of coaching, however; we simply need to think in more holistic terms and consider all of the value impacts that coaching has. Further, it's important to take into account the context and process of the coaching intervention as key inputs, as research shows there are many active ingredients that are highly influential to overall coaching success, let alone the variety of other benefits. If we consider the impact of coaching as a chain of value to be realized over time, by understanding the predictive inputs, immediate outcomes and results, we can assess value creation over time.

**Figure 29.1: The value chain**

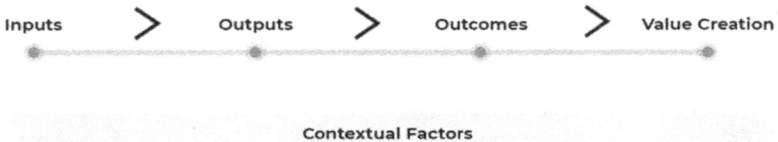

## Key inputs for success

A very common question when embarking with a coaching engagement, is "who should receive coaching?" Considering this, we can turn to the evidence. There are several key inputs for successful coaching, known as active ingredients (de Haan et al., 2013). These active ingredients are the factors that influence the impact or success of coaching. The following three inputs have been identified in research as key predictors of coaching success.

First, is *a high-quality working alliance*, meaning the strength of the relationship between the coach and coachee. When there is a higher bond between the coach and the coachee, there is a greater likelihood of realizing many outcomes of the coaching process.

Second, is *the coachee's self-efficacy.* That is, the coachee's belief in their ability to cope with stressful or challenging demands, as well as their belief that they will succeed.

Third, is *perceived coach competency.* That is, how well a coach is seen by the coachee to use a range of coaching techniques. When coaches are seen to have more of a range in their repertoire, this demonstrates credibility and, therefore, builds a level of trust in the coach.

## Coaching has benefits at multiple levels of an organization

Coaching research is coming of age and there are several studies that have shown the impact that coaching has at an individual, team and organizational level (for example, Athanasopoulou and Dopson, 2018; Theeboom et al., 2013; Sonesh et al., 2015; Jones et al., 2016). All of these levels are important if you want to gain a holistic view of the effectiveness of coaching.

*Individual outputs*

The impact on the individual is the most well-researched area. It has been confirmed that coaching has a positive impact on affective outcomes, which are changes of the individual on the attitudinal and motivational level for topics such as self-awareness, self-efficacy, reduced stress, increased job satisfaction, wellbeing and general attitudes. Coaching has the strongest positive impact on setting and reaching goals, which positively impacts the individual's performance in their organization.

*Team and organizational outcomes and value creation*

Coaching positively impacts the coachee and their wellbeing, and it is also positive for the people around them. From an organizational perspective there are a variety of indirect positive effects of coaching including increased employee satisfaction, productivity and improved leadership effectiveness.

*Holistic impact measurement*

It's clear that there are wide-ranging outcomes of coaching that are predicated on key inputs for success, as outlined in the coaching literature. Table 29.1 shows various evidence-based metrics that will help determine the overall impact of coaching at multiple levels. Many of these are leading indicators of impact, and others are lagging.

**Table 29.1: Indicators of coaching success**

| Active ingredients and coaching process | Coachee outcomes | Business/talent results |
|---|---|---|
| • Working alliance | • Goal attainment | • Job satisfaction |
| • Coachee self-efficacy | • Coachee self-awareness | • Job performance |
| • Coach quality | • Perceived learning | • Employee wellbeing |
| | • Perceived behavior change | |
| | • Coaching Effectiveness | |

Coaching is an intervention that shapes behavior and it's important to keep in mind that mindset shift and behavior change are a lifelong journey. Therefore, when looking at key measures along the value chain it is essential to examine both leading and lagging indicators – measures that can provide an immediate assessment of potential impact (leading) and others that will help assess the value of the intervention over a longer period of time (lagging). Table 29.2 offers tips to consider when determining what to measure.

## Example: Coaching for first-time leaders

Let's take, for example, coaching for first-time leaders. Many organizations provide a significant amount of resources to support this critical transition from individual contributor to new manager. There are a variety of key shifts in scope, responsibility and mindset, as well as new skills to be learned in order for this transition to be impactful and successful. Very often, first-time leaders are also attending structured learning to gain knowledge and practice new skills.

When it comes to the coaching elements of this type of transition program, there are several measures that could indicate impact, short term and long term. For example, leading indicators of the impact of coaching could include coachee self-efficacy, perceived quality and satisfaction with the coach, self-perceived learning and behavior change. Lagging indicators would include organizational metrics that indicate impact on the team and organization at large, such as team-level employee engagement, manager performance in role, multisource development feedback on behavior, team-level turnover and retention.

**Table 29.2: Tips for determining what is important to measure**

| | |
|---|---|
| 1. | Understand what the organization's objectives are for offering coaching |
| 2. | Clarify what the expected results or outcomes are, in alignment with those objectives |
| 3. | Specify what coachees need to learn and do – specifically if tied to a development program |
| 4. | Align coaching based on coachee motivation and commitment |

## Conclusion

In this chapter, we explored the importance of measurement and why it is critical to focus on a range of outcomes to assess the impact of coaching. Because coaching has an impact at an individual, a team and an organizational level, there are many different indicators that can be evaluated, not a singular number or output.

## References

Athanasopoulou, A., and Dopson, S. (2018). A systematic review of executive coaching outcomes: Is it the journey or the destination that matters the most? *Leadership Quarterly* 29(1): 70–88. DOI: 10.1016/j.leaqua.2017.11.004.

de Haan, E., Duckworth, A., Birch, D., and Jones, C. (2013). Executive coaching outcome research: The contribution of common factors such as relationship, personality match, and self-efficacy. *Consulting Psychology Journal: Practice and Research* 65: 1–18. DOI: 10.1037/a0031635.

de Haan, E., Grant, A.M., Burger, Y., and Eriksson, P.-O. (2016). A large-scale study of executive and workplace coaching: The relative contributions of relationship, personality match, and self-efficacy. Consulting Psychology Journal: Practice and Research 68(3): 189–207. https://doi.org/10.1037/cpb0000058.

De Meuse, K.P., Dai, K., and Lee, R.J. (2009). Evaluating the effectiveness of executive coaching: Beyond ROI? *Coaching: An International Journal of Theory, Research, and Practice* 2: 117–34. DOI: 10.1080/17521880902882413.

Grant, A.M. (2012). ROI is a poor measure of coaching success: Towards a more holistic approach using a well-being and engagement framework. *Coaching: An International Journal of Theory, Research and Practice* 5(2): 1–12. DOI: 10.1080/17521882.2012.672438.

Jones, R.J., Woods, S.A., and Guillaume, Y.R.F. (2016). The effectiveness of workplace coaching: A meta-analysis of learning and performance outcomes from coaching. *Journal of Occupational and Organizational Psychology* 89: 249–77. DOI: 10.1111/joop.12119.

McGovern, J., Lindemann, M., Vergara, M., Murphy, S., Barker, L., and Warrenfeltz, R. (2001). Maximizing the impact of executive coaching: Behavioral change, organizational outcomes, and return on investment. *Manchester Review* 6: 1–9.

Sonesh, S.C., Coultas, C.W., Lacerenza, C.N., Marlow, S.L., Benishek, L.E., and Salas, E. (2015). The power of coaching: A meta-analytic investigation. *Coaching: An International Journal of Theory, Research and Practice* 8(2): 73–95. https://doi.org/10.1080/17521882.2015.1071418.

Theeboom, T., Beersma, B., and van Vianen, A.E.M. (2013). Does coaching work? A meta-analysis on the effects of coaching on individual level outcomes in an organizational context. *Journal of Positive Psychology* 9(1): 1–18. DOI: 10.1080/17439760.2013.837499.

# CHAPTER 30

# How can I use coaching to support a change of culture in my organization?

Valeria Cardillo Piccolino

## Introduction

In one way or another, each of us can relate to change. Moving to a different country, beginning a new job, becoming a parent, a divorce, the end of a friendship. As human beings, we can empathize with the emotions involved in a change, be that an improvement in our life or a tough moment. As much as anything else, organizational change can generate emotional turmoil at scale! This pattern of change is felt even more so today, in an era in which the pace of change driven by technology has increased. Adapting to change has become a priority. We will see in the course of this chapter how coaching can be a support tool.

## The challenges

The majority of companies have experienced a transformation, and more than 85% of those have done so more than once (Faeste and Hemerling, 2016). However, companies often focus on the tangible aspects in making change: changing policies, procedures, logos and software systems.

It is perhaps for this reason that the majority of change projects fail. Research examining digital transformations suggested 70% of digital transformation programs do not hit their goals (Faeste and Hemerling, 2016). While tangible goals are important, the truth is that some of the most important elements of a successful transformation are the intangible ones: changing the hearts, minds and behaviors of people. One way to maximize the effectiveness of any sort of change program is to recognize the people element within the change plan (Thomas and Passmore, 2021).

# The role of coaching to support change

Dealing with emotions during an organizational change is complex, and coaching is one of the best tools to bring people on board. Internal communication can align narratives, explain the vision and dispel the myths. Training becomes a privileged moment for reflection in a group and to share the pain connected with the change. But these two tools are less effective in supporting the embedding of new behaviors over time.

How many times, while understanding that change is necessary, do we find ourselves anchored to our old ways of doing things? Coaching can unlock this resistance. Peterson (2009), in his application of Druckman and Bjork's (1991) work on learning and performance, noted that effective coaches help their clients practice new behaviors across multiple sessions. While the coachee may learn more slowly, the results last longer.

For this reason, it is good practice to target the following stakeholders with coaching as part of a culture change:

- Leadership and executive team

- Ambassadors of change

- The workforce.

Providing coaching to the leaders of an organization undergoing transformation is a valuable step to help them develop self-awareness about their own personal resistance to change and to contribute to their development as reflective practitioners (De Vries, 2008).

Dealing with change is difficult at the best of times, and for leaders in particular, who are expected to be role models, the need to cast vision and bring people on board can be tricky. When change involves entire organizations, it is very easy for some emotions to become 'contagious'. Goleman, Boyatzis and McKee (2001) remind us of the great responsibility managers have: "the leader's mood and behaviors drive the moods and behaviors of everyone else."

To understand how this works in practice, Stober (2008) draws our attention to Prochaska and DiClemente's Transtheoretical Model of Change (TTM) (see also Chapter 10: 'What should I do after my coaching ends?'). According to the TTM, people face six stages of change, and specific strategies can help individuals move from one to the next. In the 'precontemplation' stage, people are in a state of unawareness around how their behaviors and attitudes in relation to change can produce negative consequences. Employees of an organization facing a transformation might get stuck in opposing themselves to a change, overstating the cons and not recognizing the pros. Only when they move into the 'contemplation' phase do they start to realize the benefits of changing their attitude or behaviors, and become ready to take action in the stages that follow.

For example, in order to generate momentum towards the 'contemplation' stage, a coach could use appreciative inquiry, an approach that focuses on the sources of energy and motivation of the coachee, rather than on a problem or issue that requires solution. The following questions informed by an appreciative-inquiry approach would support a coachee towards an understanding of change and their role in driving it forwards:

- Which of your strengths and talents will help you lead this change?
- What are the strengths of your team that you want to leverage on, to drive change forward?
- What is working well in your organization, related to this change?
- What are the positives that you see in this transformation?

Here is where the more difficult aspect comes: leaders are the first who need to walk the talk. People are perceptive of the lack of congruence between what is preached and what is done, so leaders have to put effort into changing habits. The ability to follow through on what they say and respond positively to the change is one of the best ways to empower others to change their behaviors too.

The same type of reflection is helpful for the second stakeholder group, the ambassadors of change (which you might also call the *champions* or *change coalition*). This group will benefit from an ongoing process of understanding, explaining and focusing attention on the benefits. The key for ambassadors is therefore to equip them with the capability to understand that people may have different reactions, or might be at different stages of acceptance of a change. Most of the time, ambassadors are enthusiasts for the change, selected precisely for their can-do attitude. But this might mean that they need to control their optimism, being sensitive to the fears and anxieties of others who feel insecure in the face of transformation. It is one thing to generate energy due to the benefits and opportunities stimulated by a change, and another for blind and insensitive optimism to increase fear and anxiety associated with the unknown.

The role coaching can play here is to support ambassadors in incorporating a different perspective, developing empathy and understanding, skills that might help them when engaging people in a change. An ambassador who develops the capability to listen deeply, and then provide feedback and support in generating new solutions and perspectives on a situation, is way ahead in the task of driving change forward.

Finally, coaching is a helpful tool in supporting the workforce in contributing positively to a change. In this case, coaching provides a safe space in which people can gain confidence in their own abilities and the possibilities of a change, with the following benefits:

- Overcoming insecurities

- Understanding the role they can play in the change process

- Letting go of unhelpful false beliefs

- Shifting their focus onto the benefits and opportunities in front of them.

One example of this is the challenge that the shift towards more remote working has presented to those who have been used, for decades, to relying on physical meetings, managing others by observing their day-to-day activities or simply enjoying the human dimension of the office. People have felt lonely, disconnected and overwhelmed by technology, and while those feelings are valid, these new ways of working have also brought benefits.

In order to steer people through these challenges, providing the best technology, remote work policies and ergonomic chairs has been a necessary step. But it has not been enough. 1:1, team and group coaching have all played a part in making people feel included, increasing their empathy for colleagues, and helping them to see a bigger perspective and feel a sense of stability against a challenging backdrop.

## Conclusion

Only a systemic understanding of how multiple variables need to harmonically integrate fosters an organization's adaptability and resistance to change. To use a word coined by Nassim Thaleb, organizations need to become more 'antifragile' (2012). While fragile items break under stress, antifragile items get better under it. Coaching has an incredible power to help people navigate their fear and uncertainties, coming up with new, creative solutions, helping them develop the skills to be more adaptive and flexible.

## References

De Vries, M.K. (2008) *Leadership Coaching and Organizational Transformation: Effectiveness in a World of Paradoxes.* INSEAD Business School Faculty & Research Working paper.

Druckman, D., and Bjork, R.A. (eds) (1991). In the *Mind's Eye:* Enhancing *Human Performance.* National Academy Press.

Faeste, L., and Hemerling, J. (2016). *Transformation: Delivering and Sustaining Breakthrough Performance.* Boston, MA: Boston Consulting Group.

Goleman, D., Boyatzis, R., and McKee, A. (2001). *Primal Leadership: The Hidden Driver of Great Performance.* Brighton, MA: Harvard Business Review.

Peterson, D.B. (2009). Coaching and performance management: How can organizations get the greatest value? In J.W. Smither and M. London (eds), Performance *Management:* Putting *Research* into *Action,* pp. 115–55. Jossey-Bass/Wiley.

Stober, D. (2008). Making it stick: Coaching as a tool for organizational change. *Coaching: An International Journal of Theory, Research and Practice* 1(1): 71–80, DOI: 10.1080/17521880801905950.

Thaleb, N. (2012). *Antifragile: Things That Gain from Disorder.* London: Penguin.

Thomas, H., and Passmore, J. (2021). Coming together: A grounded theory study of the role of coaching in the mergers & acquisitions process. *International Coaching Psychology Review* 16(1): 54–66.

# CHAPTER 31

# What are the latest trends in coaching?

## Morgan Hyonne

## Introduction

The world of coaching has seen tremendous growth and changes since 1990. Coaching has become an essential ingredient for most organizations' talent and development plans. Coaching is now a multi-billion-dollar industry and continues to grow in scale and scope. The impact of the global pandemic in 2020 has seen the industry, which had been slowly creeping towards online, pivot rapidly, to see online become the standard mode of delivery. In this chapter, we explore some of the recent trends in coaching and ask what the implications are for organizations, managers and coaching commissioners.

## Trend 1: Technology-enabled coaching

It is not a surprise that all industries have been impacted by the development of technologies. A study by PwC (2020) found that 52% of companies accelerated their artificial intelligence (AI) adoption plans as a result of the pandemic. And according to the 2020 ICF Global Coaching Study, 83% of coaches increased their use of audio/video platforms for coaching, while the Trends in Coaching study (Passmore, 2021) found that most coaches who had switched to online did not anticipate returning to face-to-face delivery. What was an incremental movement from face-to-face coaching to online that had been happening over the period 2010–2020 has become a pivot, and what were once small, startup, online coaching businesses have found themselves as the new dominant players of the coaching industry in the post-pandemic world.

**Table 31.1: Online digital platforms**

CoachHub

BetterUp

Ezra

Plume

Coaching.com

AceUp

Sharpist

What are the benefits of technology-enabled coaching? CoachHub, as one example, offers coachees an overview of their strengths and areas of development prior to coaching using a guided, science-based self-assessment within the platform. Following completion of these steps, an algorithm provides the coachee with up to six recommendations of coaches to choose from. Each coaching profile summarizes the coach's experience, credentials and reviews, as well as providing a one-minute introductory video for the coachee to gauge their body language, manner and tone, to help determine their likely chemistry. All communication between coachee and coach is handled through the platform either in live video/audio sessions or through instant messaging, including options such as file sharing. There is also a virtual whiteboard accessible during the video session, where coachee and coach can communicate creatively, accompanied by learning content for the coachee to access outside of coaching sessions.

Graßmann and Schermuly (2021) have shared specific recommendations for HR professionals, coaches and developers of AI coaching programs on how AI can contribute to enhance coaching practice. For example, AI can encourage coachees when they do not progress, and help with monitoring goal achievement and sentiment trends. The researchers still recommend further investigation around the positive and negative outcomes AI coaching generates, which is a next horizon for exploration in coaching trends.

In addition to AI, virtual-reality coaching is also growing. Virtual reality (VR) creates an artificial, immersive and responsive environment in which the coaching conversation is held in real time with 3D computer-generated models. VR software has been used in a variety of functions such as training and entertainment, which can be applied to coaching, but VR is at the early stages of adoption, and more research is needed to better understand its contribution to both individual and team coaching (see Chapter 33: 'When should we use team coaching?' for more details).

## Trend 2: Coaching is democratizing

Traditionally, coaching has been reserved for senior leaders. These sessions were most often delivered face to face, and fees therefore needed to include a significant travel element, as well as the investment required for its bespoke personalization. Digitization has changed all of this.

The introduction of scalable coaching via platforms has reduced cost and increased convenience, meaning coaching can be delivered to hundreds or even thousands of coachees across multiple locations and time zones, though a single contract and a single provider, at a much lower cost than one would have historically paid for executive coaching.

According to research by the Human Capital Institute (ICF–HCI, 2020), 54% of organizations classified as high performing have a strong coaching culture, compared with 29% of all other organizations. A coaching culture is "one where an organization's people have a coaching mindset and use a coaching approach, both with each other and external stakeholders regardless of reporting relationships, to create organizational value, protect each other's wellbeing and maximize everyone's potential" (CoachHub, 2021).

The growth of digital coaching platforms has seen the scale and scope of coaching moving, with coaching being available inside more organizations and at more career grades. This trend is likely to increase, as organizations extend the use of coaching through platforms to a growing number of employees.

## Trend 3: The professionalization of the coach

With higher demands in coaching from individuals and organizations, more people are identifying themselves as coaches: 'life coach', 'business coach', 'mindfulness coach' and so forth. But this growth in numbers hides a darker truth. Not all of these coaches are trained or qualified. Many may simply be using the term 'coach' without any formal training, or have undertaken training with an unrecognized body who, on the payment of a fee, provide a certificate. Almost 20% of the coaches interviewed in an ICF study said that the biggest obstacle for coaching over the next 12 months was managing untrained individuals who call themselves 'coaches' (ICF, 2020).

While many coaches may have spent a year or more training to secure a professional qualification, the unregulated nature of coaching means it's a clear case of 'buyer beware'. In Chapter 6 we offer some detailed advice for individual coachees on what to look for when appointing a coach, to avoid appointing a coach or a coaching provider who lacks comprehensive training or professional accreditation (such as ICF or EMCC), or who does not have in place appropriate support, such as supervision.

In addition to professional coaches securing training, many organizations are also looking to build in-house coaching pools or to train their own managers in coaching skills. According to the CIPD (2015), 80% of companies based in the UK wanted their managers to coach their direct reports. The same care is needed when appointing coach trainers as in appointing coaches. The evidence suggests that developing sufficient coaching skills for managers to hold effective coaching conversations does not require merely a one- or two-day course, but instead may take a period of between three and six months, with opportunities to practice and reflect on the new skills (Grant and Hartley, 2013).

## Trend 4: Coaching as a main human and societal development tool

Organizations are facing a number of HR and societal issues. They are disrupted by globalization and changes in demographics, technology and climate, among other issues. As a consequence, companies are diversifying their workforces and developing strategies to enhance competitiveness, evolve their social responsibility and change the work environment to become more purpose-driven and create supportive environments. Alongside this, organizations are placing greater emphasis on inclusion, equity, diversity and belonging.

These aspects all require a stronger focus on emotional intelligence, specifically empathy and communications skills. These softer skills are less able to be developed through attendance at training courses, but can be fostered through coaching to develop both the mindset and the specific competencies required for reflective developmental and empathic conversations.

## Conclusion

The key emerging trends in how coaching can continue to play a useful part in addressing the challenges that organizations currently face offer opportunities and threats. Increases in the digitization and democratization of coaching expand its reach and scalability, while expansions in its professionalization and scope mean that coach buyers need to become more informed about how to implement coaching most effectively.

## References

CIPD (2015). *Learning & Development: Annual Survey*. London: CIPD.

CoachHub (2021). *Definitions, Processes and Models*. Internal Document. Berlin: CoachHub.

Graßmann, C., and Schermuly, C.C. (2021). Coaching with artificial intelligence: Concepts and capabilities. *Human Resource Development Review* 20(1): 106–26.

Grant, A.M., and Hartley, M. (2013). Developing the leader as coach: Insights, strategies and tips for embedding coaching skills in the workplace. *Coaching: An International Journal of Theory, Research and Practice* 6(2): 102–15. https://doi.org/10.1080/17521882.2013.824015.

ICF–HCI (2020). *Global Coaching Study*. Lexington: ICF–HCI.

Passmore, J. (2021). *Future Trends in Coaching: Executive Report*. Henley on Thames: Henley Business School. Retrieved 2 February 2022 from: https://assets.henley.ac.uk/v3/fileUploads/Future-Trends-in-Coaching.pdf.

PwC Research (2020). AI predictions survey. Retrieved from: https://www.pwc.com/us/en/tech-effect/ai-analytics/ai-predictions.html.

# CHAPTER 32

# What is the difference between team and group coaching?

## Sam Isaacson and Qingsong Ke

## Introduction

In addition to individual 1:1 coaching, team and group coaching are powerful development approaches that have gained in popularity in recent years as organizations seek to accelerate team performance and support individual development in cost-effective ways. In this chapter, we will offer definitions that help us distinguish team and group coaching and when each should be used.

## The emergence of team and group coaching

The past 20 years have seen an explosion in 1:1 coaching, but only more recently have team and group emerged as prominent interventions. Early writers such as Thornton (2010) focused more on the group aspects of coaching. In recent years, team coaching has become widely recognized as a specialization in itself, requiring distinctive skills and professional standards, thus separate qualifications.

Confusion around the differences between team and group coaching has led to considerable discussion of definitions and concepts (Jones et al., 2019).

## Team and group coaching defined

CoachHub, a large, global digital coaching provider, defines team coaching as "a partnering process with a group who share a common purpose, to help them reflect on themselves, their relationships and context, and to identify new insights, actions and ways of being to achieve their common purpose" (2021).

Team coaching typically involves one team coach working with a team of four-to-eight individuals, where the coaching engagement:

- Supports the team in agreeing on and achieving shared team goals

- Facilitates the development of interpersonal relationships, collaboration and communication

- Identifies and agrees on the wider stakeholder value created by the team as a diverse collective.

In contrast, group coaching is best thought of as simultaneous 1:1 coaching delivered to a small group. A group-coaching engagement:

- Supports the group in sharing experiences around common themes, rather than a common purpose

- Aids coachees in learning from themselves and others, reflecting on themes through conversation and the wisdom of the group

- Helps coachees explore and deepen a common thematic issue, finding creative solutions and develop ways of coping.

What is obvious from these definitions is that team coaching, while it may look similar in some ways to group coaching, is used exclusively when the individuals participating in the coaching share a common purpose and wish to focus on issues they share as a team, such as group dynamics, relationships within the team and how they collectively deliver value to their stakeholders.

## Implementing team and group coaching

The primary differences between team and group coaching are related to who the coachees are and the purpose of the coaching engagement. In Table 32.1, we highlight some of the key characteristics and give examples of when each might be used.

**Table 32.1: Differences between team and group coaching**

|  | Coachees are: | Purpose/ goals are: | Examples of when this might be used: |
|---|---|---|---|
| Team coaching | Team members | Common, shared | • An intact team of individual contributors reporting to the same leader |
|  |  |  | • A leadership team |
|  |  |  | • A project team |
|  |  |  | • An agile team working together for a period of time |
| Group coaching | Two or more people | Individual | • Leaders participating in a leadership development program journey |
|  |  |  | • A group dealing with a particular cultural theme on which the organization is focusing |

## Approaches to be used in team and group coaching

The skills and approaches used in team and group coaching are necessarily different. In group coaching, because the focus of the coaching is the individual needs within it, the goals for the session will be set by each individual and thus may well be different for each person in the group. In contrast, each team-coaching session will typically focus on one shared goal for the team as a whole. The skills required by group and team coaches, therefore, while similar in terms of facilitating a group alongside core coaching competencies, are not the same.

In a group-coaching setting, it is likely that the group coach will ask each participant to share their desired goal for the session, and use a variety of coaching models and techniques, drawing on the wisdom of the group throughout, while focusing on each individual in turn. Slightly tailored versions of traditional coaching models such as GROW or narrative coaching could be used for each individual, complemented by techniques to ensure that the session does not turn into simply accelerated 1:1 coaching sessions conducted with observers.

Team coaching inherently requires a different approach. The need for every team member to contribute, not just verbally but in terms of the overall purpose of the team and the team-coaching session, introduces the need for new team-coaching skills and models. This has led to professional bodies defining the team coaching skillset differently from that of 1:1 coaching. For example, in May 2020 EMCC Global launched a new Team Coaching Quality Award, and in January 2021 the ICF released its Team Coaching Competencies.

A widely respected model that draws on a wealth of research into high-performing teams and group dynamics is the PERILL model, which looks at team behaviors and mindsets through six lenses, each of which interacts with the others (see Table 32.2).

**Table 32.2: PERILL model**

| Leadership Qualities and Behaviors (LQB) | Purpose and motivation | External facing processes | Relationships | Internal facing processes | Learning |
|---|---|---|---|---|---|
| **Purpose and motivation** | LQB | Alignment of values between the team and key stakeholders | Working enthusiastically together towards shared goals | Clarity of priorities, putting collective priorities before personal | Actively seeking ways to leverage and expand team strengths |
| **External-facing processes** | Stakeholders unclear what you stand for | LQB | Strong collaborative relationships with stakeholders | Rapid and effective responses to quality issues | Rapid product and service innovation |
| **Relationships** | People pursue their own agendas | Conflict with stakeholders – disrespect of stakeholders | LQB | High level of psychological safety leads to continuous questioning of what we do | People take active responsibility for supporting each other's development |
| **Internal-facing processes** | Duplication and waste of effort | Quality issues not acknowledged or addressed | People avoid interfering in each other's territories – large 'elephant in the room' | LQB | Culture of continuous improvement |
| **Learning** | Learning focus on the individual not the collective | Slow to innovate | People hoard knowledge and expertise | Resistance to change | LQB |

(Clutterbuck, 2021)

## Conclusion

Team and group coaching are different coaching approaches, each offering distinct value. Depending on the coachee participants and goals of the coaching engagement, the appropriate approach can be selected. With these definitions in mind, the next two chapters will expand the discussion to highlight recommendations for when each should be employed.

## References

Clutterbuck, D. (2021). Why team coaching is the future. Retrieved 5 January 2022 from: https://www.grantthornton.co.uk/insights/webinar-why-team-coaching-is-the-future/.

CoachHub (2021). *Definitions, Processes and Models*. Internal Document. Berlin: CoachHub.

EMCC Global (2021). Press release: More than 1,000 team coaches become the first graduates of the world's first EMCC Global Team Coaching Quality Award Accredited Education and Training Programme. Retrieved 1 December 2021 from: https://emccdrive.emccglobal.org/api/file/download/6zuvR2lOAtE1o3kpfsU2oSasO2aMZelCeQ4IL7uK.

ICF (2021). ICF Team Coaching Competencies: Moving beyond one-to-one coaching. Retrieved 15 April 2022 from: https://coachingfederation.org/app/uploads/2021/01/Team-Coaching-Competencies-4.pdf.

Jones, R., Napiersky, U., and Lyubovnikova, J. (2019) Conceptualizing the distinctiveness of team coaching. *Journal of Managerial Psychology* 34(2): 62–78. DOI: https://doi.org/10.1108/JMP-07-2018-0326.

Thornton, C. (2010) *Group and Team Coaching: The Essential Guide*. Abingdon: Routledge.

# CHAPTER 33

# When should we use team coaching?

### Elizabeth Pavese, PhD

## Introduction

With the ever-growing collaborative nature of work and focus on results through collective team effort, team coaching has grown in popularity as an organizational intervention. Team coaching – one coach working with members of an intact team – provides tremendous opportunity for a group to grow capabilities collectively and impact organizational results in a meaningful way. Like any intervention, team coaching is useful in certain situations and not in others. In this chapter, we'll explore more deeply the benefits of team coaching and when it's most appropriately applied to realize its potential value.

## The benefits of team coaching

As previously defined (see Chapter 32: 'What is the difference between team and group coaching?'), team coaching is "a partnering process with a group who share a common purpose, to help them reflect on themselves, their relationships and context, and to identify new insights, actions and ways of being to achieve their common purpose" (CoachHub, 2021). Team coaching can be a powerful intervention to support team- or organizational-level change while simultaneously developing the individual leaders who participate in the intervention. Fundamentally, team coaching is a learning process aimed at improving performance relating to an intact team's shared goals.

While team coaching is gaining in practice, the scientific evidence to support its effectiveness as an intervention is still in its infancy. What we have learned to date through research (for example, Anderson et al., 2008; Brown and Grant, 2010; Clutterbuck, 2007) is that coachees who experience team coaching report a variety of positive outcomes for their own learning as well as team-level benefits, including increases in learning, decision making, information sharing, communication, greater team effectiveness and higher employee engagement.

## When to use team coaching

Ultimately, the results that will be seen via team coaching are based on a variety of inputs or enabling factors. Hackman and Wagemen's (2005) research that established the theory of team coaching centers on the extensive research on team effectiveness. In fact, findings from this study indicate that coaching that is geared towards enhancing interpersonal relationships rather than team functioning is less effective overall. Therefore, to make the best use of team coaching, it's important to understand the enabling conditions and team characteristics which contribute to successful outcomes (see, for example, Clutterbuck, 2007; Hackman and Wageman, 2005; Katzenbach and Smith, 1993; Maseko et al., 2019; Wageman, 2001).

### To optimize core functions of the team

There are three aspects that are essential to team functioning and which team coaching is best centered around: effort from the team, the team's strategy for accomplishing tasks, and the knowledge and skill of the team members. How a team interacts given these three characteristics will result in gains or losses for the team collectively.

For example, coaching that focuses on the effort of a team helps to elevate the motivation of team members. Here, shared commitment can be built among the team. Further, coaching that centers on the team's strategy helps the team gain clarity and focus on the tasks or goals at hand, and alignment on the approach to get the desired results. Lastly, addressing the knowledge and skills of team members helps to raise individual and collective awareness around strengths and areas for development. This brings a level of understanding on how to best leverage the unique attributes and experience that each team member can contribute towards the collective goals.

Many of the interpersonal issues that can arise within a team context, such as conflicts and miscommunications, are rooted in the core functions and dynamics of the team. A coach that focuses more deeply on the root cause of the issues can more effectively help the team grow and progress. For example, conflict issues may be a result of not understanding the complementary knowledge, background, experiences and skills within the team and how to best leverage them. Or perhaps there is a misalignment or lack of clarity in the team's direction and strategies for accomplishing their goals.

Understanding how team members align based on the core three aspects of team effectiveness, regardless of the presenting interpersonal issues, will have a more impactful outcome.

*At specific points in their lifecycle*

Every team evolves through specific stages, and as they mature in their functioning, different issues and opportunities will arise. Coaching that is applied at the right time in a team's evolution and focused on the right content makes a difference in its impact. For example, Hackman and Wageman (2005) discuss the following as key intervention points:

- Beginnings – Teams that are newly forming are focused on getting to know one another as well as understanding their goals and tasks as a group. Here, there is considerable focus on defining roles and responsibilities, and establishing how the team will work together, among other 'forming and norming' activities. Coaching that focuses on the team's effort and takes a more motivational focus is likely to be more effective.

- Midpoints – These are critical moments in a team's lifecycle, because midpoints provide a moment to reflect on how the team is functioning. This intentional pause can provide the opportunity for proactive intervention to adjust course towards specific goals. Additionally, coaching focused on the team's strategies and ways of working can have a meaningful impact at this stage.

- End points – Towards the end of major goals or deliverables is another prime opportunity for team coaching. Coaching that helps to facilitate reflection on successes, setbacks, learning and growth also helps to solidify the team's experiences and development of capabilities.

*When leaders support self-led change*

As an organizational development intervention, team coaching is focused on bringing about change, and therefore requires many supporting elements for success. Support from both the managers of teams and senior leaders can help facilitate the team-coaching experiences. Visible championship of the strategy and vision for implementing team coaching provides confidence and is inspiring to those who will go through the process. Further, engaging leaders through team coaching will help mitigate any potential barriers to success, ensure a strategic alignment of the coaching intervention to organizational goals and outcomes, and ensure that resources are allocated to optimize its impact.

*With teams that are designed appropriately*

Not all teams are created equal, and the impact of team coaching is highly dependent upon the design of the team. For example, if there are tasks and goals that are meaningful, relevant, and make use of and stretch the skills of the team, there is a higher likelihood that performance can be maximized through team coaching. Further, the size of the team can make a difference. Teams that are too large (above 8–10 team members) can generate team dynamics such as social loafing, presenting detrimental effects to the functioning of the team overall.

*When there is team readiness to engage*

Important ingredients for any coaching engagement to be successful are the motivation and commitment of the coachee involved. This remains true for team-coaching experiences. Teams who are ready to actively participate and commit to the experience will reap the benefits of team coaching. Team coaching is definitely an intervention to avoid when it is the leader of the team alone that desires the coaching to happen.

## What to consider when using team coaching

To ensure the effectiveness of team coaching, a great deal of structure is required, alongside a coach highly experienced in managing team dynamics, in addition to their coaching experience. Table 33.1 includes a few considerations when deciding whether or not team coaching is the right solution. If team coaching is deemed not to be helpful but the team still has a need for a personalized development intervention, other approaches such as 1:1 coaching for key individuals or group coaching (see Chapter 34: 'When should we use group coaching?') may be more effective.

**Table 33.1: When is team coaching the right solution?**

| | |
|---|---|
| What is the focus for the team? | Team coaching can often be initiated when the team hits – or anticipates – a stumbling block, so it's important to clarify the purpose of the team coaching experience. |
| What is expected as the outcome of the team-coaching context? | Once there is a clear purpose, it's also necessary to identify the signals for success. The results of team coaching, like any coaching engagement, can take time, so identify short- and long-term success metrics. |

## Conclusion

This chapter explored the benefits and practical applications of team coaching. Team coaching is not suitable for all scenarios as it is important to consider the needs of the team, the team's dynamics and how the team is set up to begin with in order to realize the impacts of team coaching.

## References

Anderson, M.C., Anderson, D.L., and Mayo, W.D. (2008). Team coaching helps a leadership team drive cultural change at Caterpillar. *Global Business and Organizational Excellence* 27: 40–50.

Brown, S.W., and Grant, A.M. (2010). From GROW to GROUP: Theoretical issues and a practical model for group coaching in organisations. *Coaching: An International Journal of Theory, Research and Practice* 3: 30–45.

Clutterbuck, D. (2007). *Coaching the Team at Work.* London: Nicholas Brealey Publishing.

CoachHub (2021). *Definitions, Processes and Models.* Internal Document. Berlin: CoachHub.

Hackman, J.R., and Wageman, R. (2005). A theory of team coaching. *Academy of Management Review* 30: 269–87.

Katzenbach, J.R., and Smith, D.K. (1993). *The Wisdom of Teams: Creating High Performance Teams.* Boston, MA: Harvard Business Review Press.

Maseko, B.M., van Wyck, R., and Odendaal, A. (2019). Team coaching in the workplace: Critical success factors for success. *SA Journal of Human Resource Management* 17.

Wageman, R. (2001). How leaders foster self-managing team effectiveness: Design choices versus hands-on coaching. *Organization Science* 12: 559–77.

# CHAPTER 34

# When should we use group coaching?

Elizabeth Pavese, PhD

## Introduction

Coaching itself is an organizational-development intervention – it not only provides an individual with the opportunity to support their awareness and growth towards change, it opens the door to broader organizational changes when delivered at scale or to particularly influential individuals, teams or groups. Not dissimilar from other group- and organization-level interventions, group coaching has the potential to facilitate transformation much like organizational change and development initiatives. In this chapter, we'll talk about the benefits of group coaching and when best to leverage this approach.

## What is group coaching?

Group coaching could be defined as a partnering process with a group of individual coachees, each with their own objectives, helping them reflect on themselves, their situation and context, and to identify new insights, actions and ways to unlock their potential and each become the best version of themselves (CoachHub, 2021).

As described in Chapter 1: 'What is coaching?', group coaching is not dissimilar from 1:1 coaching: it's merely facilitated in a group. Each coachee will identify their personal goals to ensure there is clarity about what they wish to attain. Being part of a group provides the coachee with additional support, encouragement and accountability by having a shared experience with others. Additionally, the group coach can help leverage the wisdom of others, which can highlight new perspectives on solutions and strategies to help each of the coachees achieve their individual goals.

## The benefits of group coaching

Similar to team coaching, the research-based evidence for group coaching is nascent, though growing. Several researchers and practitioners (for example, Anderson et al., 2008; Kets de Vries, 2005) have noted a variety of potential benefits of group coaching that span individual-, team- and organizational-level impacts (see Table 34.1).

**Table 34.1: Potential benefits of group coaching**

| Zone of impact | Example impacts |
| --- | --- |
| Individual | Understanding of self-regulation, greater awareness, improved skills and capabilities that are targeted in coaching, values and goals alignment, and sustainable behavior change. Development of enhanced coaching skills, such as asking powerful questions, reflective listening and so forth are other key individual impacts that are significantly beneficial for people leaders. |
| Group | Development of trust and support within the group, collective awareness of organizational issues, enhanced information sharing and connection across organizational silos, enhanced group energy and engagement levels, and greater awareness of group processes and dynamics. |
| Organizational | Consist of higher-performing cross-functional teams, enhanced energy and engagement levels across the organization, collective leadership development, better decision making across the organization. |

While there are a myriad of possible positive impacts from group coaching, it's not for all situations. There are some critical elements to consider when employing group coaching as a developmental option.

## When to use group coaching

Getting to real change in an organization requires a significant proportion of individuals to be involved in change processes. It also requires more systemic awareness and acting in ways that reflect systems thinking. Group coaching is well-suited to supporting individual change while shaping a broader and collective perspective of how individuals fit with the organization and impact one another (Brown and Grant, 2010), but it isn't for every situation.

*To improve collective or shared leadership*

Group coaching can promote cross-functional team building and improve leadership effectiveness (Hackman and Wageman, 2005). It helps break down barriers or silos that often exist in organizations, especially at the enterprise level, playing a key role in relationship building and raising a collective mindset to leading. Fostering a collective mindset is especially important for those individuals who lead teams with a tendency to operate in silos, where prioritizing the needs of the organization are more important than the needs of the individual or team.

*To facilitate organizational change*

Group coaching can play a key role in supporting large-scale change and cultural transformations, as it facilitates goal-focused alignment and provides a reflective space for leaders to learn together. Further, group coaching can be leveraged to overcome organizational resistance to change by refocusing from individual goals to collective, group-level thinking and problem solving (Brown and Grant, 2010). It can create a space for leaders to address concerns they have as leaders mobilizing change, as well as to discover challenges they face in times of change and uncertainty, and how to overcome them.

*To reinforce learning*

Participants in group coaching learn by doing and building from each other's experiences. Group coaching can be a powerful addition to L&D programs, as it provides an opportunity to reinforce the knowledge and skills gained from learning experiences and also to support learning from one another. Learning from peers who are experiencing a similar situation presents an opportunity to gain new perspectives, challenge assumptions and jointly identify solutions. Lastly, the group serves as an accountability anchor for participants and a support mechanism for sharing concerns, frustrations and successes.

*To build inclusive mindsets and capabilities*

Raising awareness of individual biases and experiences is certainly a bedrock in a person's growth journey. It is also a cornerstone for organizations, especially as it relates to building an environment that is diverse, equitable and inclusive. Group coaching can be leveraged to foster inclusive mindsets and strengthen capabilities that demonstrate inclusive leadership. Providing a safe space to learn knowledge around diversity, equity and inclusion issues, and to share experiences, helps cultivate a deeper empathy between people, elevating emotional and social awareness, and breaking down biases and stereotypes.

*To enhance accountability*

Sometimes the solutions to problems and goals set are emotionally and cognitively taxing. They can be difficult to navigate. Accountability is necessary in a coaching engagement, especially when pursuing highly challenging goals. Additional support and accountability from others can be incredibly powerful.

## What to consider when using group coaching

Table 34.2 outlines some areas of consideration when implementing group coaching. In a similar way to team coaching, group coaching requires more structure and a wider skillset than 1:1 coaching.

**Table 34.2: What to consider when implementing group coaching**

| | |
|---|---|
| What is the shared focus for the group? | While each participant will have unique goals, there should be a common theme or focus that the coachees can relate to during group coaching. |
| What is expected as the outcome of the group-coaching context? | Identifying the outcome will help you determine how to evaluate the impact and success of the group-coaching experience. |
| Does group coaching align with other organizational priorities? | Aligning group coaching with organizational needs may be important for success and ensuring there is the right support around the experience. |
| Do we have the appropriate set-up (i.e. tools, technology, etc.) to support the group-coaching experience? | Clarity will be needed from you and the coach to ensure that the engagement is facilitated with ultimate ease. |

## Conclusion

Group coaching is not suitable for all scenarios. It's important to consider the group size, the goal of coaching overall, as well as the needs of the coachees in order for this approach to deliver optimal outcomes.

## References

Anderson, M.C., Anderson, D.L., and Mayo, W.D. (2008). Team coaching helps a leadership team drive cultural change at Caterpillar. *Global Business and Organizational Excellence* 27: 40–50.

Brown, S.W., and Grant, A.M. (2010). From GROW to GROUP: Theoretical issues and a practical model for group coaching in organisations. *Coaching: An International Journal of Theory, Research and Practice* 3: 30–45.

CoachHub (2021). *Definitions, Processes and Models*. Internal Document. Berlin: CoachHub.

Hackman, J.R., and Wageman, R. (2005). A theory of team coaching. *Academy of Management Review* 30: 269–87.

Kets de Vries, M.F.R. (2005). Leadership group coaching in action: The zen of creating high performance teams. *Academy of Management Executive* 19(1): 61–76.

# CHAPTER 35

# How can psychometrics help a coachee's development in a coaching assignment?

Elizabeth Pavese, PhD

## Introduction

The use of psychometric tools in learning and organizational development interventions has gained popularity in the last several decades. They can be a great tool in helping a coachee gain deeper awareness of attitudes, values, motives, behaviors and so much more, depending on the focus of the tool itself. In this chapter, we'll take a look at what psychometric tools are, how they can help in a coaching engagement and issues to consider when leveraging psychometric tools.

## What is a psychometric questionnaire?

A psychometric tool is a structured framework that is meant to assess psychological characteristics or constructs (for example, personality, cognitive ability, mindsets, values, motivation, abilities, etc.) in an unbiased and standardized manner. Some tools are built to provide the coachee with in-depth self-reflection against normative scores for context (for example, the Hogan Personality Inventory or the Values in Action Questionnaire), while others provide a coachee with feedback from multiple sources (for example, Transformational Leadership Questionnaire 360). There is limited but growing research that indicates the impact of coaching combined with psychometric tools. For example, the use of multisource feedback tools has shown in a variety of studies (Jones et al., 2016; Smither et al., 2003; Smither et al., 2005) to support changes in performance over time. However, the impact found in the literature is small, even when multisource feedback is combined with coaching.

## When and how to use a psychometric tool as a part of coaching

Despite the minimal empirical evidence on the impact that coaching has in combination with psychometric tools (Batey et al., 2012), there are a number of potential benefits (Allworth and Passmore, 2012; McDowall and Smewing, 2009) from this growing body of research. Well-validated psychometric tools can provide insight into employees' competencies at the beginning, midpoint and end of a coaching assignment. Further, the results from a psychometric tool can help shape the structure of the engagement, creating a common language from which conversations can be built.

It's worth bearing in mind when selecting a psychometric questionnaire that not all psychometric tools are created equal (see Allworth and Passmore 2012 for a discussion of a wide range of coaching psychometrics). While the best tools are heavily researched, offer good reliability and validity results (i.e. the results measure what they say and are consistent over time), and their results are made public in published peer review journals or comprehensive technical reports, other psychometrics publishers are more circumspect with this data. Without open publication of research results, the claims made by test publishers (or those making other scientific discoveries) cannot be subjected to independent evaluation and thus cannot be trusted in the same way as more robust approaches. It is better to avoid such questionnaires, favoring more evidence-based interventions to ensure that your coaching programs are as effective and manageable as possible in meeting their objectives.

Let's take a closer look at some of the ways to leverage the results of psychometric tools throughout a coaching engagement.

## Beginning coaching

*Psychometrics can facilitate insight and raise self-awareness*

Psychometric tools that also provide normative data and/or give results from multisource feedback can provide great insight into relative strengths and areas for development. This depth of quantitative and qualitative data can provide a great mirror to a coachee to help them reflect and begin drawing some conclusions around their behavior and approach to the world. This of course requires a highly skilled coach to ask powerful questions and draw connections between data points to enhance the interpretation of the data.

*Widens areas for exploration or development*

Data from these assessments can help paint a broader picture of areas of strength and development. While a coachee may have embarked on their coaching journey with a specific focus area in mind, the insights that are derived through the debrief of a psychometric assessment can help uncover related areas that may also be of benefit for the coachee to explore.

*Setting goals*

When using a psychometric tool, the first coaching session is a debrief session. Insights from these discussions can serve as a springboard for goal-setting, clarifying more specific goals and setting a plan for action.

## During coaching

*Enhance understanding*

Throughout coaching, the results from these tools can help to clarify and deepen one's understanding of behavioral patterns as focus areas are explored. Further, the results of the assessment can help pinpoint specific challenges within developmental areas and perhaps provide explanations for newly discovered insights or situations.

*A mechanism for feedback*

Coaches can leverage the data in an ongoing fashion with a coachee. Data from assessments can help frame observations, be used to probe for further understanding and provide feedback in an objective manner. Additionally, having objective information can be a powerful addition in the coaching toolbox when helping a coachee manage emotions, work through an impasse or have contentious discussions.

## End of coaching

*Measuring progress*

In the short term, assessment data can be leveraged to monitor progress on goals and assess behavioral shifts.

*Evaluating the coaching process*

Longer-term behavioral change can be assessed through the use of psycho-metric assessments, especially when employing multi-rater feedback tools such as 180- or 360-degree assessments.

## Psychometrics in team coaching

Team coaching sessions vary widely in their design and delivery: no two teams are the same. Thus, psychometric questionnaires are not integral to every team coaching assignment, but can be useful for some. From our experience, psychometrics may play a role in team coaching in two ways.

*Individuals within the team*

Raising the self-awareness of each team member will give them clarity about their own values, strengths and development areas, which they bring to the team. It will uncover blind spots and surface understanding about the impact they have on others, informing how they may be limiting their own effectiveness and the effectiveness of the team.

*The team as a collective*

Using psychometrics with the team as a whole, as described above, enables the team to understand and explore the similarities and differences between each other. A strength that an individual has taken for granted might turn out to be what is most valued by others. There is an appreciation of how difference lends the team a variety of strengths, as well as acknowledging where it can cause conflict and be a barrier to performance.

## How to get started when using psychometrics

Given the growing body of literature around the use of psychometric tools, there are several evidence- and practitioner-based practices that can guide the thoughtful application of psychometrics to the coaching experience. When considering the use of psychometric tools to support the coaching process, it's helpful to keep the following principles in mind.

*Have a strategy for using psychometrics*

It's very important to have guardrails and guidelines in place that outline when, why and how psychometric assessments are to be used relative to coaching. Just because these tools can provide deep levels of insight doesn't mean that they should be used in all instances. Communication of the strategy to a coachee about the purpose for using assessments is an essential strategic element. This can help to clarify any myths about the use of such tools, providing an opportunity to reaffirm confidentiality and explain how the information will and won't be used.

### Evaluate the performance of the tool

This is directly related to issues of reliability and validity of the measure. Reliability is the overall consistency of a measure across time and contexts. We want to ensure that the results garnered from the tool are not simply due to chance or some error in measurement, and can be generalizable to other contexts and populations. Validity is the degree to which a tool measures what it claims to measure. We want to ensure that the measures we use are accurate and precise, while ensuring practicality to the situation. There are many different types of statistics and measures that are examined to assess both reliability and validity, which for a well-validated tool will be outlined in a technical manual for review.

### Consider the needs of the coachee

While it's important to consider the robustness of the tool, it is also vital to leverage tools that fit the needs of the coachee as well as the purpose of the coaching engagement. It's a delicate balance to find tools that are robust, meet the needs of a coachee and have a good user experience.

### Coachee readiness for change

As with all coaching engagements, a critical ingredient for success is the coachee's perception of a need for change and their belief that change is feasible. The use of a psychometric tool itself won't necessarily maximize the probability for changes in behavior. It is the combination of multiple conditions, including the self-efficacy and motivation of the coachee, that matters. Coaches who are ready and willing are more likely to leverage the rich data source that a psychometric tool offers.

### Have experienced coaches

Many psychometric tools require training and certification to administer the assessment and deliver feedback based on results. This ensures credibility and the appropriate application of the assessment.

**Table 35.1: Six tips to using a psychometric with your coach**

| | |
|---|---|
| What do you want to find out? | Be clear about your objectives and how these support employee development and programmatic goals. |
| Is the tool psychologically robust and rigorous? | First ask for the technical report – this is a first sign that there is some level of documentation on the performance of the tool. Another good test is to ask if the psychometric has been published in peer-reviewed journals. |
| Does the coach need to be certified? | Most tools require training or licensure to use a specific instrument. Ask your coach for evidence. |
| How does it fit into the coaching assignment? | Plan with your coach how the psychometric feedback will fit into the wider assignment. |
| Who will have access to the data? | Before you complete the test, be clear about who has access, how and when. This is particularly important for team coaching. |
| Remember, it's just one lens! | A psychometric is just one lens and what it provides is just a perspective: do avoid being defined by it. |

## Conclusion

In this chapter, we have explored the nature of psychometrics, their value as a tool in coaching with individuals and with teams. We have suggested that they have value, and can help individuals and teams gain a stronger understanding of themselves. However, care needs to be taken in selecting a questionnaire, as not all psychometrics are equal and care is also needed in interpreting the results, recognizing that the feedback is just one perspective from a single lens.

## References

Allworth, E., and Passmore, J. (2012). Using psychometrics and psychological tools in coaching. In J. Passmore (ed.), *Psychometrics in Coaching: Using Psychological and Psychometric Tools for Development* (2nd edition), pp.7–22. London: Kogan Page.

Batey, M., Walker, A., and Hughes, D. (2012). Psychometric tools in development – do they work and how? In Jonathan Passmore (ed.), *Psychometrics in Coaching: Using Psychological and Psychometric Tools for Development* (2nd edition), pp.49–58. London: Kogan Page.

Jones, R.J., Woods, S.A., and Guillaume, Y.R.F. (2016). The effectiveness of workplace coaching: A meta-analysis of learning and performance outcomes from coaching. *Journal of Occupational and Organizational Psychology* 89: 249–77.

McDowall, A., and Smewing, C. (2009). What assessments do coaches use in their practice and why? *Coaching Psychologist* 5: 42–7.

Smither, J.W., London, M., Flautt, R., Vargas, Y., and Kucine, I. (2003). Can working with an executive coach improve multisource feedback ratings over time? A quasi-experimental field study. *Personnel Psychology* 56: 23–44.

Smither, J.W., London, M., and Reilly, R.R. (2005). Does performance improve following multisource feedback? A theoretical model, meta-analysis, and review of empirical findings. *Personnel Psychology* 58: 33–66.

# CHAPTER 36

# How can a 360-degree leadership questionnaire help in coaching?

Jonathan Passmore and Laurel McKenzie

## Introduction

360-degree questionnaires have been used widely in organizations. A 360-degree questionnaire can provide useful opportunities to gather feedback from line managers, peers and team members, as well as to reflect on the behaviors or competencies included in the questionnaire, as examples of what is considered to be good leadership. In this chapter, we will provide a review of 360s, their role as a development tool, and how they can play a part in 1:1 and team coaching, and in evaluation.

## What is a 360-degree questionnaire?

A 360-degree feedback instrument is designed to provide individuals with feedback on their leadership behavior as perceived by a range of other individuals, which may include their line manager, peers, direct reports as well as wider key stakeholders.

The items included in the questionnaire are usually a list of behaviors, gathered together around a common theme. These behaviors may be derived from a number of different sources: the organization's internal competency framework, a set of generic leadership behaviors drawn from research, or a collection of general behaviors.

**Table 36.1: Example of leadership clusters**

| | |
|---|---|
| Leading and developing individuals | Showing genuine concern |
| | Being accessible |
| | Enabling |
| | Encouraging change |
| Leading the way forward | Building shared networks |
| | Networking |
| | Resolving complex problems |
| | Facilitating change sensitively |
| Leading and developing the organization | Supporting a development culture |
| | Inspiring others |
| | Focusing team effort |
| | Being decisive |
| Personal qualities and values | Being honest and consistent |
| | Acting with integrity |

(Adapted from Alimo-Metcalfe and Mead, 2012)

Internal competencies vary widely in how they are developed. Some have been rigorously researched and provide an excellent platform for development work. Others less so. The key advantage of an internal measure is that it provides consistency, with leadership programs, appraisals and 360 assessments all linked to the same framework. However, not all organizations have a well-developed competency framework. In these cases, an external questionnaire can provide the basis for assessment.

Commercial 360 questionnaires vary widely. Given that they are simply a list of behaviors, they can be relatively simple to write. The challenge is demonstrating how these behaviors are positively related to successful outcomes in a leadership role or at work more generally. If the questionnaire statements have been simply 'made up' based on observation or limited research, the feedback derived from such sources may be at best misleading and at worst damaging. Instead, the best 360-degree instruments are supported by years of research and are able to provide evidence of one or more research studies in peer-reviewed (scientific) journals. Such research can turn a simple competence framework into a psychometrically valid instrument, which provides evidence of a clear link between the behaviors included in the questionnaire and improvements in leadership.

## Using 360s as a development tool

The general assumption is that feedback is a good thing and leads directly to improvements in performance. This is often the view of most managers when they provide feedback to their team. The evidence suggests this view is naive. Giving feedback can be helpful to individuals, enabling them to understand alternative perspectives or gather evidence from different sources. This can, for some individuals, stimulate self-reflection and planning. However, the evidence suggests it is just as likely to be demotivating or confusing, and can lead to a decline in performance (Smither et al., 2003).

This outcome sometimes arises due to the mix of scores. The questionnaire will provide a self-rating (the individual's assessment of their own behaviors), a line-manager rating, as well as ratings from peers, direct reports and from wider stakeholders. Some of these people may not know the individual as well as others, some may have felt rushed and others unduly influenced by their most recent interaction with them, which means the feedback needs to be looked at in the round. Often the direct reports provide the best feedback, as they most regularly see the individuals and have the clearest evidence of their behavior. But these aspects need to be explored through a conversation, which is where many 360-degree questionnaires fail.

The risk of confusion, demotivation and inertia from feedback can be mitigated. The first step is careful management of the feedback so that it is provided in a way the manager can understand and accept. The second step is providing space to explore the feedback and make sense of what it means for the individual and their role. Finally, it requires a space for reflection and support to develop a plan of action to address the issues identified in the report. Coaching offers each of these steps in a confidential process which is focused on the developmental needs of the individual.

**Table 36.2: The good feedback test**

| | |
|---|---|
| 1. | Is the feedback technically accurate? |
| 2. | Is the feedback provided by a trusted partner in the process? |
| 3. | Is the feedback understood and accepted by the individual? |
| 4. | Is the feedback a helpful starting point for planning (reflection)? |
| 5. | Is the feedback connected to a development journey with opportunity for reflection, planning and implementing new actions? |

## The contribution of coaching to 360s

The value of 360-degree questionnaires can be considered at three levels. Firstly, the value to individuals; secondly, the value to the team; and thirdly, the potential benefit to organizations.

For an individual, coaching can bring a focus and a process to the feedback provided by a 360, enabling individuals to move beyond the confusion and inertia that can arise when feedback is provided. The coach can help the individual unpick the data: who knows them best and who do they work with most closely? The answers to these questions may vary between different competencies, as the direct report may be able to comment on their ability to show genuine concern, but may be less able to comment on their networking skills. The coach can also help the person to reflect on evidence: when did you behave like this, what informed your actions, what impact did it have and how could you achieve a different outcome? Finally, the coach can progress into exploring different ways of behaving and help the individual plan how they can develop these skills and how and when they might deploy them. With the right questionnaire, 360s can amplify the value of coaching, and while in the short term they sometimes lead to individuals realigning their self-ratings closer to the reality of their line manager or direct reports' feedback, in the medium to long term they provide a platform for leadership performance improvement.

The 360-degree questionnaire can also be useful in team development, with team members sharing their results and discussing how they experience each other, and how adaptations in behavior can lead to enhanced team effectiveness.

The final aspect for using 360s is in terms of evaluation, providing evidence of impact or development. Too often organizations have focused on ROI; while this is a useful tool for assessing investment in static objects like computers or buildings, it is a less useful measure for dynamic objects like people. The 360 is, however, a more suitable instrument for evaluation, enabling measures at the start of the coaching process, and 12 months later, to assess the impact of coaching, assuming the focus of the coaching was based around the competencies.

## Conclusion

In this chapter we have reviewed 360-degree questionnaires and identified the role they can play in coaching, helping both individuals and organizations with their wider development journey and evaluating the impact of coaching.

## References

Alimo-Metcalfe, B., and Mead, G. (2012). Coaching for engaging transformational leadership. In J. Passmore (ed.), *Psychometrics in Coaching: Using Psychological and Psychometric Tools for Development* (2nd edition). London: Kogan Page.

Smither, J.W., London, M., Flautt, R., Vargas, Y., and Kucine, I. (2003). Can working with an executive coach improve multisource feedback ratings over time? A quasi-experimental field study. *Personnel Psychology* 56: 23–44.

# CHAPTER 37

# How long should a coaching assignment last?

Gill Tanner

## Introduction

Asking how long a coaching assignment should last is akin to asking for the ideal length of a piece of string. The answer is: it depends. Coaching assignments take many forms and are used for a wide variety of reasons. Coaching has been used to help police officers learn to drive, to improve safety outcomes on oil rigs and to enhance leaders' personal awareness, decision making and wellbeing. In addition, each individual is different. Whether a coaching assignment is planned for one session or one year, what is important is to start with the end in mind. By this we mean having clear goals and measures of success. In this chapter, we will explore the question of assignment length in more depth, and consider the practical implications which can help those managing coaching programs.

## Research

A range of research pieces have explored the question of how long a coaching assignment should last. A majority of coaches in a *Harvard Business Review* study (Kauffman and Coutu, 2009) reported that their engagements lasted between seven and 12 months, with only 10% saying that the engagement lasted for less than two months or longer than 18 months. In another study, Vandaveer and colleagues (2016) reported that 65% said the typical duration of a coaching assignment was four-to-12 months. In a final example, a study exploring leader effectiveness (Thach, 2002) found that executives who received at least six months of coaching increased their effectiveness by 55% when rated by their peers in a 360-degree feedback survey.

At first glance, it looks difficult to draw conclusions from this data. There is no truly 'typical' length of a coaching assignment, despite the mode being between four and 12 months. But the fact that six-to-nine months seems close enough to the average to not stand out as different doesn't mean that it's the right length for everyone, or even for 'the average person' (whatever that might be). The right conclusion to draw, therefore, should be to keep an open mind about a typical length of coaching assignment, and think instead about what factors might influence whether the right length of coaching assignment for one particular person would be two or 18 months.

## The risk of dependency

One element of a coach's role is to empower the coachee to become self-reliant and competent. One potential danger of continuing a coaching assignment for too long is the risk of the coachee becoming dependent on the coach. Over time, the relationship develops, the trust grows and the coachee begins to use the coach more as a consultant almost to outsource their thinking. A high-quality, ethical coach will work to ensure this does not happen. One way to reduce this is to put in place periodic reviews. This might involve the coach, coachee and the line manager meeting to review progress and agree what, if anything, needs to be addressed next.

When a break like that should happen will depend on the coachee's individual circumstances. In some cases, such as coaching accompanying a leadership development program or aimed at preparing an individual for a job application process, the length of the assignment will fit the leadership or recruitment process timetable. The temptation here may be to cut off the coaching prematurely, immediately after the program ends. However, providing space for one or two sessions after the process provides space for reflection, learning and future planning.

## Internal versus external coaches

Many organizations have internal coaches, who provide coaching services as well as carrying out their main role within the business, for example as an accountant, HR business partner or line manager. These internal coaches, for example in a call center, may undertake frequent short sessions, sometimes as short as 10 or 20 minutes, helping colleagues to reflect and to enhance their skills. This role coaching may be an integral part of people development. In contrast, an executive coach working face to face may have longer sessions and, due to the increased cost and travel time, may only meet with their coachee once a month, but for a two-hour block of time.

## Frequency and length of sessions

We talk in much greater detail about ideal session length in Chapter 38: 'How long should an individual coaching session last?' The answer will also influence the number of sessions and the length of the overall assignment. For example, weekly two-hour-long coaching sessions are not sustainable for most people's job roles, while 15-minute touchpoints with a coach twice per week might be. As a general guide, more frequent, shorter sessions over a longer period will generate a better outcome, a little like going to the gym, with repetition supporting the desired behavioral change.

## Type of agreement

Whilst it is quite common to agree to a fixed timescale in which to complete the coaching assignment, this does not mean it is always the most sensible approach. In some cases, a more open-ended arrangement with periodic reviews is agreed, with a greater focus placed on outcomes being achieved than the time taken to achieve them. Of course, there are advantages to both approaches. With the former, there is a sense of urgency and drive to complete the assignment in the allotted time, while with the latter there is the assurance that the coaching will not simply stop at a given date, even if the goal has not been achieved. Furthermore, the most significant effects of coaching are often those that take time to be established, and so extending the window of opportunity may generate disproportionately more benefits.

## Abrupt ends to coaching assignments

David Clutterbuck (2014) has argued that the coaching relationship is perceived more positively by both coach and coachee if the assignment has a clear, formal ending. This is partly due to the dependency issue mentioned above, but also to the fact that it gives the coaching clear boundaries. Jonathan Passmore and Tracy Sinclair make a similar point about "starting with the end in mind" (Passmore and Sinclair, 2021). What is clear is that good coaching conversations are thought-provoking, and the thinking and reflection can last for months after the coaching has ended. This raises the concern that evaluating coaching immediately at its conclusion may not be most helpful, as the learning process is likely to continue for a period after its completion.

It also invites consideration about how the coach can support this process of ongoing learning (see Chapter 10: 'What should I do after my coaching ends?' for more thoughts on this). Many coaches encourage coachees to use a reflective journal or notebook to capture thoughts and insights, so their insights and ideas are not lost.

## The ideal length of coaching assignments

It is clear that there are a number of factors to consider when thinking about the length of a coaching assignment. In addition to what we have discussed here, there will be other aspects to consider such as cost, alignment with development programs, availability of coach and coachee, the nature of the coaching goal and the coach's expectations, amongst other things. The important point is to ensure that the coaching is effective. In order to do this, it is crucial to agree with all stakeholders the optimal format for the coaching assignment, taking into account the elements mentioned in this chapter.

## Conclusion

Whilst there is some research regarding the most common lengths of time for a coaching assignment, there is a recognition from most writers that flexibility is important, so that individual preferences and assignment needs are taken into consideration. What is central is that while taking account of the broad guidelines, all parties agree on an approach, and when starting to coach, to do so focused on its purpose.

## References

Clutterbuck, D. (2014). When does a coaching assignment really end? *David Clutterbuck Partnership*. Retrieved 1 February 2022 from: https://davidclutterbuckpartnership.com/when-does-a-coaching-assignment-really-end.

Kauffman, C., and Coutu, D. (2009). *The Realities of Executive Coaching*. Harvard Business Review. Retrieved 1 February 2022 from: https://edbatista.typepad.com/files/realities_of_executive_coaching_hbr.pdf.

Passmore, J., and Sinclair, T. (2021). *Becoming a Coach: The Essential ICF Guide*. Berlin: Springer.

Thach, E.C. (2002). The impact of executive coaching and 360 feedback on leadership effectiveness. *Leadership & Organization Development Journal* 23(4): 205–14. https://doi.org/10.1108/01437730210429070.

Vandaveer, V.V., Lowman, R.L., Pearlman, K., and Brannick, J.P. (2016). A practice analysis of coaching psychology: Toward a foundational competency model. *Consulting Psychology Journal: Practice and Research* 68(2): 118.

# CHAPTER 38

# How long should an individual coaching session last?

Omar Alaoui

## Introduction

Like the discussion in Chapter 37: 'How long should a coaching assignment last?', the length of each session is also not set in stone. There is no single magic number which always applies, but there are some useful guidelines to consider. In this chapter, we will discuss the factors that may influence the optimum length of a session.

## Typical coaching session lengths

A straw poll from any population of coaches will reveal that length of coaching session varies. While some coaches will meet coachees for 30 minutes at a time, others work with coachees for two hours, some three hours or even all day.

From our research, it's possible to observe that around half the coaching sessions that take place sit at around the 30- to 45-minute mark, with another 45 per cent lasting between one hour and two hours. Very few exceed the two-hour mark. Why are there such differences? In thinking about what length is right for you or your organization, what factors should you consider?

One factor which impacts the length of the session is the approach used by the coach. Some coaching approaches and models are designed for longer coaching sessions, because the process is more complex and the time needed to explore it is greater. For example, the GROW model is relatively straightforward and linear, exploring only behavior changes. As a result, this can often easily be conducted within 30 minutes. In contrast, a transpersonal coaching method exploring a sense of self and identity might only generate insights over a two-hour discussion. Even here there will be wide margins depending on the individual's story and style of engagement.

There is no off-the-shelf perfect recipe for effective coaching in terms of approaches. While some presenting issues might lend themselves to one approach over another, most skilled coaches will integrate different models. The best coaches will explore the issue with their coachee to find the most effective approach and pace.

Secondly, the coachee's profile, personality, individual preferences and style of engagement also play an important role in defining the duration of a coaching session. For instance, a coachee who has a tendency towards strategic thinking might benefit from longer coaching sessions, diving deeper and exploring broader horizons to get the most out of the assignment, whereas they might not be as helpful for others (for example, in terms of impact on attention span or engagement level). A coachee who is extraverted or who uses storytelling as part of their communication style will require more time to feel that they have been heard.

Thirdly, face-to-face coaching tends to also demand travel time for one or both parties involved. This is an incentive for longer coaching sessions; a two-hour round trip for a 30-minute coaching session feels like a poor use of time. As a result, face-to-face coaching would generally be longer in duration, even if the same topics are covered and the same outcomes achieved.

Finally, group- and team-coaching sessions tend to need more time, simply because the group dynamic will add time by itself. A typical team-coaching session will last half a day, while even a group-coaching session, with a small group of five participants, giving ten minutes of air time to each participant, will typically last 90 minutes (see chapters 32, 33 and 34 for more information on team and group coaching).

## Shorter coaching sessions

Coaching sessions delivered remotely, whether through audio or video, are typically shorter. Removing the time it takes to travel to and from a coaching session stimulates flexibility and focus. Coachees have the chance to book coaching sessions at shorter notice and at times that suit them, fitting around other commitments, from childcare to work meetings (for example, booking a short, 45-minute session between two morning meetings). This leads to shorter sessions and more focused conversations.

There is some research evidence that shorter and more frequent sessions can be beneficial in learning. Shorter and more frequent engagement on a topic fosters deeper learning and greater retention over time (Baddeley and Longman, 1978; Ausubel, 1965).

An additional factor for some people is that digital coaching requires focused screen time, usually with a reflective period built in. For example, by using a 45- or 50-minute session time, this allows most people 10 or 15 minutes to reflect on the learning, making notes on action points or undertaking a short reading referred to by the coach. They also offer a chance for a comfort break, a stretch and change of eye focus to a longer distance than the 50cm or so usual between face and screen.

Coaching will invite the coachee to explore broader horizons and to get out of their comfort zone. This requires a high engagement level. The longer the coaching session, the more tired the coachee becomes. For digital coaching this is also true, thus favoring shorter but more frequent sessions.

## How long should coaching sessions last?

As we've seen, there is no absolute right or wrong regarding the length of a coaching session. The relevant duration depends on the nature of the coaching program you will be deploying. Table 38.1 offers some guidelines, but these are not hard-and-fast rules; people are different, and what works well for one person may be less suitable for another.

**Table 38.1: Duration of coaching sessions**

| Coaching program characteristics | Recommended duration |
| --- | --- |
| Digital coaching | Shorter coaching sessions are probably more relevant (typically 30–50 minutes for 1:1 coaching). |
| Face-to-face coaching | Longer sessions may be more effective in this setting, mainly due to travel time (90–120 minutes). |
| | If there is no travel time for either party, shorter and more frequent coaching sessions may work best (40–50 minutes). |

| Coaching program characteristics | Recommended duration |
|---|---|
| Group coaching | Longer coaching sessions (90–120 minutes), depending on group size, with a maximum of six in a group. |
| Team coaching | Longer sessions (120–240 minutes) work well. |

## Conclusion

There are many factors to consider when deciding upon session lengths for a coaching program. While there is no universal length, we would advocate 45 or 50 minutes for online sessions, and between one hour and two hours for face-to-face sessions. But these are not hard-and-fast rules. If a coachee needs more time, they should have the freedom to book two 45-minute sessions back to back, or to ask for a half day if meeting in a team setting.

## References

Ausubel, D.P. (1965). The role of frequency in learning and retention: A cognitive structure interpretation. *Journal of General Psychology* 72(2): 359–68.

Baddeley, A.D., and Longman, D.J.A. (1978). The influence of length and frequency of training session on the rate of learning to type. *Ergonomics* 21(8): 627–35.

# CHAPTER 39

# What should we expect concerning data protection for our coaching sessions?

Jonathan Passmore and Rui Munakata

## Introduction

Discussing confidential issues with another person might be a cause for concern. We might be guarded in what we reveal in case the other person shares this information with others. We might worry about what information the other person might store about us and how secure that storage might be. How can a coachee ensure that their coaching conversations remain confidential, and that all of the data, about them and their organization, remains secure? In this chapter, we will consider the rules which cover confidentiality and data protection. What should a coachee expect when it comes to protecting their sensitive information?

## Data protection

Most coaches hold significant data on their coachees. This may be as simple as their name, email, address, job role and key relationships internally. But it often extends to highly personal information about their attitudes towards colleagues, career plans for the future and wellbeing issues. In addition, most coachees talk extensively about their role, their organization and future business decisions, everything from profit margins to new product development.

In my own role as a coach, I have coached senior government ministers, people who appeared on TV most nights of the week, as well as senior business executives, whose names appeared in the financial press. In these discussions, it was not unusual to be discussing an issue, from government policy to organizational restructures, an M&A deal or conflicts between other individuals in the public eye and then see the outcome of these events appear in the news days, weeks or months later. These clients trusted me with the most intimate details about themselves and their businesses. This is the same for most coaching conversations. To get the most out of the coaching relationship, the client needs to trust that the coach will respect the confidentiality of the information which is shared in the conversation.

Yet despite this deeply intimate or commercially sensitive data, the average coach rarely has a data-management policy or has carried out a risk or impact assessment. Research suggests that only around 11% of independent practicing coaches are registered with the relevant information bodies in their country (Passmore and Rogers, 2018). Many have not thought through or established formal processes for information management.

Sadly, the same is true for many larger coaching providers. This is made more complex as the rules for data protection vary widely between different counties, and thus compliance becomes a time-consuming and complex task.

The challenge of regulatory compliance is common across multiple policy areas (Kitching, 2006). However, the GDPR (General Data Protection Regulation) places a strong emphasis on compliance, with severe penalties for those who fail to comply. This includes fines of up to 4% of worldwide turnover of the undertaking or €20 million for serious breaches, and up to 2% of turnover or €10 million for less severe violations. In the words of Isaacson (2021), "that's 20 million good reasons to want to comply." Other national jurisdictions, such as Australia and China, have their own regulations designed to protect their residents. Coaching across borders thus becomes more complex than jumping on a Zoom call due to data-protection regulations.

There is also a growing trend among some larger providers to record calls, either to monitor standards or to use the data for analysis and machine learning. While some individuals and companies may be happy for their coaching conversations to be recorded, we suspect most are not. In some cases, these recordings are not being fully disclosed to individual coachees or companies, but are buried in the small print of a tick-box contract. It is thus worth asking explicitly and securing assurances as to whether the session is being recorded, and only proceed if you are happy with such an arrangement.

## What should organizations do when looking to employ a coaching provider?

The answer to this question depends on the size of the business. We have suggested that the individual responsible for buying might find it helpful to consider this question under three broad headings: procurement, management and end of contract. However, the attention paid to this issue needs to reflect the scale, scope and activities of the business. Which steps you take will depend on the outcome of your own impact assessment, making a judgment about what's right for your business, your employees who will be part of the coaching assignment, and possibly commercial partners, clients or customers, whose data might also form part of coaching conversations.

Most large organizations will have a 'data-protection officer', which is a good place to start when thinking through these questions. This person is responsible for planning and managing the organization's data. In larger organizations, this individual will be in active engagement with the board and the senior team to ensure systems and processes exist to ensure compliance. While different approaches may be needed with a digital platform provider, offering coaching to 10 or 1,000 managers, whether that is through face-to-face sessions or via digital, the same rules should apply.

When engaging a coaching service from a consulting company, or a coach, thought should be given to the three key stages: procurement and set up, contract delivery and contract termination, and how each stage and the data will be handled. For example, at the end of the contract, how will the provider ensure that all personal data is deleted? This is easy if it's one coach providing a service for one manager, but it becomes far more challenging when it's a team of 50 or 100 coaches, all associates, all with their own notebooks and home filing systems containing paper records. In some ways, the problem reduces when all the coaches are using the same online platform and processes, although a new set of compliance questions arise for the buyer, as to the compliance of the system with GDPR and standards such as Schrems II.

## Checklist

The following ten questions may be a useful checklist to consider when undertaking an assessment of an external provider of coaching services.

### 1. Data policy

Does the organization have a data-management policy? How is this policy kept up to date and how is compliance ensured through internal audit processes?

## 2. Access to personal data

Who will have access to the personal data of coaching clients? Is this access based on the need-to-know principle? In most instances, this will be a coaching provider and their coaches. In most firms, coaches work as associates for the coaching provider. If this is the case, consideration needs to be given to how both the provider and the associates access, hold and manage personal data. For example, if it's a face-to-face session, where does the coach store their diary, which will contain names and organizational details? When the coach writes in their coaching notebook, where is this stored? When it's a single coach providing coaching for one single manager, this is easy to manage. However, when it becomes 150 coaches providing coaching for 500 managers, it is much more complex to ensure compliance.

For those companies using platforms, many of these questions become easier. However, it's best to ask how data is stored on the platform. Where are the servers located? Finally, how does the organization ensure security of this data through its technology compliance processes? Compliance with each of the following three standards is useful: Schrems II, ISO27001 and SOC2 will be important ones to assess.

## 3. Training

The actions of employees and contractors are one of the biggest risks faced by any organization. How does the provider train its employees and its associates in its policy? Sadly, abuse by internals or human mistakes have become an ever-present danger for all organizations. This risk means digital data could be exposed. In our view, compliance training needs to be for every employee and associate, both to remind everyone with access to client data of the importance of the issue and policy, and to ensure that organizational practices stay up to date. Moreover, there should be measures in place ensuring that unauthorized accesses are detected and addressed.

## 4. Spirit or the letter of the law

Does the provider have a website and how do they use the data collected for marketing? Does the provider aim to reflect the spirit as well as the letter of the law? A further concern is when coaching providers operate in territories where policies or legislation may conflict. How do they manage these conflicts? Our view is that suppliers should aim not simply to meet the minimum standard but to comply fully with the spirit of the legislation, and do so in all jurisdictions in which they operate, meeting legal requirements in whichever territories they operate, not just the laws from the city or state where they are based or have their headquarters.

*5. Managing high-risk data*

On most projects, some of the data being held will be considered to be high risk. It may involve commercially sensitive information about a future M&A or about a new product launch which will affect the share price, or it could be personal data about an individual's health. Suppliers need to implement technical and organizational measures (ToMs) to ensure the integrity and confidentiality of the data. In addition, coaching providers need to be aware of new provisions around data-security breaches and the requirement to notify the appropriate authorities, usually regulators as well as clients, if a breach has occurred.

*6. Forget me*

The 'right to be forgotten' has significant implications for some organizations. This simply requires the ability to delete individuals, organizations and their records, but many organizations do not have such processes built into their systems. While it might appear simple for digital files, organizations can neglect back-ups, paper records, notebooks and coaching-hours logs held by individual coaches as a record of the work they have undertaken for accreditation purposes.

*7. Sharing data*

Many suppliers have multiple partners with whom they have data-sharing agreements, contained in their standard policy. It's worth asking which organizations sensitive data would be shared with and ensure you are agreeable for data to be shared with each of those organizations, rather than signing off a general agreement or a long list of names.

*8. IT security*

How does the coaching provider ensure all data from the clients is held securely and prevent others from accessing this information? Does the coaching provider have certifications on information security, such as ISO 27001 and from SOC 2? These international standards can provide the comfort which global companies expect in terms of data privacy. Finally, the best organizations employ white-hat hackers to test their defenses and identify back-door risks where they may be exposed. By ensuring a supplier has these processes in place, organizations can reduce the risk of unintended data breaches.

*9. Secure or minimize manual data*

Most organizations will also have manual data. This data needs the same treatment as digital data: to be securely held, stored and destroyed after a specific period. This means using locked filing cabinets, locked office doors, clear-desk policies and ensuring all associates keep their notebooks with client/coachee details, client/coachee files, reflective journals and supervision notes in a secure location at all times when they are not being used. This could be a safe or a locked filing cabinet. Moreover, the best practice requires a 'clean-desk' practice, as well as a no-paper policy.

*10. Don't just take it to the recycling center*

Finally, data disposal is a last risk to manage. When it comes to destroying data, simply deleting the file or the client name may not be sufficient. How does the organization dispose of its confidential waste? How does it dispose of computers? What data might be held on associated computers, and if any data is held locally, how are these data or devices disposed of? Best practice is for such data to be disposed of through a contract with a professional data-services company, which will clean computer hard drives and back-up devices, and shred paper files securely.

## Conclusion

The importance of confidentiality and data protection in coaching is difficult to overstate. The way this is implemented in many jurisdictions is through data-privacy legislation, particularly the GDPR in Europe. When organizations are engaging with a coach or a coaching provider, there is a need to validate their compliance with relevant data-protection legislation, and every individual should take responsibility for protecting all personal data with which they come into contact.

## References

Isaacson, S. (2021). *How to Thrive as a Coach in a Digital World: Coaching with Technology*. London: Open University Press.

Kitching, J. (2006). A burden on business? Reviewing the evidence base on regulation and small business. *Environment and Planning C* 24(6): 799–814.

Passmore, J., and Rogers, K. (2018). DDPR: Data Protection. *Coaching at Work* 13(4): 30–3.

# SECTION 3

# The line manager's guide to coaching

In this section, we focus on the role of managers and leaders, as well as alternative options for delivery such as VR coaching and environmental considerations.

In Chapter 40: 'How should managers lead?' Jonathan Passmore and Anna Pachenkova explore how a coaching leadership style can be combined with other elements of the management toolkit, such as being able to consult, direct, set goals and establish a future vision. In Chapter 41: 'Should I choose the coach for my direct report?' Omar Alaoui discusses why enabling coachees to choose their coach, as opposed to selecting one on their behalf, may lead to the best outcomes for individuals and organizations. In Chapter 42: 'How can I best support my direct report with their coaching journey?' Andreas Weber explores the different options for engagement, and outlines the benefits which line managers, their teams and organizations will experience when coaching is connected appropriately. In Chapter 43: 'Why do organizations need manager–coaches?' Emily Barber considers why the manager–coach approach is growing in popularity, what it means to be a manager–coach and what the key differences are between professional coaching and acting as a manager–coach. In Chapter 44: 'Which skills are needed to be a good manager–coach?' Laurène Mayer explores which are the most important coaching skills that managers need to acquire to develop as a manager–coach. In Chapter 45: 'How can I provide input into the coaching goals of my direct report?' Eliana Gialain reviews how managers can contribute to their employees' coaching goals both directly and indirectly to maximize the value achieved by the organization.

In Chapter 46: 'How can I know the budget I am investing in coaching will have a return?' Gill Tanner explores how coaching commissioners can ensure a return on their investment through a variety of measures to demonstrate the effectiveness of coaching. In Chapter 47: 'How can I build a coaching culture in my team?' Jonathan Passmore and Roxane Rath explore what a coaching culture is and how organizations can go about developing one. In Chapter 48: 'How should the line manager give feedback to support the coaching assignment?' Jonathan discusses how managers can give constructive feedback that is both challenging and supportive, as well as genuine and developmental for everyone. In Chapter 49: 'What possibilities does virtual reality offer to coaching?' Shammy Tawadros considers what VR technology usage means for coaching and how stakeholders of coaching should respond, and highlights points for practical application. Finally, in Chapter 50: 'How can we use coaching to support our corporate social responsibilities?' David Tee discusses the increased awareness of environmental, social and governance concerns within organizations and the 'global village'. David looks at the role coaches play in facilitating conversations and awareness raising for realizing organizational values and responsibilities.

# CHAPTER 40

# How should managers lead?

Jonathan Passmore and Anna Pachenkova

## Introduction

Almost every manager is now expected to be able to use coaching as part of their management toolkit. But in our view, coaching should form one of a number of ways managers lead. In this chapter, we explore how managers can foster a coaching style, while recognizing that the best managers draw on a range of different styles, to suit different people and different situations. While a coaching style might be the default style encouraged in the team, managers also need to be able to consult, direct, set goals and establish a future vision.

## Different styles of leading?

It's been said by many before that if the only tool a manager has is a hammer, everything looks like a nail. But given that people are complex, dynamic, diverse and sometimes unpredictable, it's thus not surprising that leaders need subtle, adaptive ways to communicate, engage, influence, develop, inform and direct those who work with them.

The idea that leaders should adapt their leadership styles has spawned a host of different models. This idea of varying one's leadership style, known as situational leadership, was popularized by Hersey and Blanchard (1982). They suggested that effective leaders should operate using four styles – 'telling', 'selling', 'participating' and 'delegating' (see Figure 40.1) – varying these styles based on the level of competence and commitment of their team member. While highly competent and highly motivated individuals could be managed through delegation, the low-competence and low-motivation individuals needed the 'selling' style.

**Figure 40.1: Hersey and Blanchard's Situational Leadership**

| Hersey-Blanchard Situational Leadership Theory | | |
|---|---|---|
| | **Task Behaviors** | |
| | Low | High |
| High | **Participating Style**<br>Share Ideas<br>*(Followers able, unwilling, not confident)* | **Selling Style**<br>Explain Decisions<br>*(Followers unable, willing, confident)* |
| Low | **Delegating Style**<br>Turn Over Decisions<br>*(Followers able, willing, confident)* | **Telling Style**<br>Give Instructions<br>*(Followers unable, unwilling, not confident)* |

*(Relationship Behaviors — vertical axis label)*

One of the most popular approaches to situational leadership in organizations today suggests there are six different leadership styles (Goleman, 2000). Goleman notes that none of the six styles are right or wrong by themselves; they can just be more effective in one situation than another, for most people.

1. *The directive style* may be viewed as traditional leadership, giving instructions and telling people what to do. This can achieve results and is highly effective in times of crisis – when the fire-bell rings, you need to direct people to leave the building. But the style is best used with caution. Overuse, or use as an everyday style, has a toxic effect in the modern workplace, and is likely to lead to increased conflict and employee turnover.

2. *The pace-setting style* motivates the team by setting goals and leading by example. While goals motivate (and this style is particularly effective in fast-growing entrepreneurial businesses), the drive for continuous improvement can also have a toxic effect in the long run. Employees need periods of time to consolidate; without such periods, turnover or absenteeism can rise as employees look for a break from the constant demands for higher, faster, stronger.

3. *The visionary style* aims to engage and motivate team members through communicating a compelling vision for the future. What's important is that the vision fits with the values and beliefs of the team, and is communicated in a language and style to which the team can relate. It's important for each team member to understand how their work fits into the larger vision for the organization. When giving feedback, the main criterion is how the work contributes towards achieving that vision.

4. *The affiliative style* aims to keep employees happy, creating harmony and increasing loyalty by building strong emotional bonds. The affiliative leader does this by taking their direct reports out for a meal or a drink to see how they're doing, and taking time out to celebrate group accomplishments.

5. *The democratic style* aims to increase responsibility by letting team members have a say in decisions that affect their goals and how they do their work. By listening to employees' concerns, the democratic leader learns what to do to keep morale high.

6. *The coaching style* focuses on developing each employee to their full potential by allowing team members to play to their strengths. The coaching leader encourages employees to establish long-term development goals, and helps them progress towards these goals through regular developmental conversations.

Great leaders are likely to default to the coaching style, use three other styles frequently (visionary, affiliative and democratic), and use sparingly the other two (pace-setting and directive), which if overused can have a negative effect on morale, performance and turnover.

Adopting coaching as a default style of leadership works best in professional and creative environments where the workforce is highly educated and well trained. Employees in these environments have high expectations of how they prefer to be treated; they are often highly mobile and have good ideas on how to solve the problems they face. What they need is a management style that motivates them and encourages them to take more responsibility and solve their own problems. The coaching leadership style, focused on learning and development, is ideal for these environments – though of course, coaching should not be considered the only style to be used here. A blend is almost always better.

## Five situations in which to apply a coaching style

While there are multiple circumstances in which managers can deploy a coaching style, the following five scenarios would particularly benefit from a coaching style of leadership.

1. *Developing new skills* – A coaching style could be used to help team members develop a new skill. Using coaching helps the team member to set goals, develop a plan and receive support and encouragement as they test out the new skill.

2.  *Encouraging delegation* – The style can be used to encourage greater self-responsibility. When team members come with a problem, rather than offering a solution, the leader can use a coaching style to help the team member think through the issue, come up with their own solution and implement it.

3.  *Conducting an annual appraisal* – Instead of this being a one-way conversation from manager to team member, the manager can use a coaching style to encourage the team member to review their own performance, using the previous year's objectives and evidence-based performance data (sales, etc.), as well as encouraging them to set their own goals for the coming year.

4.  *Developing self-awareness* – Part of development is helping team members to become more aware of themselves, their environment and their impact on others. The coaching style encourages team members to become more aware through encouraging a more reflective stance.

5.  *Making a decision* – The coaching style can help team members to clarify what they want to achieve, identify and evaluate alternative courses of action (with the various pros and cons of each option), and set a plan of action with milestones to track their own progress.

## Conclusion

Coaching is a powerful style for leading others and should form part of the skillset of all managers. However, while managers need coaching skills, they also need on occasions to draw on other styles of leading, from setting the vision, to directing and developing affiliative relationships with colleagues.

## References

Goleman, D. (2000). Leadership that gets results. *Harvard Business Review*, March 2000.

Hersey, P., and Blanchard, K.H. (1982). *Management of Organizational Behaviour.* Prentice Hall Publishing.

# CHAPTER 41

# Should I choose the coach for my direct report?

Omar Alaoui

## Introduction

Line managers can find it tempting to choose the coach for their direct reports. Motives may be good, wanting to make sure the right coach is appointed based on experience of having worked with the coachee, coupled with a view of the organization's objectives. There may be a genuine keenness to provide the best available coach in the market to foster the coachee's growth and development. And yet, coaching remains a partnering process between coach and coachee; taking the choice of which coach to work with away from a coachee may not be the best course of action. This chapter will focus on the impact of the coach-selection process on the quality of the coach–coachee partnership, and why allowing coachees to make their own choices will probably lead to the best outcomes for them and for their team's performance and growth.

## Why is the line manager's involvement important?

In Chapter 22: 'How can we design and deploy successful coaching programs in an organization?' we concluded that a successful coaching program will have a clear purpose, aligned with the organization's HR strategy. For most organizations, this means that monitoring and evaluation are important parts of the process. One key stakeholder in any coaching program will be the coachee's line manager. The line manager has a responsibility for supporting and championing their direct report's development, as well as for monitoring their performance. They are likely to be closely aligned with their team, and well placed to identify development needs and to have a view of the individual's performance. For this reason, it's important for the line manager to be actively involved in their direct reports' coaching engagements. Specifically, it can be helpful for the line manager to be involved in a tripartite meeting with the coach and the coachee at the start of the coaching process to agree the assignment coaching goals and at the end of the process to review the outcome of coaching (see Chapter 29: 'How will we measure the impact of coaching in relation to our strategy?' for more details). But what about their role in other parts of the process, for example in selecting the coach for their team members?

## The working alliance

The working relationship between the coach and the coachee, often called the 'working alliance', is an important part of coaching and is known to significantly impact the outcomes of coaching (Bordin, 1979). Multiple research studies have shown that the strength of the coach–coachee working alliance is also an important factor for all types of clients and all levels of coaches' expertise (Graßmann et al., 2020). That said, what factors affect the development and growth of an effective working alliance in coaching?

Three main factors appear to contribute to an effective working alliance in coaching:

1. Perceived competence – The coach considers the coachee as a resourceful person, and the coachee recognizes and values the coach's competence and expertise

2. Behavioral similarity – The coach mirrors the behavioral preferences of the coachee

3. The trust and psychological safety experienced by the coachee in the way the coach engages in their relationship.

**Table 41.1: Key factors in the coach–coachee relationship**

| | |
|---|---|
| 1. | Perceived competence |
| 2. | Behavioral similarity |
| 3. | Trust and psychological safety |

## Should the manager choose the coach for their direct report?

Given how individual perception plays a significant factor in the assessment of these attributes, it becomes very hard for one person to select another person's coach. Your perception of what needs to happen to create a space of psychological safety may be quite different to mine. As a result, while the line manager may be working with positive intent to select the best coach, they can only ever do so from their personal perspective or – perhaps worse – their assumptions about what the coachee might think. In reality, the only person who can make the best choice for the coachee is the coachee. By intervening in the match, the line manager risks increasing the likelihood of it being unsuccessful, thereby reducing the value of the coaching intervention. And it doesn't end there: there are at least four additional risks involved in making this choice for direct reports.

Firstly, the relationship with the coach may be affected. The direct report might see the coach as the line manager's messenger, not their own ally. As a result, they may choose to withhold information, present more positive information in fear it may be fed back, and generally be less open and honest in the discussion. The result is that coaching will tend to cover less ground and be a shallower conversation. In combination, this will reduce the value the coachee gets from the coaching process.

Secondly, while most managers think they know their team members well, it's almost certainly the case that the coachee will know themselves better, and thus be best placed to make their own choice as to the right fit for them. What's best may also change over time, and may depend on events both at work and at home. Some coachees want a coach who will listen, empathize and understand them, as they explore issues such as wellbeing or work–life balance. Others want a coach who will bring challenge into the conversation and help them develop a fresh perspective. A third group may want a sounding board, as they explore new ideas, innovations or plans for the future.

Thirdly, if the line manager makes the choice, this can damage the coachee's relationship with the line manager (perhaps further, if this 'interfering' behavior is common). It may contribute to resentment, anger or suspicion that the coaching conversation is not confidential; by making the selection, the line manager is signaling, perhaps inaccurately, that they cannot be trusted.

Lastly, behavioral change is usually not the only objective of coaching. Coaching often includes broader, holistic explorations, which build self-awareness, reflexivity and thus the future potential of the coachee. If the only goals set are by the line manager, who also selects the coach, this wider 'potential' aspect of coaching may be lost. Instead, the coachee needs to feel reassured that such discussions can take place, alongside the more 'performance-development' aspects of coaching. By enabling the coachee to make the selection, the line manager's own interactions with the coachee can be rightly focused on day-to-day performance, and also on the growth and development of potential, which is likely to deliver results over the person's career, not just in the following quarter.

Overall, while the line manager has an important role, the coachee should always make the decision on which coach to select. The line manager should focus their energy and effort in working with their team members; sharing their views as to development objectives as part of the coaching agenda; providing support, encouragement and praise during the coaching journey; and finally, joining the coachee in evaluating the impact of coaching when it concludes.

## Conclusion

Line managers can be tempted to take an active role in selecting the coach for their team. This risks damaging the relationship between coach and coachee, as well as negatively impacting on the relationship between coachee and line manager. The coachee is always best placed to make the choice to find the right coach for themselves. The line manager's role, in contrast, is to support their direct reports in coaching, and to be a wider sponsor for coaching in their team and the wider organization.

## References

Bordin, E.S. (1979). The generalizability of the psychoanalytic concept of the working alliance. *Psychotherapy: Theory, Research & Practice* 16(3): 252–60.

Graßmann, C., Schölmerich, F., and Schermuly, C.C. (2020). The relationship between working alliance and client outcomes in coaching: A meta-analysis. *Human Relations* 73(1): 35–58.

# CHAPTER 42

# How can I best support my direct report with their coaching journey?

Andreas Weber

## Introduction

Line managers can support their direct reports' coaching in various ways, including by becoming an active partner in team members' personal and professional development. Involving line managers in the coaching process can enhance trust and strengthen relationships, as well as improve alignment between individual, team and organizational goals.

In this chapter, we will explore the different options for engagement, and the benefits which line managers, their teams and organizations will experience when coaching is connected appropriately.

## Line-manager involvement in coaching

There are many advantages to involving line managers in the coaching of their direct reports. Line managers have valuable knowledge of the skills and possible areas for improvement of their team members, and also play a critical role in creating a working environment that enables change, supports growth, elicits feedback, and encourages trying out new approaches and behaviors. The evidence around involvement of line managers with coaching processes can be clustered into three broad areas: goal-setting, giving feedback and support, and creating the right environment. We will look at each of these in turn.

## Goal-setting

The line manager will almost always have a perspective on their team members, and be able to offer valuable insights on where their direct reports are on the journey of development, as well as their work priorities. This information can be very helpful for several reasons. Firstly, the coachee might not be aware of their development needs or their growth potential, and in many cases are not always clear about their role priorities. Secondly, the line manager will have a deeper understanding of the wider organization's needs, which can be used to ensure that the coachee's individual goals are in line with wider objectives, values and policies.

We have highlighted throughout this book the value of:

- Talking to coachees about their goals for coaching before sessions start
- Actively participating in tripartite meetings to ensure goal alignment
- Attending a midpoint review
- Engaging in coaching-assignment evaluation.

Sometimes line managers believe it is enough simply to tell their direct reports what they have to work on. But this direct engagement in the process can send the wrong signal and reduce the coachee's engagement, and is likely to lead away from the alignment everyone wants.

## Feedback and support

The line manager's involvement in the coaching process should not be limited to discussing possible goals and desired outcomes at the beginning. The line manager should be there throughout the entire journey by giving coachees continuous feedback on their progress, with a focus on catching the team member doing it right, thus providing reinforcement praise, as opposed to critical corrective feedback. The periodic 1:1 is often a good point at which to discuss coaching progress, but the feedback does not have to be limited to this; managers can give short 'in-the-moment' feedback, as well as using feedback technology tools to affirm positive progress.

This style of regular feedback encourages persistence, as well as making coachees aware that their line manager is supportive, encouraging them on their journey as they test out new behaviors and skills.

Finally, the line manager may also need to change and adjust as their team members grow and develop through coaching. The team members may expect or require greater autonomy, meaning greater delegation and different styles of leading. In this way, the line manager needs to recognize that leading is not a top-down process, but an exchange, where they too need to adjust their style as their team develops. For more detail on feedback, see Chapter 48: 'How should the line manager give feedback to support the coaching assignment?'

## Creating the right environment

Besides the individual being coached, the effects of coaching can influence a coachee's surroundings, having an impact on their coworkers and line managers. If enough employees are part of these changes, the impact can span across an entire organization. See Chapter 18: 'How can we create synergy between the organizational strategy and the coaching program?' for more information on the 'ripple effect' of coaching; the wider impacts, while difficult to measure, should not be underestimated.

Of course, learning does not stop when the coaching assignment comes to an end. Having started to use developmental reflective conversations, the line manager should continue these going forward after the coaching program. This can ensure reflection and continuous improvement are built into the way the team works together for the long term.

## The role of a line manager

So far, we have discussed the different ways that a line manager can facilitate the coaching journey for their direct reports. To be most effective, however, it is important for all of these measures to be agreed upon with the team, so that they feel included in all parts of the process. One further change, discussed in more detail in chapters 40 and 47, is the development of a coaching culture and a coaching style of leadership. This should not be underestimated, and most managers need training and support themselves to make the transition to a different style. Doing this can further help create a culture where personal responsibility and self- and situational awareness are enhanced.

## Tripartite sessions

Tripartite meetings are a good way to improve alignment and ensure that both the coachee and the organization (via the line manager and/or HR) are actively involved at each stage of the process. One key concept to bear in mind is that the role of the coach in these meetings is not to brief the line manager on how the coachee is doing, or what they have said in coaching, but instead to facilitate and hear a conversation between line manager and coachee on the focused topic of their coaching, whether this happens at the goal-setting, progress-monitoring or final evaluation stages.

## Conclusion

There can often be hesitation and uncertainty about coaching's impact on the relationship between a line manager and their direct reports. As understandable as this might be, research on line-manager involvement clearly shows that these concerns tend to disappear as soon as the coaching process shows positive effects on direct reports, their colleagues and the working environment in general. Line managers should actively support the coaching process; by doing so, they can significantly improve the outcomes. Ultimately, coaching can go beyond helping the coachee achieve their own development goals; it can also strengthen relationships, strengthen the team and have a positive impact on the wider organizational system.

# CHAPTER 43

# Why do organizations need manager–coaches?

Emily Barber

## Introduction

In an ever-changing working environment, organizations need to have a flexible approach to management and leadership styles; retaining talent and high-potential employees is key to building sustainable and effective organizations. In this chapter, we explore why the manager–coach approach is growing in popularity, what it means to be a manager–coach and what the key differences are between professional coaching and acting as a manager–coach.

## What is a manager–coach?

The manager–coach is not a professional coach. Instead, it is someone who engages with their direct reports with a coaching mindset. Adopting a coaching mindset can be a significant advantage to managers (Cox et al., 2009). Hunt and Weinberg (2002) suggest that the following characteristics are demonstrated by manager–coaches:

- An attitude of helpfulness
- Less need for control
- Empathy in dealing with others
- Openness to personal learning and receiving feedback
- High standards
- A desire to help others to develop

- A theory of employee development that is not predicated on a 'sink or swim' approach

- A belief that most people do want to learn.

The manager–coach's relationship with their staff is a reciprocal one. Manager–coaches invite their team members to reflect using open questions, listen deeply and believe in their team to develop solutions which make best use of their individual skills while delivering outcomes best suited to the organization's needs. This also means team members stepping up to demonstrate ownership and take responsibility for issues.

The key attributes of the manager–coach are:

- A positive attitude towards staff and an interest in staff wellbeing

- Being fully present when speaking with staff, removing all distractions

- Being a non-judgmental active listener and enabling staff to speak openly

- Being able to use powerful questioning to understand issues and challenges

- Being able to provide constructive feedback and establish goal-setting.

The manager–coach approach has become an increasingly important way to engage individual employees and teams, to maximize their potential and overcome issues. Tackling issues in a collaborative manner extends the benefits beyond the relationship between the manager–coach and the employee to also benefit the organization for which they both work.

## What are the key differences between a professional coach and a manager–coach?

*The professional coach*

A professional coach will be trained and accredited by one of the major coaching bodies, such as the ICF or EMCC. Working formally, the professional coach will agree a contract with their coachee, setting out how they will work together. The contract, whether documented or verbal, aims to provide a means to establish a relation of trust and create the psychological boundaries needed for in-depth reflective conversations, along with explicit agreements about how each party will behave. The professional coach and the relationships they establish are marked by confidentiality, with the coaching agenda being driven by the coachee (Gyllensten and Palmer, 2007).

*The manager–coach*

In contrast, most manager–coaches will have limited or no formal coach training and are unlikely to be accredited coaches. Research suggests fewer than one in four managers will have had any formal coach training (Anderson, 2013). For those who do receive training, it might be no more than a one-day course. As a result, the manager–coach approach may be more based around experiences of professional coaching received by the manager than any formal knowledge or psychological understanding. Research has also noted that manager–coach conversations are less formal and structured than comparable professional coach conversations. Dixey (2015) noted that development conversations led by a manager–coach may be led in such a subtle way that their direct reports are likely not to be aware that they are being coached at all.

One important aspect to note about the manager–coach's relationship with their direct reports is that it cannot escape from being a hierarchical one, even if the manager–coach approaches the relationship in a more partici-pative style. Ultimately, the manager–coach cannot change the fact that they have decision-making power over the direct report, and may have to switch at times to a more directive style. An awareness that the coach is always the line manager will impact on the openness of the coachee, negatively impacting the quality of the coaching conversation and the outcomes which can be achieved.

However, it's important to recognize that the manager–coach can add value, but that their role and contribution are different to those of an external coach. Instead, coaching in this way is more of a leadership style.

## Combining the professional coach and manager–coach

The manager–coach is not a professional coach, but can adopt a coaching mindset to support and facilitate their team members' development. Such an approach should be seen as complementary to the provision of professional coaching.

However, given the research into manager–coaches, organizations need to ensure that managers are effectively trained in coaching and communication skills. Along with using external professional coaches and training internal coaches, such steps can be important on the road towards building a coaching culture in the organization.

## Why is the manager–coach approach growing?

The workplace has undergone transformational changes in recent years, and a digital revolution has taken place to meet the demands of organizations operating in a dynamic and uncertain world. The impact upon organizational change has resulted in three main trends which are shifting the way organizations function, the role of individual employees and teams, and what is expected of managers and leaders:

1.  Employee requirements are changing, as they search for greater professional development, autonomy and work–life balance. There is an expectation that organizations must be able to provide this enhanced package of employment if they are to attract and retain talent.

2.  Teams are increasingly multi-disciplined, as cross-functional projects grow in popularity and organizations continue to move towards permanent hybrid working arrangements. This changing landscape has a direct impact on managers, who are expected to manage multi-faceted, hybrid and decentralized teams.

3.  Contemporary management and leadership skills have increased the focus of the role of managers to include being open-minded, curious, acting with emotional intelligence, and establishing a personal connection with their direct reports (Rogers, 2021).

The impact of Covid-19 accelerated the transition to hybrid working. In this new working environment, the command-and-control management approach has become far less effective. As such, managers need to engage with staff to meet their needs while also building commitment, engagement and autonomy. For example, if an individual is able to act decisively and confidently within a supportive working environment, there is a high likelihood that they will be more productive. Equally important is for the team environment to be one where employees feel equally valued, with each team member recognized and respected for their contribution to the organization's mission. Whilst there may be hierarchical roles within the teams, the focus is upon meeting business objectives. Furthermore, if managers can identify and focus upon the skillsets needed to perform roles, and subsequently grow and stretch individuals, then this should reap greater rewards for the business, as employees feel valued and are being developed.

Considering what coaching is, it is natural for us to focus upon individuals taking personal responsibility and developing deeper self-awareness. Research from Boyatzis and Jack (2018) and the ICF (2017) found the following:

- Individuals are more motivated and committed to taking action when they have found solutions for themselves, as opposed to being told what to do to remedy issues

- Helping individuals to analyze problems from the past is more challenging than supporting them to envisage a brighter future.

Coaching provides the solution to working in remote and hybrid teams, overcoming the shortcomings of the command-and-control approach. It can help team members to feel empowered to discover their own answers, devolving responsibility and unleashing potential. Therefore, in this journey towards managerial transformation, both external coaches and managers integrating coaching approaches into their management style can have a huge impact on organizations.

## Conclusion

There are important differences between a manager–coach and a professional coach; this leadership approach can support the delivery of successful organizations. In fact, the role of manager–coach is an increasingly important approach for managers and leaders to adopt in an ever-changing working environment.

## References

Anderson, V. (2013). A Trojan Horse? The implications of managerial coaching for leadership theory. *Human Resource Development International* 16(3): 251–66. https://doi.org/10.1080/13678868.2013.771868.

Boyatzis, R., and Jack, A.I. (2018) The neuroscience of coaching. *Consulting Psychology Journal: Practice and Research* 70(1): 11–27.

Cox, E., Bachkirova, T., and Clutterbuck, D. (2009). *The Complete Handbook of Coaching*. London: Sage.

Dixey, A. (2015). Managerial coaching: A formal process or a daily conversation? *International Journal of Evidence Based Coaching & Mentoring* 9 (Special Issue): 77–89.

Gyllensten, K., and Palmer, S. (2007). The coaching relationship: An interpretative phenomenological analysis. *International Coaching Psychology Review* 2: 168–77.

Hunt, J.M., and Weinberg, J.R. (2002). *The Coaching Manager: Developing Top Talent in Business*. New York: Sage.

International Coaching Federation (2017). *Building a Coaching Culture with Millennial Leaders*. Lexington: ICF.

Rogers, J. (2021). *Coaching: What Really Works*. London: Sage.

# CHAPTER 44

# Which skills are needed to be a good manager–coach?

Laurène Mayer

## Introduction

In Chapter 43, we discussed the differences between a professional coach and a manager–coach. One key aspect of adopting the posture of manager–coach is the development of a coaching mindset; a second is the development of coaching skills. And coaching skills are not innate; at times, they differ widely from the behaviors which have traditionally been ascribed to leaders. In this chapter, we will explore which are the most important coaching skills that managers need to acquire to develop as a manager–coach.

## Coaching skills for managers

Traditional management has historically placed an emphasis on setting direction, imposing objectives and telling people what to do. But the world of work is changing. The command-and-control style of leader is not effective in motivating the new workforce, which values purpose and autonomy more highly than previous generations did and is willing to leave organizations if a better offer is available. The new model of leadership is designed around unleashing the potential in knowledge-based roles, to support and facilitate employee engagement and enable individuals to come together from disparate backgrounds to collaborate, and through this create stakeholder value. Coaching is perfectly suited to this task.

But what skills do managers need to bring coaching to life in their daily interactions with employees? There are three combinations of behavioral skills which, if executed well, contribute towards building a coaching style of engagement.

*Developing presence*

The first of these is developing presence. This is about consciously being in the present moment. Overloaded schedules and endless communications and notifications can disrupt interactions. Getting away from these distractions and focusing on the present moment is key. This is particularly important in the hybrid world, where encounters take place online and the same device used for meetings is used for all other aspects of work. By turning off notifications, preparing for the meeting in advance and making best use of the technology, a manager can ensure they are fully in the present moment with their employee. Many researchers also highlight the value of mindfulness in helping managers develop presence, improving employee interactions as well as decision making and productivity (see Passmore and Amit, 2017).

*Active listening*

Developing presence will contribute to the second item on our list: listening skills. It is often said that many managers don't listen, instead simply waiting for their turn to talk. In contrast, active listening is at the heart of using a coaching approach. The manager–coach needs to truly listen to what their employee is saying. In fact, they need to do more than just listen to the words which are being communicated. They need to listen to the whole communication, paying attention to the voice tone, pace and pitch. How is this the same as, or different from, what's gone before, and how does this match the words being expressed? The manager–coach also needs to observe body language, not just overt posture and hand movements, often associated with body language, but deep body-language communication, changes in skill coloration, breathing, the amount of moisture in the employee's eye, and so on. Each data point contributes towards giving a sense of what the individual is thinking and feeling, and how this is changing over time. Finally, the manager–coach needs to listen for what's *not* being said: the missing parts of the communication and what this might mean.

Another part of listening is letting the listener know they have been heard. This involves a wide range of communication skills, including:

- Reflections – These are short interventions made by the manager–coach to the employee, like a single word of meaning or sometimes an emotion. They contain the message, "I am understanding what's important to you".

- Summaries – If reflections are the single gift of a rose to the speaker, summaries are a bouquet, drawing together a number of threads of what's been said, almost like the conclusion at the end of a chapter. They are designed to communicate a rich understanding of the message, check the meaning with the speaker, and also help the speaker spot new patterns or insights from what they have said.

- Affirmations – These are positive reflections, where the manager–coach reflects back a positive attribute they have observed to underline this attribute or achievement. Affirmations serve the purpose of strengthening the relationship, as well as building the employee's self-esteem.

*Open questions*

As with listening, managers often adopt a particular style of questioning aimed more at gathering information than at helping their employee deepen their self-awareness or better understand for themselves how to tackle the issue. Command-and-control manager questions might be considered to be enquiry questions. They are most often closed in style, leading to short informational answers: "Have you done that report yet?" "When will the data be ready for the meeting?" When using a coaching style, the purpose of the manager changes from gathering information towards generating insight. This results in a shift to open questions: "What next steps are you planning?" "What might get in your way in achieving that?" In the manager–coach's eyes there is no right or wrong answer. Their purpose is developing their employee's insights, enabling them to be more self-aware and take more personal responsibility for their actions.

On the surface, this cluster of behaviors seems simple, but years of operating in more traditional ways of engaging have shown how hard it can be for managers to avoid stepping in with advice, gathering information or listening primarily to wait for their turn to talk. In short, most managers don't have the skills to switch immediately to this new style; instead (as with any new skill) they need training and time to develop sufficiently to operate effectively as a manager–coach (McCarthy and Milner, 2013).

The outcome of this style of engagement is enhanced trust and greater openness. As the manager shares more about themselves, operates in a way that facilitates openness, and communicates that they want to listen, understand and encourage their employees to think for themselves, new relationships will blossom and new capabilities will be unlocked.

## A coaching style

In addition to these core coaching skills, the manager can reinforce certain managerial skills that they already have by infusing them with the coaching mindset.

*Delegating and empowering teams*

A key skill for the manager–coach is to be able to see the potential in others and to help them connect with their own resources to achieve their best. This skill is essential for a manager who wants to switch from being a command-and-control manager to being a manager–coach. A manager–coach will develop their direct reports' personal accountability and their autonomy. This may involve agreeing broad objectives aligned with the business plan, but delegating responsibility for how these are achieved.

*Sharing regular feedback*

Feedback is also an important part of the process (Steelman and Wolfeld, 2018). Manager–coaches with higher feedback orientation are viewed as more effective than manager–coaches with lower feedback orientation. In parallel, manager–coaches were also more likely to solicit feedback from their direct reports than more traditional managers (Ellinger, 1997). In combination, this open, feedback style of engagement contributes to greater openness and trust.

Organizations have a role to play in developing a feedback culture. This can be done by developing a learning environment that helps managers to develop the skills to provide evidence-based feedback, as well as understanding what is meant by feedback models such as the sandwich of praise–criticize–praise; it is better when the manager–coach focuses on 'catching the employee doing it right', consistently providing multiple times as much positive feedback to developmental feedback over a period of time. All of this can be enhanced through the use of 360 tools such as the Transformational Leadership Questionnaire (TLQ) or through technology tools built around capturing praise and feedback for employees.

## Creating a growth and learning environment

Creating a learning culture in an organization supports managers in the development of their manager–coach skills and coaching mindset, and more importantly creates a climate where reflective practice and continuous learning are seen as part of everyday activities (Hamlin et al., 2006). Managers can support the development of this learning culture directly by:

- Being an ambassador for the organization's initiatives and regularly encouraging discussion of L&D
- Encouraging employees to adopt a growth mindset

- Supporting employees to develop personal training or development plans.

## Conclusion

Managers have a key role to play in supporting their employees in their development. Yet according to the Gartner Manager Effectiveness Survey (2017), 45% of managers lack confidence in their ability to coach and develop employees in the skills they need today. The manager–coach approach can be one step, alongside the use of professional coaches, in helping organizations create a culture of greater personal responsibility, self-awareness and a growth mindset.

## References

Ellinger, A.M. (1997). Managers as facilitators of learning in learning organizations. Unpublished doctoral dissertation, University of Georgia at Athens, GA.

Gartner (2017). Manager Effectiveness Survey. Retrieved 4 March 2022 from: https://www.gartner.com/smarterwithgartner/fine-tune-development-spend-to-make-managers-more-effectivee.

Hamlin, R.G., Ellinger, A.D., and Beattie, R.S. (2006). Coaching at the heart of managerial effectiveness: A cross-cultural study of managerial behaviours. *Human Resource Development International* 9(3): 305–31. https://doi.org/10.1080/13678860600893524.

McCarthy, G., and Milner, J. (2013). Managerial coaching: Challenges, opportunities and training. *Journal of Management Development* 32: 768–79.

Passmore, J., and Amit, S. (2017). *Mindfulness at Work: The Practice and Science of Mindfulness for Leaders, Coaches and Facilitators.* New York: Nova Science.

Steelman, L.A., and Wolfeld, L. (2018). The manager as coach: The role of feedback orientation. *Journal of Business and Psychology* 33(1): 41–53. https://doi.org/10.1007/s10869-016-9473-6.

# How can I provide input into the coaching goals of my direct report?

Eliana Gialain

## Introduction

Coaching has grown significantly over the past two decades, as organizations increasingly look to support employees in reaching their full potential and in enhancing individual, team and organizational performance. While coaching is often seen as an individual-centered development process, line managers have an important role to play in this process. One way in particular is through three-way contracting involving the line manager, coach and coachee, agreeing the overarching goals for the coaching before the coaching begins (Ogilvy and Ellam-Dyson, 2012) in monitoring progress and in reviewing outcomes. In this chapter, we will review how managers can contribute to their employees' coaching goals both directly and indirectly to maximize the value achieved by the organization.

## The manager's role in their employee's coaching goals

Companies invest in employee development with the objective of supporting employees and also in anticipation of a positive return back to the business. This positive impact may be in terms of functional area business results, cultural transformation, helping to increase the organization's capacity to respond to change, reductions in absenteeism and turnover, and enhancing creativity and wellbeing across the workforce.

With these benefits available, one key question is what role line managers should play to optimize the benefits available, and connect individual coaching with organizational processes and goals. This activity can be viewed system-ically, connecting the individual intervention to the wider system, which is both funding the intervention and which holds expectations about its value contribution (Checkland, 2000).

Line managers can make a positive contribution to the coaching process, participating both directly and indirectly; let's look at each in turn.

## Direct involvement in setting employees' coaching goals

While some argue that coaching is personal, private and should be disconnected from line management, we should consider an alternative view. When funded by an organization, the line manager plays an important role in supporting the coachee and the coaching program as a whole. In a formal way, this can best be achieved through a three-way contracting, or 'tripartite', meeting that happens within the first few coaching sessions involving coach, coachee and line manager. The conversation may only last for 10–15 minutes, to agree organizational objectives for the coaching assignment and be transparent around its boundaries (such as confidentiality). This is not to say that the coach and coachee can't add to these objectives and work on additional personal items as the assignment progresses. During the tripartite meeting the coach might invite both parties to set out their hopes for coaching, what the focus priorities are and how these might be measured at the end of the program. The items discussed then form a baseline menu for the coaching program.

This tripartite approach to objective setting should not be the end of the line manager's involvement; it can be complemented by a midpoint check-in around halfway through the coaching. In this short meeting, the coach will facilitate a review from the perspective of both coachee and line manager, inviting both to share their perspectives on how the coaching is progressing and the perceived impact it is having. Finally, the coach invites both to review the objectives, validate that they are still relevant and explores what needs to change. This allows for realignment and ensures the coaching process stays on track.

A final tripartite could be conducted to formally close the assignment. Once again, the coach facilitates the discussion, providing opportunities for both parties to share their view on the objectives, measures of success, and perceptions on what might be good next steps for the coachee's development moving forward.

It's important to note that many line managers are interested in the coach's evaluation of the coachee, but this is not the role of the coach. Their view is in many ways irrelevant; the only data they have is what's been presented by the coachee in a confidential conversation intended for the coachee to explore their perspective.

## Indirect involvement in setting employees' coaching goals

In addition to the direct involvement described above, line managers also have an important role to play indirectly. This indirect involvement is through connecting coaching to the wider management processes, such as 1:1 meetings, performance reviews, objective setting and personal development planning. We'll look at three particular elements of this.

Firstly, the manager provides an important conduit between the coaching process and the organization in terms of its strategic objectives. By providing a view from the organization's perspective, the coachee's annual development plan and the coaching intervention itself should have a direct positive contribution towards the organizational objectives.

Secondly, and perhaps most importantly, the line manager should act as a supporter, cheerleader and accountability partner (see Chapter 14: 'How can a support team help me in making the most of coaching?'). They should explore how they can support the work being undertaken in the coaching, link the activities to possible learning opportunities, and hold the employee to account in terms of both their active engagement in coaching and their commitment to create time in their diary, to reflect and implement insights and actions emerging from the coaching conversations.

Finally, line managers should develop a coaching mindset and coaching skills so that their daily interactions better reflect a coaching style of engagement. These coaching leadership styles mirror the professional coaching the coachee is receiving, encouraging the development of greater personal responsibility and deepened self-awareness.

## Conclusion

Line managers are fundamental in enabling the transfer of coaching insights and actions from coaching room to workplace. When line managers remain passive, a significant proportion of the potential of coaching might be lost. But when active, both through direct involvement in tripartite meetings and indirectly through linking coaching conversations to the wider organization, personal development plans and through specific roles, the line manager moves from passive bystander to active agent. In this way, they facilitate the coachee's development, enabling coaching conversations to become truly transformational.

## References

Checkland, P. (2000). Soft Systems Methodology: A Thirty Year Retrospective. *Systems Research and Behavioral Science* 17, S11–S58. https://doi.org/10.1002/1099-1743.

Ogilvy, H., and Ellam-Dyson, V. (2012). Line management involvement in coaching: Help or hindrance? A content analysis study. *International Coaching Psychology Review* 7(1): 39–54.

CHAPTER 46

# How can I know the budget I am investing in coaching will have a return?

Gill Tanner

## Introduction

Evaluating the return on investment (ROI) of any learning and development (L&D) activity is always a challenge due to the difficulties in confirming that the interventions played an active role in causing the changes in organizational performance. Coaching is no exception. It is difficult to separate the success of coaching from other organizational initiatives and external factors, and in addition where a coachee leads a team and achieves results through others, it is difficult to assess how far coaching was responsible. How can we be sure that the budget invested in coaching will bring a return? In this chapter, we will explore how coaching commissioners can ensure a return on their investment.

## ROI in coaching

Many coaching writers have been critical of the obsession with ROI. Some have argued that while ROI is a useful metric for measuring static investments like IT software or buildings, it is fundamentally flawed when used for human interventions. Grant (2012) notes that there are various studies stating a wide range of ROI figures for coaching, extending from 221% to 788%, and this variability is just one of the problems of the ROI method. Firstly, it depends on whom and what you are measuring: the coach of the chief executive of a national house builder is likely to be able to demonstrate immeasurably greater financial returns than that of a manager responsible for breast-cancer care treatment in a hospital. For some roles, such as those in sales, impact can be clearly measured (although not always separated out from external factors, such as the recent global lockdowns or the decline of an industry due to disruptive innovation). The second fundamental issue is that coaching ROI is almost always not a measurement but an individual's estimate (or guess). We know from multiple research studies how unreliable we humans are at making estimates about our own performance, due to a lack of data combined with inherent biases.

At its foundation, the ROI method of subtracting the costs of coaching from the estimated value of its outcomes and expressing this as a percentage (Figure 46.1) makes sense. But given the issues noted by leading practitioners and researchers, what then is a better way to ensure that the budget invested in coaching will have a return?

**Figure 46.1: Coaching ROI calculation**

$$\frac{\text{Estimated coaching benefits} - \text{costs of coaching}}{\text{Costs of coaching}} \times 100\%$$

There is no doubt that it is prudent to monitor the spend on coaching and to be prepared to justify it; however, a more useful way to do this is to look holistically at the benefits of coaching, and not just the financial gains.

## The benefits of coaching

The benefits of coaching have been widely reported over the past decade. One particular study (Athanasopoulou and Dopson, 2018) found that at an individual level, coachees were able to overcome regressive behaviors, had increased work and life satisfaction, were able to improve their personal management and self-control, and improved their personal skills and abilities or were able to acquire new ones. On a team level, team members found their leaders to be more effective, have better communication skills, be better at managing and developing others, and have improved team-building skills. The organizations benefited because of increased employee satisfaction, improved productivity and enhanced leadership skills. Other studies have found similar positive results.

These benefits are wide-ranging and significant, and can be cited as recent evidence of the benefits of coaching, but how can coaching commissioners obtain clearer evidence to support their own budget spend on coaching?

## The impact of coaching

It is worthwhile being very specific about the needs of the organization, as outlined in Chapter 22: 'How can we design and deploy successful coaching programs in an organization?' Rather than simply outlining the benefits, a coaching commissioner might spend time focusing on the questions in Table 46.2.

**Table 46.2: Useful questions**

| Organization | 1. | What is the objective of the coaching program? |
|---|---|---|
| | 2. | How does the coaching program link to the L&D strategy, HR strategy and/or business strategy? |
| | 3. | What will it look like if the program objective is achieved? |
| | 4. | What will be the consequence if the program objective is not achieved? |
| | 5. | Is the coaching program supported by the executive team? |
| | 6. | Does the organizational culture support coaching? |
| Team | 1. | Is the line manager supportive of the coaching? |
| | 2. | How would you describe the relationship between the line manager and coachee? |
| | 3. | Is there a safe environment in the team that allows for coaching learning to be applied? |
| Individual | 1. | What is the motivation for coaching? |
| | 2. | Does the individual have a readiness for change? |
| | 3. | How much does the individual believe they have the capabilities to succeed? |
| Measurement | 1. | If ROI is problematic, what other measurements would be useful? |

The answers to these questions will assist in discovering what sort of return an investment in coaching will achieve, and how to demonstrate it within a specific organization.

It is always sensible when planning a coaching intervention to start from the end and work backwards. What is the objective of the coaching? If it is linked to the overall business or HR strategy and the objective is achieved, the spend on coaching is almost certainly justified. Even if a link cannot clearly be made between the coaching and the overall objective, perhaps the outputs justify the investment on their own (for example, improved team working, better collaboration, enhanced work performance).

## Measurement

There are various methods of measurement a coaching commissioner could consider when looking to demonstrate the value coaching is delivering. On an individual level, a self-evaluation form and line-manager feedback might be appropriate, perhaps even as an output of tripartite conversations.

To increase the quality of measurement, implementing 360-degree feedback both before and after the coaching journey can be helpful. By drawing on a wide range of perspectives, the 360 provides insights around the behaviors which the coachee needs to develop, and also tracks their journey through a stakeholder-centered approach.

From an organizational standpoint, a range of metrics become available, from strategic commercial targets like net promoter score (NPS) results and sales figures through to more people-focused metrics such as employee engagement survey results, employee promotion and retention rates, and absenteeism figures. Every organization is driven by different objectives, and measuring the impact of coaching on metrics that will incentivize high-quality coaching will ensure it has the greatest relevance.

## Coaching and other L&D interventions

In addition to thinking about the benefits and impact of coaching in isolation, it is worth considering the effectiveness of coaching when compared to other L&D initiatives. Few organizations track the impact of their leadership programs or measure the value of their performance review scheme, for the same reasons that we uncovered at the beginning of this chapter. While the board may like to ask the questions about ROI for any investment, collecting meaningful data about this for any human intervention, whether that's training, appraisals, leadership development or something else, is at best tricky, and without significant cost and time, near impossible.

Beer, Finnstrom and Shrader (2016) noted that while American companies spend billions of dollars on training and education, there is little evidence they can demonstrate a good return. Similar points have been made about learning: that it frequently fails to lead to behavioral change as individuals slip back into old habits and behaviors. It is worth turning our attention as we close this chapter, therefore, to a study (Rekalde et al., 2017) that looked at whether coaching was more effective than other methods, including long external courses, short external courses, in-house courses, day schools, seminars, conferences, job rotation, e-learning, outdoor training and mentoring. The study concluded that coaching was more effective than the other methods in delivering sustained behavioral change. If coaching commissioners feel the need to demonstrate the ROI of coaching, it would make sense to validate the ROI of a raft of other people interventions first. Similar results have been found when comparing coaching and traditional instructional learning, showing coaching led to both better outcomes and reduced learning times (Passmore and Rehman, 2012).

## Conclusion

Research demonstrates that coaching is a highly effective method for people development and can contribute to wider benefits for the organization. Whilst organizations can use ROI, managers need to be aware of its weaknesses and that, at best, these numbers are estimates. Other metrics can provide a more sophisticated and nuanced evaluation of the impact of coaching, and as a general rule coaching delivers a greater ROI than other interventions.

## References

Athanasopoulou, A., and Dopson, S. (2018). A systematic review of executive coaching outcomes: Is it the journey or the destination that matters the most? *Leadership Quarterly* 29(1): 70–88. https://doi.org/10.1016/j.leaqua.2017.11.004.

Beer, M., Finnstrom, M., and Shrader, D. (2016). Why leadership training fails – and what to do about it. *Harvard Business Review*, October 2016. Retrieved 3 March 2022 from: https://hbr.org/2016/10/why-leadership-training-fails-and-what-to-do-about-it.

Grant, A. (2012). ROI is a poor measure of coaching success: Towards a more holistic approach using a well-being and engagement framework. *Coaching: An International Journal of Theory, Research and Practice* 5(2): 74–85. https://doi.org/10.1080/17521882.2012.672438.

Passmore, J., and Rehman, H. (2012). Coaching as a learning methodology – a mixed methods study in driver development using a randomized controlled trial and thematic analysis. *International Coaching Psychology Review* 7(2): 166–84.

Rekalde, I., Landeta, J., Albizu, E., and Fernandez-Ferrin, P. (2017) Is executive coaching more effective than other management training and development methods? *Management Decision* 55(10): 2,149–62. https://doi.org/10.1108/MD-10-2016-0688.

# CHAPTER 47

# How can I build a coaching culture in my team?

## Jonathan Passmore and Roxane Rath

### Introduction

Coaching is now widely used across organizations. But having a coaching culture is more than just using coaching inside the organization. High-performing organizations successfully integrate coaching into the wider HR strategy. They understand how coaching can leverage improved performance and support wellbeing, whether this is through growing high-potentials or supporting the wider workforce through a 'coaching for all' strategy. In this chapter, we will explore what a coaching culture is and how organizations can go about developing one.

### What is a culture?

The term 'culture' is widely used, but, like coaching, it has a wide variety of definitions that are applied by different leaders, organizations and sectors. One of the clearest and shortest defines culture as "the way things get done around here" (Deal and Kennedy, 1982). Terence Deal and Alan Kennedy's simple definition has resonance and has been widely used by many organizations, recognizing the fact that culture has many faces, from formal processes, such as policy statements, mission and values, to the informal rules about how people dress, greet one another or where you can park in the staff parking lot.

A more academic definition is offered by Edgar Schein. Schein suggested culture is

> a pattern of shared basic assumptions that was learned by a group as it solved its problems of external adaptation and internal

integration, that has worked well enough to be considered valid and, therefore, to be taught to new members as the correct way you perceive, think and feel in relation to those problems.

(Schein, 2004: 8)

As with culture, there are a range of definitions as to what is a coaching culture.

Peter Hawkins has argued that a coaching culture exists in an organization when a coaching approach is a key aspect of how the leaders and staff engage and develop all their people and engage their stakeholders in ways that create increased individual, team and organizational performance and shared value for all stakeholders (Hawkins, 2012). Drawing on this thinking, CoachHub, a digital coaching provider, offers the following definition of a coaching culture:

> An organization that aims to maximize the potential of all who work for it, be they employees, associates, or suppliers, through their use of coaching both informally as the default style of leadership and formally through the contribution of trained coaches, creating a workplace where individuals are supported and challenged to become more self-aware, [and] take greater responsibility in creating organizational value and protecting each other's wellbeing.

To bring a new culture alive, organizations need a planned approach. One way of delivering culture change is through the three Cs approach:

- Common mindset – A shared view about the role of coaching within the organization, from the senior team in the C-suite to supervisors managing local teams.

- Champions – A cadre of leaders from across the organizational hierarchy who see bringing coaching alive as their personal responsibility.

- Coaching in many organizations is disconnected from broader organizational activities and the HR strategy. This approach to coaching is typified by a number of common features:

## The old-style approach to coaching

While coaching has been actively used by managers for more than three decades, in many organizations it has remained a personal perk, almost like a personal parking space. Coaching in many organizations is disconnected from wider organizational activities and from the HR strategy. This approach to coaching is typified by a number of common features:

- The 'why' of coaching – The organization understands that coaching is valuable, but not how to integrate it into the wider HR strategy or why it should be used.

- Appointments – The selection of the coach and their appointment is undertaken by the individual manager, often without due process and frequently based on personal relationships.

- Assignment focus – The assignment's focus is decided by the individual manager with little or no reference to the broader organizational perspective or objectives.

- The coach – The coach is seen exclusively as an external contractor, responsible for their own development and standards, which are unrelated to the organization.

- Evaluation – The evaluation is based on the perceptions of the manager as to how they felt the coaching went, with little consideration of metrics or alternative perspectives, such as that of the line manager.

It is clear that while 'personal coaching' may suit the individual manager, it offers little to the organization. Greater value can be gained by linking the coaching process more closely to the organization's needs and objectives through a coaching culture.

## The coaching culture model

Passmore's (2021) coaching culture model is a framework that can help organizations to move away from the approach of personal coaching to a more integrated approach, and is informed by earlier work on coaching culture (Passmore and Jastrzębska, 2011). The model suggests that to develop a coaching culture, organizations can consider their coaching approach under four headings or zones. Each zone contains a checklist that the organization can apply to evaluate its progress towards full implementation of a coaching culture.

### Zone 1: Leaders – Managed access to external coaches

In this zone, the focus is on how the organization uses coaches to develop and support its top talent, specifically the board and directors. This is usually achieved through the engagement of external executive coaches. The framework suggests ways that executive coaches should be appointed, managed and evaluated to deliver maximum organizational value.

*Zone 2: Everyone – Democratizing coaching*

In this zone, the focus is on how coaching can be extended from the top team to all managers, supervisors and employees. One common way of achieving this goal is through using a digital coaching platform. The framework suggests ways the partner can be selected, managed and evaluated.

*Zone 3: Approach – Coaching as the default leadership style*

In this zone, the focus is on how a coaching style of management can be developed as the default leadership style of the organization. This requires coaching skills to be an integral part of all leadership, management and supervisor training programs, helping managers to understand what coaching is, when to use it and how to use it to best effect within a line-management role, alongside other leadership styles.

*Zone 4: Distributed – Coaching across organizational boundaries*

In this zone, the focus is on extending coaching beyond organizational boundaries. Most organizations now work with multiple partners, suppliers and agents to deliver their services or products. In this zone, the organization looks for ways to extend a coaching style to these relationships. For a public-sector organization, this may mean creating cross-boundary coaching delivery. In other sectors, it may mean adopting a win–win development approach to project delivery, where project issues are worked through using a coaching style that adds value and seeks to build long-term relationships with key partners, agents and suppliers.

## Ten steps to developing a coaching culture

Creating a coaching culture is a long-term commitment for any organization. It is a journey which may take five or ten years. At a practical level, what can organizations do to move closer to a coaching culture?

Here are ten steps that organizations can consider to help them move forward:

1. Integrate coaching into your HR strategy, stating how and where coaching can support the business objectives

2. Commission, manage and supervise coaches

3. Democratize coaching, making coaching available on demand for all

4. Managers choose their coach

5. Coaching provider's pool should reflect the organization in terms of technical skills, age, gender, race and languages

6. Evaluate coaching's contribution to organizational goals

7. Train all managers in coaching skills

8. Encourage coaching as the default management style

9. Use team coaching to develop team performance

10. Develop a coaching style of working with key partners and suppliers, focusing on win–win styles of working.

## Conclusion

Understanding of what is meant by the term 'coaching culture' has developed over time, and it is now possible to identify several character-istics demonstrating that an organization has a coaching culture. Adopting a coaching culture is a maturity step that follows the democratization of coaching and requires a structured, long-term plan to realize in practice.

## References

Deal, T., and Kennedy, A. (1982). *Corporate Culture: The Rites and Rituals of Corporate Life*. San Francisco: Perseus Books.

Hawkins, P. (2012). *Creating a Coaching Culture: Developing a Coaching Strategy for Your Organisation*. Maidenhead: OUP.

Passmore, J. (2021). *Coaching Culture: Practical Actions for Auditing Your Organization*. WBECS. (Online) 28 October 2021.

Passmore, J., and Jastrzębska, K. (2011). Building a coaching culture: A development journey for organisational development. *Coaching Review* 4(2): 123–7.

Schein, E. (2004). *Organisational Culture and Leadership*. San Francisco: Jossey Bass.

# CHAPTER 48

# How should the line manager give feedback to support the coaching assignment?

Jonathan Passmore and Rosie Evans-Krimme

## Introduction

Managers are expected to give feedback to others, helping their team to stay on track and to develop. Many leaders find this difficult and avoid the feedback opportunity or default to a 'praise only' response. Yet we know that regular feedback can enhance relationships within a team, as well as improve performance. In this chapter, we will explore how managers can give constructive feedback that is both challenging and supportive, supporting their team members' development as part of a wider coaching culture. We will also explore how managers can secure genuine feedback on their working style and build a culture in their team where open genuine feedback is part of 'how we do things around here', which helps everyone to grow and develop together.

## Providing feedback

There are few better ways to improve performance than providing feedback. While feedback should be a regular part of working within a team, too often it is limited, with many managers trapped in one of three modes:

- Mode 1: The 'no feedback' mode – In this mode the manager gives no feedback to their team members.

- Mode 2: The 'warm platitudes' mode – In this mode the manager gives feedback but this feedback is limited to insincere praise: "Great job everyone". This feedback is often unrelated to specific incidents and is lacking in evidence, making it hard for team members to understand what exactly they did well and what behaviors they should repeat.

- Mode 3: The 'critical voice' mode – In this mode the manager is often silent for long periods of time, providing no feedback until things go wrong. Then they become hyper critical, often blaming individuals for poor performance, but lacking the supportive element to help develop a plan for improvement.

Over my own career I have experienced managers who have used all three modes. One episode in particular sticks in my mind, even though this was over 30 years ago. On this occasion I was a departmental director with a team of around 150 staff. I wrote a report for my boss, which came back with one word on it: "CRAP!" Apart from this being demotivating, I was left asking myself a series of questions: what was 'crap' about the report? What needed to change to meet my boss's expectations? What could I learn or improve for the next time I needed to write a new report? In summary, I had little or no evidence on why the report was judged to be in need of improvement; with no guidance on how I could improve, I was left confused.

Pretty much everyone wants to do a good job and wants to learn how to get better. Without feedback on our current performance and guidance on what could be changed, it can be hard to improve. The effect of the 'critical voice' mode of feedback makes good people leave.

Instead of seeing feedback as a chance to vent feelings, a more useful way for managers to think about feedback is as help. When feedback is delivered with empathy, understanding and encouragement, feedback can be a powerful tool to help improve performance.

Feedback should be a vital part of the coaching process, beginning even before a coachee begins a coaching relationship. By providing feedback, the manager can provide the coachee with clarity on what needs to be improved and thus help contribute to setting the coaching agenda (i.e. the goals). One of the best ways of doing this is through the tripartite commissioning meeting, attended by the coach, coachee and the coachee's line manager. In this meeting, everyone can have a say about the goals and agree on the priorities.

In Table 48.1 we suggest possible reflective questions for an initial meeting, prior to the first coaching session. You will notice that instead of starting with feedback, the coachee should adopt an evidence-based evaluation, and do this from multiple stakeholder perspectives. One of the challenges we face in feedback is that if it's not owned by the individual, little progress is made. Most people are fairly accurate when they take the time to think critically about the evidence. The important part is to get them to focus on the evidence. With this in mind, more detailed evidence-based questioning often brings individuals closer to the perspectives shared across the team.

**Table 48.1: Reflective questions to use before coaching starts**

1. Before you start the coaching assignment, I thought it might be helpful if we spend some time together reviewing your performance and what might form some of the goals you set for your coaching program. Let's take a few minutes to reflect. How do you see your performance over the last year/quarter?

2. What have you been most proud of?

3. What has gone less well?

4. What learning did you take away from those episodes?

5. Next, thinking about external stakeholders, what do you think [name a stakeholder] would think about your performance this year/quarter? What evidence would they draw on?

6. What do you think my perspective might be on your highs and lows over the period?

7. What patterns have emerged for you from these pieces of feedback?

8. Given these reflections, what goals do you want to explore with your coach?

9. How can I best support you during the coaching process?

10. How can I best supplement the coaching with other interventions?

In addition to encouraging reflection before the start of the coaching assignment, it's helpful to review performance throughout the coaching, with two particular points highlighted. The first of these is around halfway through; at this point, the line manager and coachee can reflect on the goals and the progress being made. This also provides an opportunity for the line manager to discuss additional goals or areas of development with the coachee. The second point is at the end of the coaching assignment, where a review meeting to evaluate the impact of the coaching is helpful, for the line manager to provide feedback on the successes made and comment on what the next steps might be in the coachee's development journey.

**Table 48.2: Reflective questions to use at the close of coaching**

1. As you come to the end of the coaching assignment, I thought it might be helpful if we spend some time together reviewing your performance and what you have learned from your coaching program. Let's take a few minutes to reflect. How do you see your performance over the last year/quarter? What have you been most proud of?

2. What has gone less well?

3. What difference has the coaching made to you over the past months?

4. What learning or insights did you take away from your coaching sessions?

5. Next, thinking about external stakeholders, what do you think [name a stakeholder] would think about your performance this year/quarter? What evidence would they draw on? (Repeat this for two or three key stakeholders – it can also be helpful to have gathered information from stakeholders in advance.)

6. What do you think my perspective might be on your areas where you have developed most, and areas where you are hoping to make further progress?

7. How can I best support you during the coming period?

8. What other development activities do you need to progress towards these goals?

Of course, all line managers should be giving continuous feedback, with similar conversations taking place in all 1:1 sessions with direct reports. These discussions work well when they are focused around a specific incident, such as a bid or a key event. In Table 48.3, we have suggested a structure for managing feedback in response to a specific incident or situation.

**Table 48.3: Giving situation-based feedback**

1. Ask permission to explore the topic.

2. Invite the person to review the situation and their behavior from their own perspective and then from an independent viewpoint.

3. Ask permission to give your feedback and make it clear that this is a viewpoint.

4. Focus on behaviors, as opposed to the individual.

5. Use specific evidence, such as evidence you have observed (never third-hand information) or feedback from a 360 or psychometric test.

6. Provide the opportunity for multiple interpretations, while encouraging the person to reflect on this feedback.

7. Encourage the person to commit to some action – for example, to reflect further or develop a plan of action.

It's worth remembering that any feedback from any single stakeholder, or even the line manager, is not the whole truth, it's just a perspective. It's simply how that person experiences the situation or the behavior. What is most helpful is to look for patterns. When inviting others to give feedback, capturing the feedback word-for-word can be really helpful. Secondly, gathering feedback from a range of three-to-six different people who work with the person regularly also helps. For most, the same themes come up time and time again. It's these which should be the focus for future development.

## Negative versus positive feedback

Sadly, many people see feedback as a negative process. This does not have to be the case. In fact, many argue we should give five times as many positive statements as developmental (negative) statements, and this number increases the closer the relationship (aim for 10:1 ratios or greater at home!). I call this 'catching people doing it right'. It's based on the simple belief that most people want to do a good job, and if we can simply encourage people to repeat more positive behaviors, poor behaviors will diminish. Ask any experienced school teacher and they will tell you, what works best is to find the one child out of the 30 in the classroom doing what you want, and praise them. One by one, the other 29 children will start to copy the behavior of the child which has been praised.

## Receiving feedback

It's important too for line managers not only to give feedback but to proactively invite others to provide them with feedback. Feedback can provide the opportunity for everyone to learn. What works with one team member may not work with another, and thus receiving feedback and adapting leadership style is often the best way leaders can serve each of the individuals in their team. As before, focusing on patterns which emerge in the feedback reveal what a line manager might need to change for the whole team, and should become the focus for their personal development plans.

## 'Feedforward'

Marshall Goldsmith, a leading executive coach, prefers to use the term 'feedforward' as opposed to feedback (2015). He argues that we don't need to think about what we did less well yesterday or an hour ago; instead, we need to focus on what we can do better tomorrow. This future-focused developmental conversation can be incredibly powerful. It shifts the focus from what we did wrong towards what we can learn to do right; a shift in thinking from a static mindset to a growth mindset (Dweck, 2016).

A simple question can start this process: "If there is one thing that I could do to be a better leader, what one piece of help would you give me?" We can explore this through further questions, but what is critical is that the person receiving the feedback simply express their gratitude, by saying 'thank you', and does not in any way challenge the feedback which has been given. All feedforward help is a gift. Whatever the person giving the feedback says, positive or negative, the rules we should all observe are: never argue, never justify, never defend behavior, simply offer thanks, taking the gift away to reflect, consider and possibly explore with a coach.

## Conclusion

Developing a feedback culture in a team can be a powerful tool as part of a wider coaching culture. Feedback can help inform coaching through a tripartite meeting and contribute to the coaching goals for the coachee. It can also be useful to review what progress has been made, both providing evidence-based positive feedback and next development steps. However, the very best line managers will use feedback as a regular way of working:

'catching people doing it right'. Providing supportive, evidenced feedback is all part of creating high-performance workplaces where everyone can thrive.

## References

Dweck, C. (2016). *Mindset: The Way You Think to Fulfill Your Potential.* London: Robinson.

Goldsmith, M. (2015). *Triggers: Sparking Positive Change and Making it Last.* London: Profile Books.

CHAPTER 49

# What possibilities does virtual reality offer to coaching?

Shammy Tawadros

## Introduction

Back in 2010, video conferencing seemed to need a dedicated room with on-hand technical support to make it happen. By the 2020s it has become a primary form of communication for many, now used by almost all organizations as a result of the global pandemic. Ten years ago, virtual reality (VR) was in the same state; it needed expensive hardware and sometimes knowledge of computer programming. Then, in 2021, the Facebook holding company rebranded as Meta revealed that it had invested more than $10 billion in VR and associated technologies that year. The 2020s may witness a seismic shift in VR technology usage. In this chapter, we'll consider what that means for coaching and how stakeholders of coaching should respond, and highlight some points for practical application.

## Coaching and communications technology

During the 2010s, it wasn't uncommon to hear coaches claiming that coaching couldn't happen remotely. Yes, telephone coaching was an option, but it, along with video coaching, was considered by many to be inferior and somehow incomplete. The events of 2020 changed that perception forever. There's an argument to be made for the unique experience of meeting in person, but the additional investment of time and cost, and the impact on the natural world, would negate most if not all of that added benefit (Isaacson, 2021). The vast majority of coaches, and most coachees, would now be extremely comfortable if video coaching were the only option available.

The truth is that coaching and communications technology are intertwined. As one method of meeting becomes the primary option for people, coaching needs to follow suit. The reason for this is the foundational coaching principle of rapport. If a coachee is most comfortable meeting using a particular tool, a coach refusing to use it risks breaking the trust that the relationship is built on. In order to mitigate that risk, those with an interest in coaching should keep half an eye on the development of communications technology.

The trajectory of communications technology is towards the metaverse, a concept of reality overlaid by an internet-worth of digital content using augmented reality (AR). This could be a visual warning of traffic hovering over a particular road, projected through a pair of glasses or contact lenses. It could be the seamless ability to compare prices of a product online by taking a photo of it on a smartphone. Or it could be a life-size hologram of a friend, generated as a live reflection of their movements and facial expressions. As convenient as video coaching is, the act of staring into a 2D screen feels unappealing in comparison. This hasn't fully arrived yet, but in the meantime a halfway house is available: donning a VR headset and meeting in a virtual space through avatars, in tools like AltspaceVR, MeetinVR or vTime XR.

## The impact of VR meetings on coaching

VR locations are always carefully designed spaces. They're pleasant and predictable – great for psychological safety – and there are no distractions. While a VR headset feels more high-tech than a laptop, the technology is much less present; in contrast to a PC screen with its keyboard, mouse, and endless menus and background windows, VR simply contains you, the space and the person you're meeting.

This focus on the space might have downsides. Claims have been made that learning in environments away from the workplace makes learning less effective, and VR locations can certainly feel different from the day-to-day. But those claims aside, the ability within VR to select locations can be powerful. A coach and coachee might meet somewhere in nature to escape from the intensity of their city. Or they might travel into orbit to consider the wider systems at play from a macro level (Isaacson, 2020).

It goes without saying that VR experiences are designed to be immersive. The trick that 360-degree sound and visuals play on the mind is indecipherably convincing for the most part, and this grounds a coach and coachee in the conversation much more than video coaching does. The limits to potential interruptions accelerate a sense of presence, and this makes the experience far more embodied than the natural tendency of video coaching to gravitate towards the purely cognitive.

This is perhaps best demonstrated through the experience people have of gesticulating much more naturally in VR than via video, and gesticulation has been shown to increase a tendency to learn (Novack and Goldin-Meadow, 2015). There's also evidence that VR increases physiological awe, which is defined as the emotions that arise "when one is confronted with something vast that transcends previous knowledge schemas" (Chirico et al., 2018) and characterized by goosebumps, making mindset-shifting insights more likely.

Overall, therefore, we can conclude that VR holds potential to increase the effectiveness of coaching. We've spent some time thinking about using VR for remote meetings, which it does well, and there are also opportunities to use it when coaching in person, which we'll look at now.

## Other uses for VR in coaching

VR offers two superpowers more than any other: the ability to travel anywhere in reality or fantasy, and augmented virtual abilities. Several VR tools have emerged in three broad categories that may prove useful for coaching.

The first of these I'll call guided meditation apps. The intensity of the typical day can get in the way of coaching sessions, so it's not uncommon for a coach to use mindfulness techniques from time to time. VR has the power to cut through the noise of life, by transporting the user to a place where the distractions of the day become irrelevant, and the use of the headset can inject the ingredient of playfulness into the time, laying a foundation for experimentation as a partnership. One example of this sort of tool would be Tripp, an audio-visual experience in which the landscapes the user is presented with are designed to invoke a sense of calm. Psychedelic colors shift around, encouraging conscious breathing and increased awareness. A more advanced option would be DEEP, a tool that incorporates biofeedback into the experience, allowing a user to explore a fantastical space purely through their breathing.

The second category would be experiential learning tools, through which the user performs a relevant task, enabling self-reflection in the tool itself, accompanied by questions from a coach. One example of this would be VirtualSpeech, through which the user is placed on a stage, complete with notes, slide decks and an animated audience. They can deliver a presentation, experiencing what it's like to do this in front of a crowd, and then receive a dashboard analyzing their performance. A coachee wanting to improve at public speaking couldn't get a more relevant experience live in a coaching session. Another example would be BodySwaps, through which the user experiences social interactions such as a job interview or delivering difficult feedback. After having walked through the interaction, the perspective is changed to that of the person on the receiving end, increasing self-awareness (Slater et al., 2019).

A third category contains what I'd broadly describe as creative tools. These might allow the user to explore a coaching issue using more than just cognitive processes, breaking through limiting ways of thinking, in the same way that an in-person coaching session might make use of picture cards to bypass language in expressing a dilemma, or physical objects to represent a systemic constellation. One example would be Tilt Brush, an advanced 3D painting tool. A coachee could use this to express their current situation visually. The real power in a tool like this is the ability to entirely change perspective and see things in a new way, giving real opportunities for insights. Another example would be Cosmic Sugar, a simple tool allowing the user to manipulate millions of particles as if controlling gravity in a vacuum; a coachee could introduce their own shapes and explore different forces to find ways through situations they find hard to express otherwise. And then there are examples like Fujii, a creative gardening app complete with fictional plant and insect life, encouraging nurturing of new seeds and exploration of virtual gardens.

With the right coachee and the right coaching issue, a coach could skillfully facilitate a VR experience that enhances a coaching session and offers chances for joyous disruption.

## How to be prepared

The VR products available are many and varied, each with their own capabilities and constraints. Their similarities, however, make the best way to prepare for using VR to just start using it! The fundamental principles of selecting, teleporting and gesturing might operate slightly differently from one tool to another, in the same way that the bullet-point button is located in a different place in different word-processing tools; but at least knowing that these features should be possible gives a level of helpful intuition.

Headsets are expensive, but not prohibitively so, costing about the same as a mid-range smartphone. But a cardboard kit available online for the price of an expensive coffee will, when plugged into a smartphone, turn into a headset that at least lets people dip their toe in. There's no excuse not to at least try out the world of VR, and the first experience is likely to pique anyone's curiosity.

In advance of launching a full-scale VR coaching intervention, it's important that everyone has a chance to get comfortable with the tools. Set aside time purely for learning the ropes and 'playing'. It's pleasant to have a conversation in VR, but if there's an object in view, a user might want to have a look before they leave the space; give that chance early on.

Physiology is important, so ensure a safe, comfortable space beforehand. This includes making sure no-one is going to accidentally knock over a vase of flowers when they reach out their hand, and having drinks and bathroom breaks before the session starts, because a need to remove the headset halfway through a deep conversation is best avoided.

Technical issues also need addressing. Depending on the tool, the environment may be unintentionally disruptive. I once coached someone in a virtual boardroom, past which a helicopter periodically flew – something impossible to miss. In another location, a billboard was in view advertising recent updates to the VR tool we were using; helpful as a user, but not helpful in a coaching session. Another important element is privacy features – from a broad perspective as far as personal data is concerned, and from a narrower perspective when thinking about friend invites popping up in the middle of a conversation (Isaacson, 2021). Most of these are settings that can be configured and so it's worth identifying them beforehand.

## Conclusion

The metaverse is a hot topic. Exploring ways that VR could enhance the delivery of coaching seems innovative and prudent, and it's increasingly an accessible option. The potential for accelerated insights and increased self-discovery is notable. Experimentation is justified, and a recommended approach would be to incorporate coaches trained in the use of VR as much as possible.

## References

Chirico, A., Ferrise, F., Cordella, L., and Gaggioli, A. (2018). Designing awe in virtual reality: An experimental study. *Frontiers in Psychology* 8, Article 2351. https://doi.org/10.3389/fpsyg.2017.02351.

Isaacson, S. (2020). Coaching in virtual reality. Retrieved 2 March 2022 from: https://www.linkedin.com/pulse/coaching-virtual-reality-sam-isaacson.

Isaacson, S. (2021). *How to Thrive as a Coach in a Digital World: Coaching with Technology.* Open University Press: London.

Novack, M., and Goldin-Meadow, S. (2015). Learning from gesture: How our hands change our minds. *Educational Psychology Review* 27(3): 405–12. https://doi.org/10.1007/s10648-015-9325-3.

Slater, M., Neyret, S., Johnston, T., et al. (2019). An experimental study of a virtual reality counselling paradigm using embodied self-dialogue. *Scientific Reports* 9, 10903. https://doi.org/10.1038/s41598-019-46877-3.

# CHAPTER 50

# How can we use coaching to support our corporate social responsibilities?

David Tee

## Introduction

Corporate Social Responsibility (CSR) is being increasingly considered by companies across multiple sectors for many reasons. An increase in interconnectivity across the global village brings the impact of our choices more visibly to home. CSR is becoming less of a differentiator and more of an expected norm across a number of industries, with younger generations of talent differentiating between potential employers based on their values and policies on issues such as the environment. Whether it is in place for strategic or purely ethical reasons, what role might coaching play in helping your business advance its CSR agenda?

## What is CSR?

Many organizations have moved from simply having economic goals since at least the 1960s (De George, 2011). The span of interests and activities and the motivations that CSR covers are argued to be broader than mere corporate philanthropy, with the concepts of CSR succinctly defined as *"International private business self-regulation"* (Sheehy, 2015: 625). Carroll (1991) built on an earlier 'three concentric circles' model of organizations' corporate social responsibilities to suggest it has a pyramid with four levels, as follows:

- The pyramid apex concerns philanthropic responsibility, such as contributing resources to the wider community

- Next, ethical responsibility involves ensuring the business does no harm and feels an obligation to be a force for good

- Legal responsibility is concerned with compliance with the law, as well as a broader determination to 'play by the rules of the game'

- At the foundation of the pyramid, economic responsibility, the need to be profitable, is argued by Carroll to be a necessary enabler for executing the other three responsibilities.

Since the 1990s, organizations have become increasingly aware of their responsibilities with regard to the natural world, and the four dimensions have (entirely appropriately) been expanded (see, for example, Stobierski, 2021).

## Why does CSR matter?

A number of reasons as to why CSR is important – or why you might want to consider how you can use coaching in your business to leverage your CSR agenda – were stated in this chapter's introduction. To revisit one of these, Gen Z forms a large percentage of the working-age population and CSR matters to them. This influences their brand choice as consumers, but also career destination (Luther, 2016). To a greater extent than other generations, Gen Z favors employers with CSR policies that align to their own beliefs and values. A strong CSR agenda can therefore aid talent attraction, development and retention.

There is also evidence regarding the direct link between CSR and business performance and profitability. Positive Organizational Scholarship authors argue for the link between positive leadership behaviors such as organizational virtuousness (a very similar idea to the 'philanthropic responsibility' dimension within the CSR pyramid above) and financial performance (Cameron, 2003), with further evidence of this link emerging within wider research (Saeidi et al., 2015). This all suggests there need not be a trade-off between CSR and profitability. Cameron (2021) goes further by stating businesses that uncommonly outperform their competitors (his term: *"positively deviant"*) are characterized by pursuing their social responsibilities as worthy endeavors in and of themselves, rather than as a hoped-for catalyst for financial benefit, talent recruitment or other end goals.

## The role of coaching

As has been explored elsewhere in this book, coaching is conceptually distinct from other related interventions. At the heart of this distinction is the notion of coaching as a non-directive, facilitative intervention; the coach is there to "Ask – don't tell" (Whitmore, 1992), even if they [think they] know the answer to the client's problem. It is this central tenet of not advising, guiding or informing that serves to raise client self-awareness, along with responsibility, problem-solving and ownership of the solution. How then might coaches stay in this non-directive space and yet serve the organization's CSR agenda?

## The financial crash and beyond

Peter Hawkins, one of the pioneering thinkers within the field of coaching, challenged the received truth of the coach as unwaveringly neutral in 2009, when he issued the challenge *"What were the coaches doing while the banks were burning?"* (Hawkins and Turner, 2020: 2). It was a matter of record that many of the financial institution casualties during the crash of 2008–2009 had been using coaches for their executives in the run-up to their demise. What were the awareness-raising activities, the constructive challenges, that took place within those coaching sessions that might have allowed those leaders to act to change course? What are the artfully constructed questions that a coach might put to an individual client or, maybe in team coaching, to the C-suite collectively, to at least enable them to purposefully consider and adopt a chosen stance or strategy on the issues that typically fall under the CSR remit?

One can readily see that having permission as a coach to raise these questions is markedly different to acting as a consultant or mentor and advising as to the actual solution. With this approach, the client is still empowered to think through and determine solutions for themselves, with the coach – staying neutral – as a powerful catalyst. Adopting this approach, at the very least, rules out the option of leaders being (willfully?) blind to such matters and, more optimistically, enables desired changes, advancing CSR policy and demonstrating how coaching can be purposefully deployed as a CSR leverage tool.

Coaching as a profession has increasingly responded to Hawkins' rallying call. To give one example, since the financial crash, we have seen the climate emergency resulting in the establishment of a formal body, the Climate Coaching Alliance (CCA, 2022), with its founders advocating for coaches to 'play midwife' to the creation of a healthier relationship between client organizations and the environment. To give another example, Passmore, Liu and Tewald (2021) have pointed to the lack of awareness and action regarding race and sexual orientation within the coaching profession, and called for greater positive steps from coaches in relation to the 'Diversity and Inclusion' agenda. Other coaching groups are also emerging in relation to different social responsibility topics.

## How specifically might an organization use coaching to advance CSR?

Let's get more practical. There are a number of options detailed here, but it's important to be creative and think beyond these initial suggestions.

A direct approach would be to target coaching spend and activity on staff members that wish to use their coaching for a topic related to the CSR strategy. Purposefully prioritize coaching goals aimed at realizing your environment policy, your diversity policy, your community engagement policy or other relevant policies. Build in an evaluation strategy that purposefully tracks and captures data about the successes that coaching is generating around these topics.

A more indirect approach would be to consider the skills and behaviors evidenced to drive CSR activities. For example, Abdullah, Ashraf and Sarfraz (2017) identified the relationship of factors such as creative self-efficacy and organizational identification on CSR. If coaching is used to build these characteristics within employees, the business can then tap into these attributes when advancing more formal CSR activity.

Use your CSR priorities as a consideration when selecting and bringing in external coaches to affect the impacts of your coaching program. This comes with a warning, however: please check that coaches specializing in these areas are not really offering consultancy in disguise, fashionably badged as coaching but actually with a prescribed tool or solution. Instead, professional coaches knowledgeable and skilled in these areas should be putting the provocative questions and challenges to your staff on the topics that matter the most. A coach with a public, formal affiliation to a body committed to these issues, such as the CCA, would be a very useful starting point.

Beyond individual coaching, choose to use both team and group coaching for CSR purposes. With team coaching, maybe the coach could work with the team in your company that is able to set the CSR strategy. With group coaching, built around shared themes rather than interdependent roles, bring together champions and change agents from different directorates and departments to cross-pollinate and build upon best practice. Furthermore, using the internal communications strategy to promote the fact that this is where development spend is being prioritized may also result in some vicarious learning and wider raising of the CSR agenda across the workforce.

Finally, it is important for the coaching commissioner to be an exemplar. An organization with in-house coaches should not use them solely to facilitate the performance and development of its staff, but also as a force for social good. Look for partner organizations in the community, such as prisons keen to use coaching to help people successfully transition from serving their time to becoming productive citizens, or organizations helping military veterans find a new role and purpose. These are just two examples where coaches are already known to have done effective work, but think of a cause related to your organization's context, community and values where your coaches can step away from staff coaching and be part of the organization's wider CSR contribution.

## Conclusions

CSR is important and relevant for many reasons, and there is a helpful role that coaches can play in advancing it. Alongside any consultants, advisers and internal expertise, your coaches can be having the conversations, putting forward the pertinent questions and raising awareness throughout your employees and leaders at every level. This way, coaching can be used as a very powerful catalyst for realizing the organization's values and responsibilities.

## References

Abdullah, M.I., Ashraf, S., and Sarfraz, M. (2017). The organizational identification perspective of CSR on creative performance: The moderating role of creative self-efficacy. *Sustainability* 9(11): 2,125. https://doi.org/10.3390/su9112125.

Cameron, K. (2003). Organizational virtuousness and performance. In K.S. Cameron, J.E. Dutton and R.E. Quinn (eds), *Positive Organizational Scholarship*, pp.48–65. Berrett-Koehler.

Cameron, K. (2021). *Positively Energizing Leadership.* Berrett-Koehler.

Carroll, A. (1991). The pyramid of corporate social responsibility: Toward the moral management of organizational stakeholders. *Business Horizons* 34(4): 39–48.

CCA (2022). *Why the Climate Coaching Alliance?* Climate Coaching Alliance. https://www.climatecoachingalliance.org/about/.

De George, R.T. (2011). *Business Ethics* (7th edition). Pearson.

Hawkins, P., and Turner, E. (2020). *Systemic Coaching.* Routledge.

Luther, S. (2016). *Why Your Company Should Start Focusing on Gen Z.* Lucas Group. https://www.lucasgroup.com/your-career-intel/forget-millennials-gen-z.

Passmore, J., Liu, Q., and Tewald, S. (2021). Future trends in coaching. *Coaching Psychologist* 17(2): 41–51.

Saeidi, S.P., Sofian, S., Saeidi, P., Saeidi, S.P., and Saaeidi, S.A. (2015). How does corporate social responsibility contribute to firm financial performance? The mediating role of competitive advantage, reputation, and customer satisfaction. *Journal of Business Research* 68(2): 341–50. https://doi.org/10.1016/j.jbusres.2014.06.024.

Sheehy, B. (2015). Defining CSR: Problems and solutions. *Journal of Business Ethics* 131(3): 625–48. doi:10.1007/s10551-014-2281-x.

Whitmore, J. (1992). *Coaching for Performance*. London: Nicholas Brealey.

www.ingramcontent.com/pod-product-compliance
Lightning Source LLC
Chambersburg PA
CBHW071327210326
41597CB00015B/1375